The
Last Good
Time

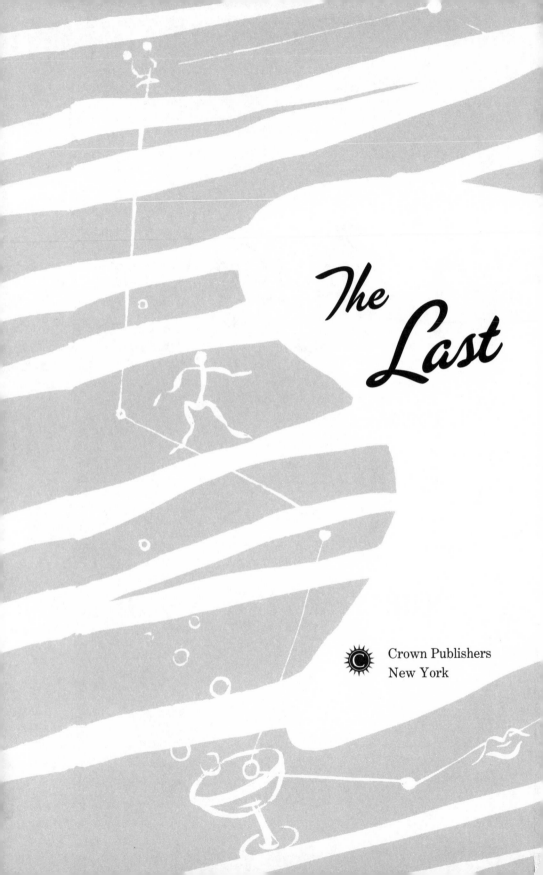

The Last

Crown Publishers
New York

Good Time

Skinny D'Amato,

the Notorious 500 Club, and

the Rise and Fall

of Atlantic City

JONATHAN VAN METER

Unless otherwise noted, all photographs are courtesy of Paulajane D'Amato.

Published by Crown Publishers, New York, New York.
Member of the Crown Publishing Group, a division of Random House, Inc.
www.randomhouse.com

CROWN is a trademark and the Crown colophon is a registered trademark of Random House, Inc.

Design by Lauren Dong

Printed in the United States of America

Library of Congress Cataloging-in-Publication Data

Van Meter, Jonathan.
    The last good time : Skinny D'Amato, the notorious 500 Club, and the rise and fall of Atlantic City / Jonathan Van Meter.—1st ed.
        p. cm.
    1. Atlantic City (N.J.)—History—20th century. 2. Atlantic City (N.J.)—Social life and customs—20th century. 3. D'Amato, Skinny, d. 1984. I. Title.
    F144.A8 V36 2003
    974.9'85043—dc21   2002154783

ISBN 0-609-60877-0

10 9 8 7 6 5 4 3 2 1

First Edition

To Andy

The
Last Good
Time

✴ *Prologue*

This is a book about a man named Skinny D'Amato and all the great and terrible things that happened to him. It is a story about the beginning and the end of a very particular time and place in America. Skinny appeared, for all intents and purposes, out of thin air—and then rose steadily to a level of exceptional prominence in Atlantic City, a profoundly American beach town that has always wanted to be a Big City. Along the way, and perhaps unbeknownst even to Skinny, he became one of the most quietly influential figures of the twentieth century.

With all the tragedy that has befallen the D'Amato family and the city that Skinny loved so much, it's hard to know where to begin. Perhaps it's best I get right to the man himself, the extraordinarily generous and talented gambler and nightclub impresario and his glamorous wife, Bettyjane. I could tell you about how the two of them—dapper Italian and elegant WASP—reigned for a time in their hometown like proletarian royalty until Bettyjane died of a brain aneurysm at forty-six. Or do I start by telling you about Skinny's notorious 500 Club, the place in Atlantic City where Dean Martin and Jerry Lewis became a team, where a young Sammy Davis Jr. got an early break and Frank Sinatra played three, four, five shows a night every summer until the early 1960s. Would you believe me if I told you that Skinny D'Amato—not Humphrey Bogart—was the real father of the Rat Pack?

I suppose I could begin with Skinny's oldest child, Paulajane, who grew up in the 1950s living in an apartment above the 500 Club. She's the strong one, the survivor, the blond leggy beauty pageant queen and former model, the one who's obsessed with the D'Amato legacy and will not stop until her father's flag is planted firmly in the present. Or perhaps it's best I begin with myself—the writer—the year I arrived in Atlantic City and the day that I first stumbled upon the D'Amato mansion just as it was being ransacked by the public and sold to the highest bidder.

Actually, the *very* beginning of the story came a few months earlier, when I first saw Paulajane D'Amato. She walked into a restaurant where I was waiting tables, and when I laid eyes on her I was instantly fixated. Who *is* that woman? I wondered. She was tan, freckled, and all smile—the picture of breezy confidence. She did not look or dress like anyone I had ever seen in Atlantic City, and I just assumed she was famous. She moved like a famous person, carried herself like someone who was used to being stared at. She acted like a woman who was accustomed to getting what she wanted.

I had moved to Atlantic City the day after Christmas 1985 into a basement apartment on Bartram Avenue in a neighborhood called Chelsea, once very exclusive and mostly Jewish, but now very mixed, just south of the Pacific Avenue casino strip. I was twenty-one, six months out of college, and impossibly excited about being on my own in the world; earlier that year, I had landed a summer internship at *Atlantic City* magazine that eventually turned into a real job that paid all of $11,000 a year. I spent the first several months updating nightclub and restaurant listings for the guide in the back of the magazine. Occasionally I got to write a random little story about some local peculiarity or an advance in slot machine technology.

My apartment was a small one-bedroom for $300 a month, where I lived with a roommate, Louis, who had dropped out of college to join me in my adventure in Atlantic City. His first job was as a bus greeter for Caesars, which meant that when the masses rolled into town from New York or Scranton or Baltimore, it was Louis's face—handsome, unlined, and full of promise—that the bored, slot-machine-obsessed senior citizens saw first.

Louis and I were so broke that, more nights than I care to remember, we ate popcorn for dinner. Or scrambled eggs on a roll from the Atlantic City Italian Bakery. For cheap fun, we used to smoke pot—or, if we were lucky, pop a Valium—and walk the ten blocks to Steve Wynn's Golden Nugget, ride the escalators, and watch all the freaks throw away their money. I would occasionally drop $10 in a slot machine, but that was the extent of my gambling. In the whole three and a half years I lived in Atlantic City, I probably spent no more than $150 in the casinos.

One strangely warm Saturday morning, January 11, 1986, I woke up, got the paper, saw an ad for an estate sale, and convinced Louis to walk to Suffolk Avenue to check it out.

VENTNOR TAG SALE
Paul "Skinny" D'Amato
ESTATE SALE

Memorabilia
Photographs
Furniture
Clothing
Etc.

Friday and Saturday
JANUARY 10 & 11
10 am–6 pm
12 So. Suffolk Ave.
CASH ONLY

I had a vague idea who Skinny D'Amato was; my parents talked of going to the 500 Club in the 1950s when they were young, as almost anyone of a certain age who lived within three hundred miles of Atlantic City had. I remember my mother telling me that she and my father and some friends drove to Atlantic City late at night after her prom, still in their evening dresses, white gloves, and tuxedos, and stood on the street in front of the club, begging to get in. Thanks to a soft touch on the door that night, they prevailed. It was 1955, at the height of the club's popularity, when on any given night the corner table in the front room might be occupied by Joe DiMaggio or Walter Winchell or Elizabeth Taylor and Mike Todd or just about any star you can think of from that time. The detail that has always stuck out from that story is that it was the first time my mother had ever seen ultra-violet light, the kind that turns zebraskin bar stools into a near halluci-natory experience.

My excitement about going to the estate sale on that muggy January day was dampened by the fact that I had so little money. I didn't imagine there would be anything I could afford. But as soon as I walked through the door of the house—built on a man-made hill, a little higher and a little bigger than all the rest—I felt the rush of history; finding a bargain was no longer the point. It was as if I had passed through a rent in time and crashed right into a fabulous, exclusive party. I had become obsessed in college with anything that looked as if it had come from the fifties and sixties—especially modern lamps and ashtrays—and here, at the D'Amato house, I had found nirvana.

Just inside the door, there was a bucket of orange Cal-Neva Lodge pens for sale for fifty cents apiece, left over from the hotel-casino that Skinny, Frank Sinatra, Dean Martin, and (perhaps) Sam Giancana owned together in Lake Tahoe in the early 1960s. I remembered read-ing in one book or another about how Sinatra lost his casino gaming license in Nevada because Giancana, the Chicago mobster, was caught hiding out in a bungalow up at the Cal-Neva, visiting with his girl-friend, Phyllis McGuire of the famed McGuire Sisters. Frank had to sell the place in 1963. It's one of those facts that sticks in my head because it happened in my birth year, the year Kennedy was assassinated and Frank Sinatra Jr. was kidnapped.

The house on Suffolk Avenue was a huge, white, three-story Dutch Colonial affair with more than twenty rooms and seven bathrooms. The outside was adorned with crisp orange canvas awnings with white fringe. Inside, there was great style in evidence—a kind of sixties mod-

ern, Hollywood daring—all oranges and whites and browns and camels
and taupes. The huge formal dining room, with wall sconces and a fireplace, was dominated by a long oak table and twelve tufted ivory
leather barrel chairs. I learned years later that the set was formal
boardroom furniture given to Skinny and Bettyjane as a housewarming
present by Robert and Joan Tisch of the Loews Corporation. Throughout the house there was pale orange wall-to-wall carpet. The den, just
off the living room, was like a luxurious cave—the ceiling and walls
were covered with thick, dark-brown-and-orange paisley fabric matching the heavy drapes. In the back of the house there was a big open
kitchen with dark wooden cabinets and custom-made appliances and
bright orange Formica countertops. (Orange, it turns out, was both
Frank Sinatra's and Skinny's favorite color.) Upstairs, there were three
bedrooms for the children: Paulajane, Cathy, and Angelo. In the
sprawling master bedroom, two chandeliers hung from the ceiling, and
there were "His" and "Her" bathrooms, one in black and the other in
white—both dripping with gold fixtures. Skinny's huge dressing room
looked like the men's department of Saks—hundreds of beautiful
custom-made silk suits and dinner jackets in every color, gorgeous
button-down shirts, dozens of pairs of Italian suede loafers and tuxedo
pumps, all of it meticulously organized, the hangers equidistant from
one another.

Downstairs were all manner of black-and-white photographs of
Skinny and the Rat Pack, each one for sale. (I bought three things: a
pair of Skinny's white suede loafers that fit perfectly and that I wore
nearly every day the following summer; an orange plastic boomerang-
shape ashtray; and a Cal-Neva pen.) As I was poking around the house,
I turned a corner, and there was Paulajane. Even in sweats, she was
glamorous. Like Skinny, she has an erect bearing and an indescribable,
innate quality, a natural and powerful charisma, that draws people to
her. She and her sister, Cathy, were hosting the sale that day, greeting
old and new friends as well as total strangers as if it were a holiday
party. Perhaps it was their way of not having to face the facts. In reality, they were having an open house for the public, allowing them into
their famous father's inner sanctum so that they might pick through the
family's things. People showed up and stood on their front lawn hours

before the sale started, anxious to see the inside of the house where the famous had tread—and where Skinny's only son, Angelo, had brutally murdered and partially dismembered a young man in the basement ten years earlier.

✦

If the D'Amatos—or what's left of them—are (or were) Atlantic City's own, strange version of a royal family, then, like most royals, they seem cursed with misfortune. In the late 1960s, Bettyjane discovered she had a brain aneurysm and slowly went mad. In 1972, after years of seizures and an addiction to pills related to her illness, she died in her sleep. A year later, the 500 Club burned to the ground; it was front-page, above-the-fold news in *The New York Times*. In 1974, Skinny barely survived a massive heart attack and never fully recovered. Cathy, a year and a half younger than Paulajane, would later move as far away as she could—to Hawaii. And in 1976, Angelo murdered his friend Ronald Bodanza. He served only thirty-three months of a ten-year sentence thanks to a plea bargain that was so controversial, the Atlantic County District Attorney's Office had to hold a press conference to explain it to an outraged public, most of whom assume to this day that Skinny or one of his famous friends pulled some strings or paid off the judge.

When Angelo got out of jail at the age of twenty-one, a job was arranged for him with the construction company that was building the new Playboy Hotel & Casino at Florida Avenue and the Boardwalk. He tried to return to the spoiled, pampered life he had known before, but he quickly became a compulsive gambler, stealing from his own family to feed his habit, falling in with a crowd of lowlifes. Eventually he was caught embezzling thousands of dollars from the construction company and went back to jail. In 1983, while he was serving an eight-month sentence, the remains of the body of Keerans "Kerry" Carter, a girl who had come to Atlantic City from Atlanta, Georgia, washed up in the marshes along one of the boulevards connecting the mainland to Absecon Island, and Angelo was indicted for a second, even more gruesome murder. His family was dragged through two painfully lurid trials that brought to the surface the dark side of the *new* Atlantic City, a town that had, as always, an underbelly of drugs, gambling, political corruption, prostitution, and crime. Less than a year after Angelo was sentenced to twenty-seven and a half years, Skinny—the man everyone called "Mr. Atlantic City"—died of a massive heart attack at the age of seventy-five.

The week before he died, a representative from a publishing house in New York, accompanied by two lawyers, went to visit him in his bedroom on Suffolk Avenue, to see if they might be able to talk Skinny into writing a book. In the last ten years of his life, after the 500 Club burned down, Skinny's bedroom became one of the busiest places in town. It was there, in that outsize room with daffodil yellow walls that held photographs of Frank and Sammy and Dean and Jerry, that he conducted all of his business, smoked his five packs of cigarettes a day, and kept a restaurant-size coffee urn next to his bed so that he didn't have to go too far to feed his caffeine addiction. He drank dozens of cups a day, always out of a glass, always with a spoon in it "so the glass won't crack." When the sun went down, Skinny played cards with an ever changing cast of characters nearly every night. Sometimes the stakes were high enough that an Atlantic City cop would hang around to make sure nothing too terribly shady went down. (One night, a guy won a big pile of money, leaned over to scoop it up, and promptly died of a heart attack—slumped across the card table in Skinny's room.)

When legal gambling came to town in the late 1970s and the casinos were built, the entertainers who once performed in Skinny's club on Missouri Avenue began returning to the resort, to play the big, plush new showrooms of Resorts, the Golden Nugget, and Caesars. And when they did, more often than not they made a pilgrimage to Suffolk Avenue to pay their respects to Skinny. As one woman who lived across the street from the D'Amatos when she was a little girl said, "I thought they had a restaurant in their house. There were always these great big cars—Cadillacs and Lincolns—gliding up and down the street. Limousines were constantly parked out front. Sinatra's limo would pull up, usually around the holidays."

But on that afternoon in late May 1984, when the big black car carrying the publishing executive and his two lawyers pulled up, they had no idea that theirs would be the last limo, that this would be the final meeting Skinny would take in his silk paisley robe. "Listen, Skinny," said the guy from New York. "Eddie Fisher said marvelous things about you in his book. Myron Cohen had a whole wonderful section about you in his book, and Jerry Lewis swore his undying affection to you in his autobiography. You could talk about your relationship with Frank, Dean, Jerry, Sammy, the Kennedys, Grace Kelly. You know what I mean?"

"Yeah," said Skinny. "The only trouble is, you don't want me to write nice things about them, do you?"

"Think it over," said the publishing exec.

"Yeah, okay, thanks," Skinny muttered, trying to be polite to his visitors but knowing he'd never change his mind.

Almost exactly a year after Skinny died, I began my internship at *Atlantic City* magazine, and a few months after that, I stumbled into the D'Amato estate sale. In 1987, I wrote a cover story on Paulajane called "Skinny's Kid." It was the best-selling issue in the magazine's decade-long history. A year later I left Atlantic City, but I remained fascinated by the resort where so many people—including the D'Amatos—made and lost their fortunes and where by 1990 four out of the previous seven mayors had been indicted on one criminal charge or another. I found myself pulled back to the resort, again and again, and often wondered how I could write a book about this little city-by-the-sea. One night, out of the blue, my phone in New York rang, and it was Paulajane. We talked about her father and of her dream of opening a new 500 Club in one of the casinos, and suddenly . . . it clicked. Skinny would lead the way.

But how to write a book about a man whose greatest accomplishment was to inspire uncommon loyalty from great men by never telling anyone anything? His own children could not provide me with the most basic facts of his beginnings. Indeed, they hoped that *I* would be the one to finally answer the question that has haunted them their entire lives: Was Skinny in the Mob?

I spent hundreds of hours with Paulajane. I visited Angelo in prison on three separate occasions, spending a total of ten hours with him in an ugly, brightly lit conference room at East Jersey State Prison in Rahway. I had dinner on two occasions with Cathy, who does not enjoy talking about the past. I went to Vegas, south Florida, Lake Tahoe, Philadelphia, Pittsburgh, Los Angeles, and all over south Jersey tracking people down. The Rat Pack is dead, unfortunately, as are many of the people who might have been able to help. But there were a few— and just a few—people who really understood a thing or two about Skinny. Hundreds of people—thousands, maybe—"knew" and "loved" Skinny.

The best way to begin to acquaint oneself with Skinny D'Amato is by looking at the town where he was born and raised, and where, even today, his presence can be felt in nearly every aspect of society. If there had not been an Atlantic City, there would not have been a Skinny D'Amato. In turn, if there had not been a Skinny D'Amato, Atlantic City would not have survived to become the East Coast gambling mecca that it is today. The new Atlantic City is, in many ways, a resort created in Skinny's image. He was born at the tail end of the stifling Victorian era and came of age at the height of Prohibition and he somehow intuited, long before most, that the compulsive nature of human beings was irrepressible. He knew, as sure as the tide would come in each day, that people of every class, race, and religion are going to drink, gamble, fuck, smoke, take drugs, stay up all night, waste money, and worry about the consequences some other day.

Chapter **One**

Atlantic City has always been an extraordinarily weird and misunderstood place. My Atlantic City of the late eighties was, in many ways, not all that different from the resort that Skinny lorded over for thirty years, beginning in the early forties. The city itself sits at the northern end of Absecon Island, a narrow, ten-mile-long strand separated from the mainland of New Jersey by seven miles of water and wetlands. Four towns make up the island—Atlantic City, Ventnor, Margate, and Longport—all of them accessible by causeways and bridges. One of the things many first-time visitors miss when they go to Atlantic City is the rest of the island, which is lovely and, in certain places, swanky. I have come to think of Ventnor and Margate as the Beverly Hills of south Jersey, as both towns are choked with block after block of huge mansions built over the last hundred years in every imaginable architectural style. "Atlantic City slammers" is the excellent phrase I once heard someone use to describe these hulking beauties.

When I arrived in Atlantic City I knew very little about the island, with its odd mixture of booming, new-money casino culture, blighted urban landscape, picturesque beaches, wealthy cloistered neighborhoods, and vibrantly seedy black and gay communities. I grew up at the Jersey shore in the seventies, just thirty miles south of Absecon Island, yet I had been to Atlantic City exactly once by the age of twenty-one. There was almost no reason to bother, as the city was a crumbling ghost town. I was in the marching band in high school, and during my sophomore year, in 1979, we marched in a parade on the Boardwalk. By that time, the referendum on gambling had passed and Resorts International had opened its doors, but the city was still mostly just sad.

I will never forget the strange and intoxicating feeling I had that day, a feeling of being suspended in time, with the beautiful empty beach on one side of us as we marched down the Boardwalk and the once majestic, now rotten city on the other side. The rides, arcades, stalls, and shops were padlocked, and the famous Steel Pier had been closed for years. It was as if the Apocalypse had finally come and we in the parade and its meager bystanders were the only people left.

My grandfather played the trumpet in a big band in nightclubs all around the Northeast when he was young; he spent a lot of time in Atlantic City in the thirties and forties, and I had heard stories about the fun he had had there in the sprawling supper clubs and the back-alley speakeasies and the people who came from hundreds of miles to dance to the swing bands. I had heard about—and had seen old black-and-white photographs of—the Easter parades that rivaled Fifth Avenue's and drew hundreds of thousands to the Boardwalk in their suits and hats, the dancing in expansive ballrooms that jutted over the ocean on huge piers.

By the time I was a teenager, though, all that was gone. The resort began its slow and inexorable decline as early as the late 1940s, with the gradual bankrupting of the railroads and the growth of cheap jet travel to warmer, more exotic places, like Miami and the Caribbean. Because Atlantic City had been built up over the first half of the century in the frantic ad hoc manner of most seashore resorts, its buildings, under constant assault from the salty sea air, were beginning literally to crumble. The city had reached its nadir by the early 1970s. The whole urban center had been transformed into one great big slum, with most businesses closing and young people bailing out, leaving the blighted remains to the senior citizens and poor blacks, who couldn't afford to escape.

But when I came to work at the magazine in 1985, things were looking up. Along the Boardwalk, modern towers were rising as quickly as Donald Trump, Steve Wynn, and Hugh Hefner could build them, but there were still traces of the old Atlantic City. The gigantic, turn-of-the-century "wedding cake" hotels, the rooming houses along the beach, and Club Harlem on Kentucky Avenue were still standing, as was the White House Sub Shop, Angelo's Fairmont Tavern, Tony's Baltimore Grille, Dock's Oyster House, the Irish Pub & Inn, the Knife & Fork Inn, and a handful of other institutions from the old days (many of which have pictures of Skinny hanging prominently on their walls). Up near the Inlet—a burned-out neighborhood not so affectionately called "South Bronx–by-the-sea"—stands what remains of the redbrick Chalfonte–Haddon Hall. Once one of the largest hotels in the world, the structures were built by Quakers who for decades refused to sell alcohol on the premises. After a multimillion-dollar renovation, the building, painted white, is now home to Resorts International, the first casino to open after New Jersey legalized "gaming" (christened as such in a vain attempt to imbue the new industry with a sense of good, clean fun).

Set back from the Boardwalk, with scrappy little Brighton Park splayed out before it, stands the Claridge, the last and most austere of the great Atlantic City hotels. Built of red brick in 1930, it was at the time the tallest hotel in the resort. Today, it's the only one that's been somewhat faithfully restored to its original luster—at least on the outside. Like Resorts, Bally made use of part of the shell of an old hotel—the Dennis—but you can barely tell what it once looked like, as it was partially demolished to make way for a huge purple-and-silver glass tower that is lit like a plastic Christmas tree.

There are certain things about Atlantic City that newcomers learn very quickly. There are no supermarkets or movie theaters in the city; you have to drive offshore or "downbeach," as they say locally, to buy groceries or see a film. Until recently, there was not a single miniature golf course, which is strange for a Jersey shore town. In lieu of normal public transportation, Atlantic City has jitneys, little pale blue buses that look like bread trucks, which run up and down the island, picking up and discharging people as they go. Stranger still are the Boardwalk's rolling chairs, the resort's answer to the rickshaw, imported from Philadelphia's centennial celebration of 1876. Bars are allowed to stay open around the clock, and many do, which lends an air of desperation to certain parts of town. New York Avenue was once a thriving gay mecca, though today there's not a single gay bar left on that strip. The rest of the gay community has scattered to the winds.

The city has its traditions, too. The most famous and most bizarre is Miss America week in September, considered sacred by many of the locals and duly celebrated with parades and parties and drag shows and, of course, the event itself, which continues—even as the pageant tries to reinvent itself—to bring out Atlantic City's crusty, odd society to their reserved seats. The pageant has been held since 1921 in Atlantic City and since 1929 in Convention Hall, a building that spans seven acres (two city blocks) and—with no pillars—was for many years the largest unobstructed room in the world. It seats forty-one thousand people and features the world's largest pipe organ. In 1973, Miss America was flown around inside the huge room in a helicopter.

Most of the middle- to upper-middle-class white population live in Chelsea, or farther downbeach, in Ventnor, Margate, and Longport. The black population, many of whose families have been in Atlantic City since the Civil War, live uptown or in the Inlet. At the turn of the century, 25 percent of Atlantic City's population was black (compared with 2 percent in New York); today, more than half of the population is black. Throughout the eighties, "the World's Playground," as it has been called since the early 1900s, was the most visited resort in the country—more than Las Vegas, more than Disneyland—with nearly thirty million visitors a year. When I moved to town, Atlantic City was in the midst of a boom. There were already eleven hotel-casinos doing business to the tune of $2.15 billion a year in total earnings—just slightly less than the total earnings of the over *one hundred and thirty* licensed establishments in and around Las Vegas.

Even today, everywhere you look in Atlantic City there are signs of what used to be, the ghostly outline of a nightclub or a hotel on a block that was once teeming and fabulous. Everywhere else you look you see the potential of what's to come, a city trying so hard to reinvent itself that you can practically hear the local officials' collective heaving. It is impossible to experience the *now* of Atlantic City, however, because the whole place is suspended somewhere between the past and the future.

It is no longer what it was, and it is not yet what it will one day be. And it is this quality—the rotting, tarnished city of yore, improbably yoked to the glittering temples of corporate ambition—that gives Atlantic City its frisson. It is a gorgeous and haunted place.

✦

Like any well-meaning addict who tries and fails to get clean over and over again, Atlantic City *wants* to be a better and different kind of city, but the forces aligned against it are just too great. In spite of the extraordinary success of legalized gambling, the resort has had a very difficult time reinventing itself and bouncing back to life. One formidable obstacle is its lack of attractive natural resources. Most of the world's resorts—Miami, Rio, Monte Carlo—exist in such physically spectacular locales that even if they fall on hard times, their intrinsic value can never be diminished. Someone will always come along to rediscover or "save" them.

Atlantic City was built on an unremarkable ten-mile-long strip of sand. There is a beach, but the character of the island before it was transformed in the late nineteenth century was one of windswept isolation, with a landscape of fine, white sand dunes that reached as high as fifty feet, cedar oak and holly trees, duck ponds, swamps, and briar thickets. In the summer, the place swarmed with mosquitoes and greenhead flies. Black snakes, foxes, rabbits, muskrats, and mink infested the island. Not exactly a paradise in waiting.

But that is precisely what made Atlantic City's first heyday in the Victorian era so incredible—it had created so much from so little so quickly. All of Atlantic City's resources—what drew so many people to the island—were *un*natural, which is to say man-made. The machine— the railroad—was what made Atlantic City possible, and then the Boardwalk, the colossal hotels, the gigantic piers, and the crowds followed.

The uninhabited island was known as Absegami, or "Little Sea Water," to the Lenni-Lenape Indians, who used it in the summer months, traveling over a five-mile trail through the marshlands and then rowing across the bay. The Lenni-Lenape gave up their rights to all of south Jersey in a trade with white colonists for things like iron kettles, hoes, knives, and axes. The earliest white landowner was an Englishman named Thomas Budd, a Quaker farmer who arrived in Atlantic County in the late 1670s. The colonists dubbed the strand "Further Island." In 1678, Budd bought fifteen thousand acres of land in Atlantic County—some of it on the island—from William Penn and a group of Quakers, who had received it as payment of a debt owed to them. Budd was basically swindled; the land was, at four cents an acre, practically worthless.

The first official residents were the Leeds, led by the reclusive odd-ball Jeremiah, who built a log cabin around 1785, the first permanent structure on the island at what is now Missouri and Arctic Avenues (almost exactly the spot where Skinny D'Amato would be born and raised and would build his nightclub over 150 years later). Jeremiah's tiny cedar cabin eventually grew into Leed's Plantation, where corn and rye were farmed and cattle raised after he and his ten children cleared the land. He slowly bought up every parcel he could get his hands on, and by the time of his death he owned all but 131 acres (just 1 percent) of what he had called Absecon Island. Jeremiah's sons, Robert and Chalkley, grew up to become the city's first postmaster and mayor, respectively, in 1854. After Jeremiah died in 1838, his second wife, Millicent, got a license to operate Aunt Millie's Boarding House, located where Baltic and Massachusetts Avenues are today. "Board-inghouse" was a bit of a misnomer—Absecon Island's first business was, for all intents and purposes, a bar.

In 1833, the *New Jersey Gazeteer* compiled an index of the resorts along the Jersey shore. Of the eight places listed—including Toms River, Tuckerton, and Somers Point, all of which advertised and took in guests for the season—only Cape May to the south and Long Branch to the north had boardinghouses dedicated exclusively to summer guests. Both of those towns were on the mainland, easily reachable by steam-boat and stagecoach lines from Philadelphia and New York. Speculation about developing Absegami—or any of the other barrier islands dot-ting the one-hundred-plus miles of the Jersey shore line—was almost always met with skepticism about whether a roadbed could be built and maintained through the swampy meadows that separated the island from the mainland.

By 1850, there were seven houses on Absecon Island, and all but one belonged to descendants of Jeremiah Leeds. But the big bang creation moment of Atlantic City was just around the corner. Dr. Jonathan Pitney had been a resident of Absecon village on the mainland since 1820. He had represented Atlantic County at the state constitutional convention in 1844 and had run for Congress in 1848. For twenty-some years Pitney, who owned land on the island, had nursed a fantasy of building a railroad from Philadelphia to the coast with an eye toward developing the wilds of Absegami into a retreat for Philadelphians. He described the climate of the island as "salubrious" and imagined a "health resort" on its shores. The mainlanders dubbed his scheme "Pitney's Folly" and joked about the "railroad to nowhere." After writing a series of letters to Philadelphia newspapers, he assembled a group of landowners and manufacturers from south Jersey, including Samuel Richards, whose family was among the largest landowners in the eastern United States; Richards's holdings included a glassworks and fifty thousand acres in Camden County, which would have to be sliced in half by the railroad. Incidentally, Richards later admitted that when he first saw Absecon Island, he thought it was "the most horrible place to make the termination of a railroad" that he'd ever seen.

Pitney and his new partners enlisted the help of Richard Osborne, a nationally known civil engineer who was born in England and educated in Chicago, and had seen the power and wonder of towns booming in the West. He had also seen how easily fortunes could be carved out of virtually nothing simply by building a railroad. He predicted that "Pitney's Folly" would one day overtake Cape May as the nation's premier ocean resort. "The work worn artisan shut up in the close and debilitating shops of the city," he declared, "whose limited means prevents a long absence from his calling, will find here the rest and recreation that he cannot now obtain." Cape May—which was, believe it or not, America's first seashore resort—catered exclusively to wealthy businessmen from Philadelphia and Baltimore and until the Civil War had been a regular vacation place for the elite planter families of Virginia and Maryland, as well as the summer retreat for a few presidents. Frederika Bremer, a travel writer and novelist from Sweden, reported back to her people at home about this strange new sport, "seabathing," that she witnessed in Cape May. "Men, women and children, in red, blue, and yellow pantaloons . . . go out into the sea in crowds, and leap up and down in the heaving waves amid great laughter and merriment." But seabathing was a curious new custom that was available only to those who could afford to get to—and stay in—Cape May; there was no such thing as an ocean resort for the lower and middle classes. Though Pitney had planned to build a resort that would compete with Cape May, Osborne had intuited that cheap railroad travel to the Atlantic Ocean was going to create a distinctly different kind of watering hole.

One day in 1852, Osborne led a group of Philadelphia capitalists to the island to share with them Dr. Pitney's vision of the future and to convince them to invest in the railroad company they would eventually form. Pitney coaxed a charter for the railroad out of the New Jersey State Legislature in March 1852 and, with the help of Osborne, persuaded his backers that the risk was minimal. The Camden & Atlantic Railroad was formed, and in June 1852, ten thousand shares of stock were sold in one day to thirty-eight investors at $50 a share. By this time, Jeremiah Leeds was long gone and his heirs were no longer interested in farming, so Pitney and Richards were able to buy most of Absecon Island. The Leeds demanded $25 per acre but ultimately settled for $17.50. After the railroad was finished, some of these same parcels sold for $300 per acre, beginning in earnest Atlantic City's peculiar relationship to real estate speculation. Osborne confidently announced that the seaside village would one day become "the lungs of Philadelphia."

Several potential names for the future resort were suggested— Ocean City, Seabeach, Surfing, Strand, and Bath—until one day Osborne unfurled a map of the town survey for the investors with the words *Atlantic City* emblazoned across the top of it. Twenty-five years later, Osborne recalled, "I have ever claimed, and do so now, that this name created in the minds of men throughout the Union a certain interest in the city, and this interest it was sought to further secure by giving to each state its own avenue."

Naming things is always tricky business, especially when there's no thing yet. It is an inherently hopeful, forward-looking act. The right name can sometimes seem to make all the difference in the perception of a new enterprise. The name Atlantic City is wonderfully generic, but at the same time it has a whiff of rosy, can-do optimism about it—like Universal Pictures or Standard Oil. The fact that the city was, at the outset, designed with broad avenues running parallel to the ocean—named Pacific, Atlantic, Arctic, Baltic, Mediterranean, Adriatic—with the streets cutting across given the names of the states, only added to the sense that its founders had high hopes. Their new resort was going to be a kind of Oz on the ocean, and they purposefully encoded into its DNA a grandiose, if cloying, Americanism, hoping that Atlantic City would one day become a symbol of the lower- and middle-class yearning to lighten up and live a little. (And, in fact, that is precisely what happened: some seventy years after the resort was founded, Bruce Bliven wrote in *The New Republic*, "When Americans dream of that perfect society which is some day to be, what form does that imagining take? Atlantic City, New Jersey.")

The fact that the resort would one day become the inspiration for Monopoly, the most popular board game in history, threw the crass symbolism of America at play into high relief. Today you can almost wonder which came first, the city or the game. When I lived in Atlantic City and would, from time to time, find myself *noticing* that I was on Park Place or Baltic or Marvin Gardens, I would laugh out loud, because it could suddenly seem so absurd. I wasn't in a "real" place; I was living on a board game.

✦

On March 3, 1854, the governor of New Jersey approved the city charter, and on May 1, 1855, the city was incorporated. The first train from Camden to Atlantic City took two and a half hours and arrived on July 1, 1854, with six hundred people, including members of the press, Philadelphia dignitaries, and a brass band. Richard Osborne later recalled that the train—nine cars long—left Camden at nine-thirty A.M., and by noon guests were steaming up Atlantic Avenue toward the nearly completed United States Hotel—the largest in the nation at the time. The six hundred guests gathered in the large saloon of the hotel and listened to self-congratulatory speeches. So there you have it: The future unholy city of the hoi polloi exists where it does for the most boring of all possible reasons. It lies at one end of a perfectly straight line, the shortest distance between two points—Philadelphia and the Atlantic Ocean.

A train to Atlantic City made it possible for the first time for people to get to the ocean from Philadelphia in the morning and return later that evening. Day-tripping was born. The resort became a place where people could go for very brief vacations. Within the next few years, wood-frame buildings began to sprout up in the northern end of the island, among them a few dozen houses, three churches, a lighthouse, a market, several railroad structures, the Surf House, the Mansion, and Congress Hall. Accommodations were fairly primitive, with no running water or indoor plumbing. The roads remained ungraded while pigs, cows, and goats roamed free on the island. First-time visitors, expecting the relative luxury of Cape May, were often painfully disappointed.

By 1855 there were seventy-one structures, mostly boardinghouses, but the fledgling resort was suffering from bad publicity. In August 1857, a nor'easter sent visitors scampering back to Philadelphia before the season was up. During the winter that followed, severe storm tides flooded the battered, eroding island and left unusually large, shallow ponds of stagnant water—a perfect breeding ground for insects. During the 1858 summer season, all hell broke loose. Horses covered hoof to mane with bloodsucking flies rolled in the streets for relief, and cattle waded into the surf to flee the hungry insects. Island visitors wore nets over their faces and begged the railroad conductors to take them back early. The panic of those two summers nearly wiped out the railroad, which offered $1 round-trip fares in an effort to recover.

By 1860, the year of the first census, Atlantic City had a year-round population of 687 and a capacity to accommodate 4,000 tourists. While the city had established itself with well-off Philadelphians—especially Quakers—the resort was not exactly taking off in the way its founders had hoped. It was nothing more than a village of cottages and boardinghouses. The start of the Civil War brought the city's growth to a grinding halt, and it didn't really recover until ten years later, when the first boardwalk was built, in 1870. Although the 1870s were a time of economic depression in America, this was precisely when Atlantic City began to boom as a popular resort, thanks largely to the growth of industrial society.

Two critical steps led to the surprising and explosive growth of Atlantic City. William Sellers, a Philadelphia industrialist, the president of the Franklin Institute, and a world-class manufacturer of machines, was, quite plainly, the man who realized that the screw in one machine shop ought to be the same size as the screw in the next machine shop. Standardization was a simple but very big idea, and it changed the world in many ways, leading to, among other things, the Pennsylvania Railroad, which was the first to adopt his standard.

Standardization also put Philadelphia in charge of the industrial process and transformed it into a vital urban center—a position that is hard to imagine today, given the city's current backwater status. Sellers had an adopted nephew named Frederick W. Taylor, who worked in one of his plants; through his revolutionary management and efficiency principles, many of which are still in use today, he increased productivity in Sellers's steel plants even further and, in so doing, increased the workers' salaries. By raising wages, the factory owners encouraged labor harmony. So even though the work became numbingly boring, the workers all looked forward to the weekend. Standardization of industry created the modern worker-as-consumer, whose goal was no longer a more pleasant and equitable workplace, but more money in the paycheck so that he could buy new furniture on Market Street and spend a week in Atlantic City. The working-class demand for leisure was born.

By 1872, the Camden & Atlantic had improved the ride—it was now faster and smoother, and there were windows on the cars to keep out the dust and soot. Two years later, five hundred thousand people made the trip to Atlantic City. Then, in April 1877, construction began on the newer, cheaper, narrow-gauge line; fifty-four miles of railroad were laid down in just ninety days. When the first train of the new Philadelphia–Atlantic City line left the station, the price of the trip had fallen from $3 round trip on the Camden & Atlantic to $1.50 on these new "excursion" trains, making the trip affordable to hundreds of thousands of new people.

While the average Joes of Philadelphia were being transformed into vacation-loving consumers, the wilderness of Absecon Island was being tamed and turned into an urban wonderland at the beach. Until the Boardwalk came along, Atlantic Avenue had been the center of resort activity. Except for a few hours in the morning, the beach was empty and forbidding, littered with rotting shipwrecks. At night it was terrifying, described by one visitor as "a scene of desolation, dark in the moon shadows of tufted hummocks, and sinister with the sounds of crawling crabs and the clank of their snapping claws." Lounging on the beach and swimming in the ocean were not yet popular leisure activities. Initially, people traveled to Atlantic City mostly for the novelty of taking a train to the ocean in a couple of hours. But the novelty quickly wore off, and the burgeoning city was becoming a place where people went not necessarily to look at the ocean and, perhaps, dip their toes in, but to stroll along an esplanade and socialize, show off and people-watch, with the ocean and beach as mere backdrop. In fact, most benches along the Boardwalk, then as today, face the city, not the ocean.

Boardwalk in Atlantic City is a proper noun—a street address. It's not the boardwalk. It's simply . . . Boardwalk. Or *the* Boardwalk. The structure itself grew in height, length, and width in five stages. The first was a temporary walk laid down in twelve-feet-long sections at the beginning of every summer to keep sand out of people's shoes—and out of the carpets back at the hotels. At the end of the season, it was packed up and put away for the winter. The second boardwalk, also temporary, was built in 1880 and was a bit longer and wider. By 1883, over one hundred businesses had permanent, capital-B Boardwalk addresses. In 1884, a storm demolished the walkway, so the next incarnation was built on pilings five feet above the beach. A hurricane destroyed that structure in 1889, and by the following spring, a fourth boardwalk appeared, this one twenty-four feet wide, ten feet high, and nearly four miles long, with railings along each side. An expanded fifth and final structure was built by the Phoenix Bridge Company in 1896, supported by steel pilings and girders forty feet wide—essentially the same Boardwalk that exists today.

Like seemingly everything else in Atlantic City, the Boardwalk came into existence for the most prosaic of reasons (keeping sand out of the shoes and carpets) and then grew almost immediately into an institution—and the city's raison d'être. People came from all over the country, but mainly from the Northeast, to experience this Boardwalk—the Champs-Élysées of New Jersey. The ocean was upstaged by the spontaneous and ever shifting social event that the Boardwalk became. Whenever I look at old pictures of the well-dressed—seemingly all in black—throngs on the Boardwalk from Victorian America, it is obvious that they are having an experience unavailable to us today: the thrill of being caught up in a radically different way of gathering together as humans. They all look surprised.

As Charles Funnell wrote in *By the Beautiful Sea*, a wonderfully dry and rigorous dissection of Victorian Atlantic City, "The thousands of different people who flocked to the city shared an extraordinary community of feeling which could not exist under normal urban conditions, because, unlike the conventional city, Atlantic City had a single purpose. The Boardwalk was a stage, upon which there was a temporary suspension of disbelief; behavior that was exaggerated, even ridiculous, in everyday life was expected at the resort. The rigidities of Victorian life relaxed, permitting contact between strangers and the pursuit of fantasies.... The town was a gargantuan masquerade, as visitor deceived visitor.... And people wanted to be deceived, to see life other than it was, to pretend to be more than they were."

Though this particular aspect of Atlantic City was born in the Victorian era, it came to define the place for decades afterward. In fact, it was this very quality—the gargantuan masquerade—that would allow Skinny to one day reinvent himself from a poor kid with street smarts to the ultimate connected guy. The success of his nightclub would hinge upon this basic human craving in regular folk to "pretend to be more than they were."

✦

As the Boardwalk became the city's main thoroughfare, nicely framing the ocean view, the next stage of Atlantic City's development seemed intended to obliterate nature altogether. Colonel George Howard built the first public amusement pier in 1882. It was 650 feet long, and it floated away in a nor'easter two months later. He built another, and a storm-tossed schooner destroyed it. In 1884, James R. Applegate built a pier at the foot of Tennessee Avenue. It was stronger than the first two, multitiered, and 625 feet long, and it featured a large pavilion suspended over the water into which Applegate booked vaudeville shows and concerts. It also housed a large public icewater fountain that used a ton and a half of ice daily. In 1887 came the thousand-foot-long Iron Pier, which was bought twelve years later by H. J. Heinz, who installed a gigantic illuminated "57" (as in varieties) sign that loomed out over the Atlantic Ocean—the resort's answer to New York's smoking Camel sign—until the pier was destroyed by a hurricane in 1944. And then more piers, each longer and bigger and more elaborate than the last, kept coming: Young's Ocean Pier, where Sarah Bernhardt made her Atlantic City debut in a performance of *La dame aux camélias* (Camille); Young's Million Dollar Pier, where Harry Houdini entertained thousands by "disappearing" and where Bull Moose candidate Teddy Roosevelt gave a campaign speech; Steel Pier (which eventually became known as the "Showplace of a Nation"); then Steeplechase, Garden, and Central Piers.

If the pier developers were trying to build out atop the ocean and extend the city over it, they nearly succeeded. You could dine, dance, bathe, shop, go to church, and, in one case, *live* on the piers and the Boardwalk. In 1908, Captain John Young built a flagrant Italianate villa from imported marble on his Million Dollar Pier and hired his lifelong friend Thomas Edison to design the pastel lighting concept for the sculpture garden that surrounded it. The address? Number One, Atlantic Ocean. Eventually the hotel owners on the other side of the Boardwalk, whose ocean views were being ruined by these monstrous stationary cruise ships, threw up a stink, and further development was stopped. Laws were passed that said no more structures could be built on the ocean side of the Boardwalk.

Ironically, the ocean view was never really in danger of disappearing; it was the hotels that were, though not until many years later. Their destruction is, without question, the biggest crime Atlantic City has ever committed and the saddest thing that happened to the resort, a loss on par with the destruction of the original Penn Station in New York in the early sixties. When you look at pictures of these lost hotels, it wrenches the heart. And while there were many exceptional hotels along the Boardwalk, only two were truly important pieces of architecture, both designed by the great Philadelphia architect William Price.

Following the lead of Cape May, Atlantic City's first hotels were long, modest wood-frame structures with verandahs surrounding the entire ground floor to catch the "healthful" salt air. (Atlantic City, perhaps trying to corner the market on hype and quackery in those days, deceptively billed itself as a curative wonderland; much was written about the city's magic "ozone," which was purported to rid people of nearly any disease or ailment.) Because land was at a premium, the hotels were built perpendicular to the beach, usually in an L shape. But as more competing railroads began to steam across New Jersey and the cost of the journey decreased, more and more tourists came to the resort and the hotels got bigger, fancier, and in some cases just plain bizarre, especially along the prime Boardwalk sites. At the turn of the century, there were hundreds of boardinghouses, but the major Boardwalk hotels were the original Traymore, the Seaside, the St. Charles, the Chalfonte–Haddon Hall, and the Shelburne—all spindly firetraps of a conservative Victorian sensibility. Price's first Atlantic City hotel was the shingle-style Marlborough, more modern than the others but not quite the breakthrough that was about to come.

In the first decade of the 1900s, Price changed the face of the Boardwalk by constructing his two great reinforced-concrete hotels, the Blenheim and the new Traymore. Both structures were the culmination of fifty years of development throughout the country, and they rose like cathedrals at the edge of the Atlantic Ocean, making something more permanent of the resort and solidifying its status as not just hucksterville, but also a cosmopolitan destination for the wealthy—the so-called city-by-the-sea. The Blenheim, with its English aura (it was named after the Blenheim, the home of the Duke of Marlborough), magnificent dome and towering chimneys, and modern conveniences (it was the first hotel to have a private bath in every room), cost $2 million and was completed in 1906; it touched off a luxury hotel boom that lasted for nearly thirty years. The Blenheim was followed by the Dennis and the Chalfonte–Haddon Hall. Finally, the mother of all hotels, the new Traymore, was completed in 1915 to the tune of $4 million—a soaring concrete-and-steel colossus that could accommodate over three thousand guests. In fact, it was the first art deco building ever, the very model for the skyscrapers that rose ten years later in New York. It was also the first building with a branded identity: everything from the menus and cocktail shakers to the sleek modern furniture and sculpted interior walls was orchestrated by Price to be part of a larger, single identity. Its most remarkable feature was the Submarine Grill, a supper club designed to look as though you were under the ocean. Above the lounge, on a roof deck, was a fish pond with a glass bottom that doubled as the lounge's ceiling. At night, the lights that were beamed through the pond cast shadows of fish onto the dance floor. The Traymore became one of the first great landmarks in America. Pictures of it showed up on candy boxes and purses and other souvenirs that visitors to Atlantic City brought home so they could say to their friends: "I've been to the Traymore . . . I've seen the modern world."

✦

What has always separated Atlantic City from every other East Coast resort is its scale. It is a "big city" in a small beach town—an anomaly. One is constantly struck by the juxtaposition of these two very different cultures. On one block, you could experience the very worst aspects of New York City—honking traffic jams, bus fumes, junkies, street hustlers—and on the next block, you could see a family in their bathing suits and flip-flops, headed for the beach.

This, of course, is where Atlantic City's other insurmountable obstacle lies. It's not city enough for some and not beach enough for others. The only other place in America where the beach and city are so close together is South Beach, Miami, but that analogy fails when you consider that the downtown business center—the actual city of Miami—is several miles from the shoreline, on the mainland. *Everything* in Atlantic City is on the island, literally steps to the beach.

This seems mostly to do with the fact that Atlantic City was built as an extension of Philadelphia. It's as if, instead of escaping from the city, Philadelphians decided to bring the whole damn thing—including noise, dirt, and chaos—with them to the shore. Unlike Coney Island, which was built as a commuter amusement park for New York City, Atlantic City wanted to be more like Newport, Rhode Island. In other words, the resort was just the right distance from Philadelphia to be considered a retreat; though it was a short trip, it was a journey nonetheless, so psychologically it made visitors feel as if they had traveled to *somewhere*. They could leave their working-class lives behind for the weekend and live differently in Atlantic City for forty-eight glorious, decadent hours.

If Atlantic City held itself above other shore towns with boardwalks for reasons to do with size and grandeur, it had another legitimate reason to be a little full of itself: It was becoming a vital stage in the development of American entertainment. In the late 1800s, vaudeville thrived in Atlantic City and then quickly evolved into a considerably more mainstream showbiz staple: the variety show. By 1900, one of the most successful acts in town was John Murphy and his Original Murphy's Minstrels, featuring none other than W. C. Fields as "America's Greatest Comic Juggler."

The first *Ziegfeld Follies* debuted in Atlantic City in 1906 and moved to Broadway the following year. In fact, the city became Broadway's most important incubator—throughout the first third of the twentieth century, more than 1,100 plays had their "out of town" opening in Atlantic City. The first movie house, the Bijou, opened on Atlantic Avenue in 1903, and by the 1920s, there were a few dozen movie theaters around town—some of them palatial. In 1929, Harry Warner spent a fortune building the Warner Theater on the Boardwalk—from its terra-cotta facade and terrazzo floors to the gilt-framed mirrors and twinkling lights embedded in the fresco on the domed ceiling, the place was plush and huge, seating over two thousand people. (The gorgeous facade remains and has been incorporated, somewhat awkwardly, into the Boardwalk frontage of Caesars.) Indeed, Atlantic City went movie mad during the Depression, and scores of Hollywood premieres unfolded on the Boardwalk.

The same year the first movie theater opened, 1903, John Philip Sousa and his band were booked into Steeplechase Pier and spent the next twenty summers setting up shop on the Boardwalk, partly because Sousa married a local girl. Irving Berlin spent summers writing songs in Atlantic City, and George Gershwin started out plugging *his* songs on the Boardwalk. It is astonishing to realize just how many of the icons of early-twentieth-century entertainment either got their break or spent time polishing their acts in Atlantic City.

By 1890 the year-round population of Atlantic City was 13,000. Ten years later it had more than doubled, and by 1910 it was at 46,000, reaching an early, first peak in 1915 of 51,667. Beyond this explosive growth was the huge and ever expanding weekend population who poured into town on frequent and cheap trains. For example, *The Philadelphia Inquirer* estimated that 100,000 people traveled to Atlantic City on August 27, 1893, on a day or weekend excursion. One of the most telling sets of statistics from this same era is that at the turn of the century, Philadelphia had 1,203 saloons, or 1.15 per 1,000 population; New York City had 7,579, or 5 per 1,000 population; Atlantic City had 190, or *14.55 per 1,000*!

The combination of so many saloons and show business culture had turned Atlantic City into a kind of Times Square at the beach. And where there are show folk and booze, prostitution is usually lurking just around the corner. "What community would hail, as a blessing, or as evidence of prosperity, the establishment of a vile brothel in its midst?" wrote the *Philadelphia Bulletin*. "There are more than one hundred of these dens of infamy in Atlantic City. Just think of it—one hundred such places in a city of this size!" The *Bulletin* was Philadelphia's most well-read newspaper, and in August 1890, they began publishing a series of front-page exposés on prostitution in the resort that caused a sensation. Initially, there was no red-light district per se in Atlantic City. The brothels were mixed in with the rest of the community, but eventually Chalfonte Alley became well-known as the place to go to pay for sex. This was mostly shrugged off by the neighbors; in fact, many saloons and restaurants had an entrance marked "Ladies," where respectable women could avoid prostitutes and their customers.

Shortly after the turn of the century, Atlantic City's personality began to split, and the Boardwalk represented a physical and psychic boundary between the two halves. On one side, there was the beach and the ocean and all the recreation that went with it, which was to say good, clean family fun. There were tacky souvenirs and games; there were early versions of Boardwalk rides, including a precursor to the Ferris wheel, one of the world's very first roller coaster, and a gigantic sliding board. There were dance contests and pageants and any number of cruel absurdities passed off as entertainment that the city became famous for (boxing cats! the diving horse! a girl with two heads!). On the other side of the Boardwalk, down dark, narrow side streets like Westminster Place, known as Snake Alley, the city was a banquet of temptation: sex, gambling, booze, drugs, gay bars, and black speakeasies. It had also become—as it remains—one of the first and only twenty-four-hour cities in America. Even today, you can say that of only New York, Las Vegas, and New Orleans. Other great cities with a lot of nightlife—Miami, Los Angeles, Chicago—all have relatively sane bedtimes.

"Atlantic City is not a treat for the introspective," wrote James Huneker in the *New Cosmopolis* in 1915. "It is all on the surface; it is hard, glittering, unspeakably cacophonous, and it never sleeps at all. Three days and you crave the comparative solitude of Broadway and Thirty-fourth Street; a week and you may die of insomnia."

✦

Skinny D'Amato was born on December 1, 1908, just a few months after one of the most unsettling and defining summers in Atlantic City's history. That August, the newly elected governor of New Jersey, John Franklin Fort, took up his campaign promise to promote civic virtue by enforcing the Bishops' Law (so-called because of the four Catholic and Episcopalian bishops who lobbied for the bill), a three-year-old, largely ignored bit of state legislation that was intended to curb Sunday operation of saloons. On August 12, Atlantic County prosecutor Clarence Goldenberg, in an effort to throw the state a bone, made public a list of sixteen known gambling houses—eight frequented by whites and eight by blacks. It backfired. Fort—with his Excise Probing Commission behind him—decided to make Atlantic City ground zero in his war against vice; he demanded of Goldenberg that "gambling houses, opium joints and dens of similar character" in Atlantic City "be wiped out."

Shortly afterward, an Atlantic County grand jury failed to indict several saloon keepers in flagrant violation of the Sunday closing law, and on August 27, Governor Fort went ballistic, threatening to call out the militia to rule the streets of Atlantic City by martial law if the resort didn't clean up its act. Then he took his campaign to the press:

> *To the People of the State of New Jersey:*
>
> *The State Excise Commission in session in Atlantic City on the third day of August, last, took testimony and heard statements which it can safely be said astonished all good citizens of the state. . . .*
>
> *No one in office or before that Commission questioned the fact that street walking, gambling, houses of ill-fame, people of ill-repute, and obscene pictures and open violation of the excise laws existed in Atlantic City. A leading citizen said before that Commission: "The citizens are alarmed that it is as it is now, and conditions are something terrible right here at the present time in this city. Never in the history of the city has it been worse. Never have the notorious street walkers been worse than they have been recently. Never has gambling been more open and more of it in the city than right now. . . . The police department and officials of the city all know it; they are all aware of it, or could find out if they wanted to. . . ."*

The predictable cracking down on vice and what must have seemed at the time as the outrageous threat of militia crawling up and down Atlantic and Pacific Avenues was not, in and of itself, a defining moment for Atlantic City; a similar, if less hysterical, effort had been made some years earlier at forcing temperance on the decadent beast that the resort was becoming. Rather, it was the city's *reaction* that marked the beginning of something big, which was that the business owners, law enforcers, and politicians closed ranks and decided to agree among themselves who would be sacrificed on the altar of virtue to please the state legislature and reform movement prudes led by Evangelical Protestants. For example, a grand jury indicted some token proprietors of blatantly offensive establishments and a vendor of "immodest postal cards." A few speakeasies were raided, and gambling folk were warned to lie low for a while. In other words, Atlantic City would *pretend* to care about the law and who was breaking it, but the business of providing forbidden pleasure would remain priority number one. Atlantic City's self-deception—Sin City masquerading as a family resort—was too embedded in its character for it to change. Enoch L. "Nucky" Johnson—a man who would come to rule Atlantic City with a corrupt iron fist, but who was at this time merely the county sheriff—spoke for nearly every hotel, saloon, brothel, and gambling hall owner in town when he said that "thousands of people would never come here again if the soldiers were in possession of the resort for even so much as one Sunday."

Even Reverend Sydney Goodman opposed the Sunday restrictions. Admittedly, he was not your average man of the cloth; Goodman was pastor of the "Men's Church," where he encouraged the single young men who attended his services to smoke during the sermon. In the middle of the militia controversy, one that was covered gleefully by all the Philadelphia newspapers, Goodman delivered an audacious reprimand titled "Fear Not, Atlantic City," in which he posited that the public did not expect Atlantic City to be "a paragon of virtue and pose as an example for the entire State and Nation . . . the laws should be adjusted to meet the views of the communities to which they apply." Gambling, he added, was a vice as old as dirt and an unavoidable outgrowth of "cosmopolitan" life.

✦

Is it possible that a newborn baby could absorb the hubbub in the air around him so completely that it would come to define his entire life? That Skinny was born during the year Atlantic City was forced to wrestle with its psychic split—family resort versus Babylon—seems almost too neat. But it is an irresistible fact nevertheless. The way Atlantic City chose to deal with the conflict was to have its cake and eat it, too. How else to explain Skinny?

He was born Pasquale Emilio D'Amato on Willow Avenue, a little side street off Arctic Avenue in the back bay neighborhood of Atlantic City that would come to be called Ducktown. Pasquale was changed to

Paul when he was still a child, because his father had a falling-out with his best friend, Pasquale, who he had named his first-born son after; his boyhood chums tagged him "Skinny" when he was thirteen and already nearly six feet tall. (His friends also called him "the Dart," a nickname he detested.) Skinny's father, Emilio, was an immigrant from Naples, and his mother, Maria, had been born in Atlantic City. Skinny liked to brag that his family had been in Atlantic City for six generations, "the oldest Italian family in town," he claimed. All told, Maria gave birth to eight children: Marie, Rose, Skinny, Emil (whom everyone called Willie), Columbia, Antoinette (whom everyone called Pat), and two Josephs, one of whom died shortly after birth and the other when he was seven (he fell at school, hit his head on a desk, and died two days later).

Emilio D'Amato was a barber; he rented space on the ground floor of a fairly big apartment building on the corner of Missouri and Arctic Avenues and ran his shop there until he bought a bar with a small restaurant. A hard worker, Emilio must have been ambitious as well, working his way up the scale of proprietorship. He was well liked in the close-knit neighborhood dominated by Italians, but that also included Jewish and Irish working-class families. His best friends were the other business owners (butcher, grocer, and tailor) who all belonged to the local social clubs—the Garibaldi, the Royal Order of the Moose, the Sons of Italy—where they played card games learned back in the old country.

Maria DiSanti D'Amato's great-grandparents had immigrated to America from Naples in the 1800s and settled in Atlantic City, and her grandparents eventually came to own several row houses on North Texas Avenue. Maria's mother was a crank—everyone in the neighborhood was afraid of her. Maria, however, was "loved by everyone" according to a neighbor, Anna Bunting, who was best friends with Skinny's sister Columbia. "Mrs. D'Amato used to play the piano by ear and we would sing our hearts out," said Bunting. "She taught me all those songs: 'When Your Old Wedding Ring Was New' and 'I Want a Girl (Just Like the Girl That Married Dear Old Dad).' She used to play the Italian songs for me because I speak fluently and none of her children did. But both of Skinny's parents spoke beautiful English, and I used to like to be around Maria because of that. She was a sweetheart, and she was so nice to all of us neighborhood kids. And very pretty."

Around 1920, the D'Amatos built and moved into a two-story, six-room row house on Missouri Avenue, half a block from their previous home on land given to them by a DiSanti relative. Downstairs, there were a living room, dining room, and kitchen; upstairs, there were three bedrooms. According to Skinny's sister-in-law Grace D'Amato, Skinny started running away from home and playing hooky from school around the time they moved to Missouri Avenue.

When he was in school, he ran craps and card games in the playground. All the Italian kids in the neighborhood attended St. Michael's, a Catholic school and church that are still standing on Mississippi Avenue. "Skinny used to like to gamble behind St. Michael's church with my brother Frankie," said Bunting. "All of the boys used to go back behind St. Michael's and shoot craps. They *loved* to shoot craps. I remember my father would chase them." Skinny often put Frankie's kid sister on lookout. "I used to have to tell my brother, 'Poppy's coming!' I know my father wanted to kill them for gambling."

When he wasn't in school, Skinny set up his games anywhere he could: in vacant houses, on the train platform, or at street corners. Whenever he was caught, Emilio punished his wayward son severely, which led to his running away again. Skinny's brother Willie knew where all of his hideouts were, and Maria would send her younger son with clothing and food.

There are very few photographs of Skinny as a boy, but two have survived from 1922, both of them taken on the beach in Atlantic City just before Skinny's young life would be shattered by tragedy. In one picture, there's a group of about twenty kids, all of them in their midteens, equally mixed among boys and girls. There's something about the way they're all hanging on one another that suggests there was a natural intimacy, that this was a close-knit group of friends. Skinny is lying in the sand in front of the group wearing a black, one-piece tank bathing suit. He's lounging in a graceful, almost seductive pose and has the unmistakable air of someone with an excess of confidence. He is already slyly handsome. Behind the group, you can see the Traymore looming ominously, like a sleeping dinosaur.

Around the time this photograph was taken, Skinny began working for his father, who had opened up his café, Emilio's, on Missouri Avenue, no more than five hundred yards from where Skinny was born and right on the very spot where he would one day own his nightclub. The café became a favorite take-out joint for a few gangsters who spent the summers in Margate, and Emilio would dispatch Skinny and Willie to deliver food to them by trolley car. No one has ever suggested that Emilio had any connection to the Mob, and, in fact, it seems very unlikely, considering his reaction to Skinny's gambling and his strict, hardworking aspect. (Though he was arrested once in 1923 for a violation of Prohibition.) But one can only imagine that Skinny, who had already rejected his father's values and had assumed his role as street-smart leader—the kid in the picture on the beach, in charge of his group—must have been thrilled to make these deliveries.

In 1923, when Skinny was thirteen, his father died of a stroke. Emilio was only thirty-eight years old, and he left his family with a debt-laden business and a house with a lien on it. Apparently, Emilio was a soft touch for the down-and-out and had lent a lot of money and bailed several people out of jail—expansive gestures that often went only one way. This, alas, would become one of Skinny's hallmarks—and the root cause of his downfall. Every single person who knew Skinny has a story about how obscenely generous he was and how he lent money to people from every corner of his life. As his daughter Paulajane said, not a little bitter, "If I had all the money that was owed to my father, I'd be a millionaire."

Atlantic City mythology has it that when Emilio died, Skinny—a thirteen-year-old with only a second-grade education—became the man of the house and the breadwinner. But according to his sister-in-law Grace D'Amato, Skinny moved out of the house on Missouri Avenue after his father died and *Willie* took over the responsibilities of supporting the family, quitting school when he was ten so that he could work as a delivery boy for John Capone's meat market and giving Maria all his earnings at the end of every week.

Shortly after Emilio died, Maria met and started dating a police officer, but before long, she too died at the age of thirty-eight. There's a bit of mystery surrounding her death. Paulajane had always been told that

Skinny's mother died from appendicitis. But when Anna Bunting was asked how Maria died, she said, "I would rather not say about that. I wouldn't want to do that to her memory." Antoinette Norma Malone, the daughter of Skinny's oldest sister, Marie, said, "She died from her teeth! She didn't take care of her teeth, and poison went through her system." An abscess left untreated can spread to the heart and the brain and ultimately lead to death. It's not hard to imagine how there could be shame attached to such a pointless and unnecessary loss of life, which would explain the mystery, to say nothing of why the song "Mamma" would reduce Skinny to tears for the rest of his life.

There are conflicting stories about what happened next. At some point during Skinny's teenage years—perhaps after his father died, or maybe after his mother's death—he went to live in South Philadelphia. Skinny once told a reporter that after both his parents died, "I was shipped off to some relatives in Pennsylvania for a couple of years, but I got back to Atlantic City by the time I was fifteen." Dolores Del Raso, who lived next door to Skinny years later in Ventnor and became very close to him, said, "The family he lived with were relatives—an aunt or something—and their name was Caputo. They lived between Twelfth and Thirteenth Streets on Ellsworth, right on my street. That was his connection to South Philly. He stayed there for a couple years and then came back to Atlantic City when he was still a kid."

By the time Maria D'Amato died, Skinny's older sisters were beginning to live their own lives. Marie married Joe Ravielli, a barber and musician, and they moved into one of their grandmother's apartments on North Texas Avenue, where they had two daughters. Rose was a lesbian who opened a speakeasy during Prohibition in the Inlet—on the very last block, facing the seawall; called Topsie's, it was known for decades as a gay bar. Columbia married John Scannapieco and, according to Bunting, "had bad times." Years later, when Skinny became successful, "he used to pay her rent, send coal there. She had four children, and Skinny worried about her. She and John married when they were very young and they never had anything."

And there was Pat, the baby, who was twelve years younger than Skinny and, according to Antoinette Malone, "absolutely gorgeous. When you walked with her you thought you were with Hedy Lamarr."

When Maria died, Pat, who was just a baby, was sent to live in Cleveland with her aunt Dirna D'Amato. Pat's son, Al Cohen, who is today the vice president of Local 54, the hotel and restaurant union in Atlantic City, said, "There's a lot of D'Amatos in and around Cleveland. My uncle Vito was a cook, and he was part owner of a restaurant in Cleveland called Quinn's. Apparently they all ended up doing very well." But as far as shedding any further light on his mother's young life, forget it. "She was doing *something* out there," he said, "but it was always kept very, very quiet. No one talked about it. My mother *never* talked about it."

At one point, said Paulajane, "my father found out that Aunt Pat was working onstage as a showgirl, and he drove all the way to Cleveland and pulled her off the stage. I remember Aunt Pat telling me that when she saw him she was onstage doing her little two-step and he walked into the back of the room and she almost dropped her drawers. He walked up to the edge of the stage and snapped his fingers, and she got right off."

Skinny, said Cohen, apparently objected to Pat's lifestyle, and he went there to get her and bring her home when she was about seventeen. Not long after she arrived back in Atlantic City, Pat met and married a businessman, Sammy Cohen, who was seventeen years older than her. They eventually settled in Margate, had five kids, and opened two bars in the late 1940s—the Gables, which was on the bay, and the White House, near the ocean on Atlantic Avenue. Skinny and Pat were, said Cohen, "the closest of all of the brothers and sisters," which would explain why Skinny objected so strenuously to her being a showgirl.

It is worth noting that Skinny himself had a brief flirtation with the stage. On the corner of Missouri and Atlantic, just across the street from where the 500 Club would one day stand, was the Earle Theatre, a place that featured mostly vaudeville through the twenties and thirties. One night a week they had an amateur contest, and Skinny, who was a naturally talented dancer, entered the contest a few times and performed a tap routine. If he ever nursed any real fantasies about being the center of attention, these forays into show business must have disabused him of the notion, because he got onstage only twice more in his entire life.

When he was fifteen, Skinny felt that he'd at least have to *try* to honor his father by getting a real job. He lied about his age and landed a spot working on a construction site, but all it took was one life-threatening moment—he was nearly blown off a very high scaffolding—and that was the end of that. Right then and there, Skinny gave up altogether on the idea of an honest, workingman's life and set about launching himself down a road that he must have thought was more promising than construction—or at least more fun. He borrowed $40 from his uncle John DiSanti and, with it, rented out the ground floor of a tenement at 2209 Arctic Avenue, a building that is, remarkably, still standing. (It's in a part of town that has been eviscerated by urban blight as well as the construction of a new entryway to the Atlantic City Expressway and the $330 million tunnel to the Marina District that was completed in 2001 and bitterly fought over by Donald Trump and Steve Wynn.)

"It was only a sawdust joint," Skinny once said. "Nothing classy. Sawdust on the floor and lots of betting in the back of a cigar store. I never did sell a single cigar there. Never even had 'em there. I opened the place for $40 that I borrowed from my uncle. The pool table we shot craps on cost $10, the dining room table that we used for cards cost $10. I just cut the middle out of the table so the dealer could stand in it and deal blackjack. And the rest paid the rent, which was cheap in them days. I used to run little craps and card games there. Nothing big. For $3, anyone could get in the game. But as time went on, I'd get a bigger joint and then a bigger joint. I had a following, people who liked me, so I did all right."

There was a pool table in the back of the cigar store because Skinny's first real expertise wasn't playing cards—he was a pool hustler. But he quickly realized there was more money in cards, and before long he had become known as the "master shuffler," a nickname that referred not just to his skill with a deck, but also to his unerring ability to mix together people from different walks of life. "He uses a lavender touch," an old-time bookmaker once said of Skinny. "You don't have a chance. He can take your pants off before you realize what's happening." Skinny's friends sensed he was going places and—some happily, some begrudgingly—fell in line behind him.

✳

One evening, I drove to Toms River to have dinner with Joe DiSanti, Skinny's cousin, the son of the man who gave Skinny the $40 that helped launch him into history. Joe lives with his wife in a palatial Victorian house in a neighborhood called Island Heights. Their house sits right on Toms River Lake, one of the most desirable locations in all of south Jersey. Joe DiSanti has a degree in engineering, and he specializes in prefabricated concrete; he has helped build, for example, the Tropicana in Atlantic City. On the night that I visited, Joe junior, who works with his father, slaved over the stove and waited on us hand and foot, serving up a delicious four-course meal as if he were hired help. Much red wine and Sambuca flowed. The two Joes talked about how the fifteen-year-old Skinny took an old dining room table and scooped holes in it to hold the poker chips. Joe junior showed me a photograph of Skinny standing in front of his first joint. He's wearing an ill-fitting suit, a pair of scuffed-up shoes, and a white driving cap. Many years later, Skinny told a journalist that shortly after that picture was taken, he "started wearing tailor-made suits, because if they tried to take in the standard kind, I was so skinny that the pockets met in the back." On the window of the storefront the following words are stenciled:

SKINNY'S
2209
Cigars—Cigarettes

There's a sign that reads "Drink Coca-Cola in Bottles 5 Cents." A few Optima cigar boxes are displayed just beyond the sign. "Several years ago," said Joe senior, "when Skinny was still alive, I was going through my father's things and I found a business card. It was longer and thinner than the standard business card, and all it had printed on it was the word *Skinny's* and the address. Well, I happened to be going to visit Skinny, and I handed it to him and said, 'Does this mean anything to you?' Like a child, he said, 'Can I keep it? Can I keep this, Joey?' He was real quiet, and he kept turning it over and looking at it. He said, 'Your father gave me forty bucks to open up my first joint. This is the place.' And then he tucked it in his pocket."

Chapter Two

Around the time that Skinny D'Amato was opening his first gambling parlor on Arctic Avenue, Nucky Johnson, the man who would become his role model, quasi mentor, and connection to the New York Mob, was nearing his zenith as the political boss of south Jersey. Oddly enough, Nucky's thirty-year reign began in 1908, the year Skinny was born. Right in the middle of the flap over the Sunday closing laws and the governor's threat of loosing the militia on Atlantic City, the voters in Atlantic County chose the twenty-five-year-old Enoch L. Johnson to be their sheriff—the youngest ever to be elected in the state. They could not have known that they were handing the reins to a man who would put Atlantic City on the map while setting it up for the inevitable fall from grace. In some ways, the resort still has not recovered from the damage Nucky did.

He was born in 1883 in Smithville, a bayside village on the mainland just north of Atlantic City, to Scotch and English parents and raised on a diet of politics. His father, Smith E. Johnson, and mother, Virginia Higbee Johnson, were the descendants of two old south Jersey families—hardworking, thrifty, and honest—typical Revolutionary stock. Smith was a produce farmer, and Virginia, an elegant but tough lady who was well-known around town, drove the produce wagon to market alone, wearing high boots decorated with metal toeplates. Smith, who had political inclinations, ran for sheriff, and to everyone's surprise he won—and quickly became one of the acknowledged Republican leaders of Atlantic County. He served as sheriff every other three years from 1890 to 1908, because state law prohibited a sheriff from succeeding himself.

When Nucky graduated from Atlantic City High in 1900, his father made him a sheriff's clerk and then, at twenty-one, the undersheriff. In 1908, when his father could no longer serve, Nucky was elected sheriff, and the first thing he did after being sworn in was to appoint his father as ... deputy sheriff. Nucky, who had been reading books about oratory, political science, and government, instantly blossomed into an effective leader. He wore spats and patent-leather shoes, and he organized a Young Men's Republican Club and had himself elected chairman. He had jurisdiction over the various local police departments, and he quickly instituted an even *more* lax policy of law enforcement in order to allow gambling and prostitution—and therefore Atlantic City—to thrive. In fact, he had a great deal to do with the resort becoming the tangy, bustling metropolis that it was in the early part of the twentieth century. He went around to all the Boardwalk hotels and encouraged the proprietors to launch national advertising campaigns, and sure enough, tourists from all over the country began pouring in. Extra train excursions were added by the railroads, fancy New York clothing and jewelry shops opened branches on Atlantic Avenue and the Boardwalk, and then the luxury hotel boom began, bringing ever wealthier customers to the resort—many with plenty of money to gamble.

Eventually, Nucky landed a spot on the Republican County Committee, an organization headed up by one Louis Kuehnle, a great big rumpled fellow known to all as "the Commodore" or "the easy boss." Kuehnle was a never married millionaire who owned a yacht and traveled everywhere with his scruffy little dog, Jerry. He was the head and/or founder of half a dozen prominent civic organizations and the muscle behind the building of much of the city's early infrastructure; he was also the owner of the Corner, a hotel and saloon at Atlantic and South Carolina Avenues, right next to the train station, which functioned as the unofficial county seat. Kuehnle and Nucky's father spent most of their time running the city and the county from the front porch,

handing out patronage—and lecturing their young pupil, Nucky, on the ways of governing in south Jersey.

Once Woodrow Wilson—a Progressive Reformer and Presbyterian moralist—was elected governor in 1910, Kuehnle's days were numbered. Speaking at the original Traymore, Wilson pronounced that the city was living under "a reign of terror." He said, "There are policemen at the door who would lay hands on me if they dared. . . . It is a question of emancipation from everything that is disgraceful and rotten." Wilson, the southern son of a minister who loathed the machine politics that prevailed among the educated northern elite, assigned a special Supreme Court justice to hear cases in Atlantic County, and he ordered his attorney general, Edmund White, to institute a grand jury investigation.

Kuehnle, the original corrupt Atlantic City boss, soured on politics thanks to Wilson's relentless campaign and retreated from power, vacating his position as head of the Republican County Committee. He was eventually convicted of graft, sentenced to a year of hard labor, and fined $1,000. Nucky, who would engage in every imaginable kind of election fraud over the next thirty years, was indicted for illegally removing registration books and official election returns from the county clerk's office, but he was acquitted. Emboldened by his ability to outfox Wilson—and encouraged by his father—Nucky seized control of Kuehnle's political machine, and no one challenged him. During Woodrow Wilson's successful run for president in 1913, he bragged about "cleaning up" Atlantic City; in reality, the only thing he accomplished in the resort was to spread Nucky's fame beyond New Jersey by turning him into a figure of national political intrigue.

In 1914, the Atlantic County Board of Freeholders honored Nucky by electing him county treasurer, an office he held for thirty years. He never actually performed any of the duties of his position, and it was widely known that he used the county treasurer's office merely as his political headquarters. Nucky had learned a valuable lesson, one that Skinny would perfect years later: To wield real power in a place as corrupt as Atlantic City, one must fly just under the radar—and play both sides of the fence. In order to command the respect of politicians, the bigwigs, *and* the criminals, a certain trilinguality was necessary. For

example, at one point on his way up, the Republican powers-that-be in New Jersey offered Nucky the state chairmanship, but he turned it down. "Let someone else have the throne," he said. "I'll take a seat at a ringside table."

In 1916, Johnson expanded his base of power beyond the county by managing the gubernatorial campaign of *Atlantic City Press* founder Walter E. Edge. When Edge, a Republican, made it to the New Jersey Governor's Mansion—in a year when the voters tilted toward Democrats all over the country—he awarded Johnson by naming him clerk of the State Supreme Court of New Jersey. Suddenly, the gravel-voiced boom of Nucky Johnson could be heard in the Trenton State House, where he was given a grand office. During that period, Johnson was not only the absolute boss of Atlantic City and Atlantic County, he was part of a triumvirate of Republican leaders who controlled the state that included David Baird of Camden County and Morgan Larson from north Jersey. In 1921, Nucky helped Warren Harding get to the White House and was rewarded with an invitation to sleep in the Lincoln Bedroom. Harding also gave Nucky two interstate highways for Atlantic City—Routes 30 and 40, known locally as the Black Horse Pike and the White Horse Pike.

In 1928, Johnson's power reached a crescendo when he backed Morgan Larson for governor and Hamilton F. Kean for United States senator and both were elected. Kean attributed his excellent showing with voters in south Jersey solely to Nucky. Describing a campaign meeting there, Kean said, "Every speaker began his talk by declaring that he was devoted to God and Enoch Johnson." From this point on, Nucky had a hand in the appointment of every state and federal officeholder in New Jersey. The candidates for the Atlantic City Commission, the Atlantic County Board of Freeholders, the New Jersey State Senate, and the county judgeships were all chosen personally by Johnson rather than the Republican organization. No political boss in America had ever wielded as much power in one state as Nucky Johnson did in New Jersey.

The root of Johnson's awesome power lay in the fact that he controlled Sin City. Atlantic City's population mushroomed to 66,000 during the 1920s; by the middle of the decade, nearly half of the 160,000

people of Atlantic County lived in Atlantic City, and fully one-third of those people were black. Unlike most famous political machines of the early twentieth century—those in New York and Chicago, for instance—Atlantic City's was run by Republicans. This had less to do with any deeply felt principles than with pragmatism. Atlantic City had the largest black population of any city north of the Mason-Dixon Line. (As a point of comparison, the black populations of most northeastern cities at the turn of the century amounted to no more than 2 percent.) After the Civil War, thousands of southern blacks flocked to Atlantic City because of the prevalence of service jobs and menial labor in the resort's huge hotels and restaurants; these jobs carried with them a small measure of dignity because all such workers were considered actual employees—a part of something—and not just servants. Atlantic City hotels paid blacks more than anywhere else in the country. And until Franklin D. Roosevelt came along, most blacks, in gratitude to Lincoln, voted Republican.

Johnson controlled the "Negro vote" through the appointment of black precinct captains in Atlantic City's predominantly black Northside to whom he personally distributed "loyalty" money. The fact that they appeared to have a kind of autonomy over their communities kept them happy—and voting for those whom Nucky wanted them to. But buying the black vote wasn't enough to win every election. Padding the voter registration lists was a matter of course during the Johnson regime. (At one point, the Atlantic County League for Better Government went through the lists, knocked door-to-door in Atlantic City, and came up with fifteen to eighteen thousand fraudulent names out of thirty-eight thousand registered voters!) From June to September, the transient population ranged from fifty thousand to three hundred thousand, many of whom were seasonal employees; some of them registered to vote to ensure they got their jobs back the following summer. Entire casts of burlesque shows sometimes registered en masse, just to show their appreciation of the city's loose morals. On election day, voters were bused in from Camden and Philadelphia and led to the polls. And, of course, Johnson could always count on gamblers and prostitutes to cast sufficient illegal votes for his candidates, fortifying the black and transient vote. Throughout his career, Johnson allowed the proprietors of speakeasies, whorehouses, and gambling dens to operate with virtual impunity—as long as they voted for his ticket and paid him "tribute." The income that he exacted from the underworld was enormous. This money was used to further grease the wheels of his sprawling political machine throughout the state—and to support his over-the-top lifestyle.

As Nucky grew more powerful with each passing year, he also became more outrageous. When his wife, Mabel Jeffries Steelman, died in 1912 from tuberculosis, Johnson was only thirty. Just six months after her death, he threw the first of his infamous "annual parties," distinguished by an astonishing intermingling of high society, politicians, underworld racketeers, and several dozen Broadway "cuties" whom Nucky hired through a chorus girl agency in New York. The parties were usually staged at the Ritz-Carlton, taking over a couple of floors, with a dozen bottles of champagne and cracked ice in the bathtubs of every room. The first one lasted three days, which predictably led to rumors of orgies taking place; not long after, two women filed "breach of promise" (to marry) suits, and one woman alleged she had been raped. The press, of course, were not invited, and Nucky had his henchmen stationed at the gates to make sure no one slipped by. (Skinny and his future pal Frank Sinatra and *his* future pal John F. Kennedy would hold remarkably similar parties in Atlantic City, Los Angeles, Miami, and Las Vegas some thirty years later.)

Sometime in the mid-1920s, a cabdriver named Louie Kessel began waiting outside of nightclubs for Nucky. When he emerged, Louie—a former wrestler who spoke with a thick German accent, stood five feet five, weighed 260 pounds, and waxed the tips of his huge mustache—would pick up the drunken Nucky, take him home, undress him, and put him to bed. Nucky rewarded his new man servant—whom everyone called "Roly-Poly" Louie—by making him his valet and bodyguard. For the next fifteen years, Nucky and Louie were rarely seen apart, and Nucky transacted a lot of his business through Louie. The two men developed a strange routine. Nucky woke up every afternoon at four, at which point Louie would give his master's pink, fleshy body a pounding rubdown. Nucky would take a shower, and then Louie would dry him with towels. At five P.M., a black maid would bring Nucky his standard breakfast of twelve scrambled eggs, which he would eat in bed. Louie would then help him into one of his more than one hundred handmade suits, and the two men would walk to the Boardwalk, lean against a railing, and pass out dollar bills, political advice, instructions, and favors. After a couple of hours, Nucky and Louie would take a rolling chair ride down the length of the Boardwalk, and then, by eight P.M., they would eat dinner at one of any number of the hotel restaurants. Johnson ate nothing but lobster, steak, and caviar and deigned to drink only champagne and eighteen-year-old brandy. By ten o'clock, Nucky was out on the town, gambling and drinking until five or six A.M., when the cycle began all over again.

Nucky was as famous on Broadway as he was on the Boardwalk. A New York gossip columnist once wrote that Nucky and the millionaire Guy Loomis were "among the most liberal and careless spenders of the present day." The columnist noted that he wasn't happy unless he had an army behind him and that he would drag his acolytes from one night-club to another, footing all the bills along the way. Once he gave a waiter $5 for handing him an extra napkin, and his tips ranged as high as $100. He was known to buy whole rows of ringside seats for championship fights and invite all his friends and cronies; on occasion, he would bring the entire cast of a Broadway show to Atlantic City on the weekends to entertain himself. When celebrities came to town, he elected himself host, taking them to the nightclubs and gambling parlors and keeping them out all night.

He was so flamboyantly generous that no one ever forgot it; one year at Christmas he received five thousand cards and over seven thousand telegrams. A small army of messenger boys was dispatched to his suite with groaning sacks of notes from well-wishers. He was a heavy-set man who stood over six feet tall, had a shiny bald head, and always wore round, horn-rimmed glasses. During winter, he walked the boards in a $1,200, full-length raccoon coat. Every day of the year, he pinned a fresh red carnation to his lapel—a sartorial flourish that remained his signature till the day he died.

Nucky was known for dating showgirls—including Hilda Ferguson and Evelyn Nesbit. His most famous line—"Every time I kiss a blonde I taste a saxophone"—was uttered one night at the Silver Slipper in

Times Square after he found out that his latest girl was cheating on him with a musician. Eventually he fell in love with Flossie Osbeck, a *Ziegfeld Follies* girl, and he moved her into his two-story Spanish-style stucco bungalow near the Boardwalk. Just down the street on Iowa Avenue stood the Ritz-Carlton; there Johnson maintained a suite on the seventh floor, where he held his lavish, all-night parties and kept a closet filled with cash that Louie counted every day. He eventually bought the Ritz outright and became known as the "Czar of the Ritz-Carlton." For Flossie's convenience, he kept an apartment in Manhattan at 128 Central Park South. At one point, he owned two Cadillacs, a Lincoln, a Rolls-Royce, and a Ford, which he kept in operation for Flossie and his friends and constituents. He himself was driven around town by Louie in a $14,000 powder blue Pierce-Arrow limousine.

✦

Prohibition provided the rocket fuel for Skinny D'Amato's early ascent. By the time he was twenty, he had more than a dozen "sawdust joints" not unlike the original Skinny's at 2209 Arctic Avenue, though each one grew a little bigger, a little more elaborate. He not only had a huge following in Atlantic City, but he was by now setting up traveling games in Vineland and Hammonton, two towns in New Jersey on the way to Philly; whenever a fraternal organization or fire hall wanted a game, they called Skinny. But in Atlantic City, he was benefiting from the loose, wide-open resort that Nucky had created. And now he was big enough that he was on Nucky's radar, paying him off to run his gambling interests and impressing him with his extraordinary touch with people from all walks of life.

It was through Nucky's late night carousing and gambling that he first met Skinny, and the two began a relationship that would last until Nucky died in 1968. It was also through Nucky that Skinny would begin his lifelong association with the Mob. Under Nucky's rule, it became an open secret in the underworld that Atlantic City was neutral ground for mobsters from New York, Philadelphia, Baltimore, and Chicago and a safe haven for criminals of any stripe—provided they paid Nucky for protection. When Lucky Luciano was on the lam and hiding out in

Atlantic City, Nucky asked Skinny to take care of him. The way Skinny got to know Luciano was through Nucky; and the way Nucky became acquainted with Luciano was through Prohibition.

Just as Skinny was opening his first sawdust joint in 1922, Charles "Lucky" Luciano, a decade older than Skinny, was well on his way to becoming "the King of Booze" in New York, as Al Capone famously anointed him. In 1917, Luciano had become friends—and teamed up—with Frank Costello, Meyer Lansky, and Benjamin "Bugsy" Siegel. The four young men—along with Capone in Chicago—would change the face of America over the next twenty years by radically transforming the Mafia from a kind of loosely organized secret society imported from the old country to the purposeful, menacing, greedy corporation that it eventually became.

During World War I, Luciano and Co. began to solidify their positions as head thugs in charge in Manhattan. There was a lot of money around, and they found a way to get their percentage of it, mostly through burglarizing jewelry stores and pawnbrokers. By the time the Armistice was signed in 1918, they had pulled together a gang of more than twenty people and began to rule the streets of downtown Manhattan, where Luciano, Lansky, and Siegel had all grown up and still lived, as well as the East Harlem territory of Frank Costello. They held up banks, robbed warehouses, and made life miserable for a lot of people. Slowly but surely, they worked their way into the illegal gambling business.

It was through gambling—a vice that was generally tolerated by society—that they learned an important and early lesson: The investment in protection from law enforcement and public officials to ensure the continuation of their operations was well worth the cost. With protection from the right people, there was no end to the fortunes that could be made from gambling.

On January 17, 1919, the Eighteenth Amendment to the Constitution of the United States was ratified, banning the manufacture, sale, or transportation of intoxicating liquor. Nine months later, in October, over the veto of President Woodrow Wilson, Congress passed the Volstead Act, clarifying the language of the Prohibition amendment and setting up the bureaucracy for its enforcement.

Criminals are nothing if not pragmatic about human nature. The lessons Luciano and Co. had learned from the gambling underworld— that people would gamble whether it was illegal or not, and *somebody* ought to provide it—were perfectly applicable to Prohibition; Luciano and others like him predicted that the nation would now slide into deep and protracted denial about an even more pervasive vice.

It didn't take a genius to figure out that the demand for liquor was insatiable and the supply now severely limited. Meyer Lansky said to Luciano one fateful day: "If you have a lot of what people want and can't get, then you can supply the demand and shovel in the dough. In other words, that's what we ought to do with whiskey—get plenty of it, good, uncut stuff right off the boat, and then sell it at a high price to a bunch of people who don't have the brains enough not to drink it."

The first deal that Luciano ever made to buy a shipment of liquor to sell in Manhattan was in 1920. He and his three partners ponied up $35,000 to purchase a carload of 100-proof rye from Irving Wexler, aka Waxey Gordon, a bootlegger from Philadelphia. It was the first of many deals between Gordon and Luciano; but, more important, it was the beginning of the interconnectedness of the tristate Mafia. The cooperation among gangsters from the boroughs of New York to the cities of New Jersey, like Newark and Fort Lee, and on to Philadelphia quickly grew into an intricate, organized web of like-minded criminals. Today, their names are nearly all household: Dutch Schultz, Albert Anastasia, Vito Genovese, Joe Adonis, Carlo Gambino, Abner "Longie" Zwillman, Willie Moretti, and Arnold Rothstein, to name just a few.

Much of the good whiskey was being purchased from Canada through Samuel Bronfman, who was head of the Distillers Corporation–Seagram and one of Canada's richest and most charitable citizens. It was either trucked in or brought down on a fleet of ships owned by Luciano's pal Longie Zwillman, "the Al Capone of New Jersey," who operated out of Newark. His ships picked up liquor from the French islands of St. Pierre and Miquelon off the coast of Canada, and much of it wound up coming ashore in or near Atlantic City. Scotch and rum originated, obviously, in Scotland and Cuba, and those deliveries were made by ships that stopped offshore. Speedboats painted gray and totally darkened would meet the ships and make the dangerous trips back to shore to various illegal ports along the East Coast.

Atlantic City had become the headquarters for the nation's most notorious rumrunners. Rum Row, some thirty miles offshore, supplied the entire country with its hard liquor. The notorious Dougherty brothers of Philadelphia; Harry Fleischer, head of the so-called Purple Gang of Detroit; and George Remus, the Ohio lawyer and bootleg king, had speedboat fleets operating out of Atlantic City under Nucky's protection, and they all competed viciously for primacy.

In and around Atlantic City, a fleet of trucks would pick up the liquor from wherever it came ashore and haul it to the distribution warehouses. Longie Zwillman employed Atlantic City cops to escort his cargo, but he was never afraid to do the dirty work against rival bootleggers himself. Zwillman was arrested five times over a two-year period in the late 1920s on assault and battery charges. He was convicted only once, which led to the only time he ever spent behind bars—he served six months in 1928 for savagely beating a rival runner.

Luciano quickly figured out that Zwillman's shipments of Scotch or rum or whiskey could be cut with cheap grain alcohol and sold for top dollar as the real, pure thing. Because of a loophole in the Volstead Act, a certain number of companies around the country were permitted to produce grain alcohol for industrial purposes. Several of those companies were in Philadelphia, and they were immediately infiltrated by Waxey Gordon's crew. Luciano's and Gordon's interests dovetailed nicely to form an extraordinarily profitable and mutually beneficial partnership that lasted for several years. Luciano would get his shipments from Canada or Scotland or Cuba and his grain from Gordon in Philadelphia, then arrange to have them blended, rebottled, and relabeled in Gordon's Philadelphia and south Jersey plants and stored in warehouses, many of them near Atlantic City.

✦

Lucky Luciano and Nucky Johnson met for the first time at a boxing match in New York City. On September 14, 1923, heavyweight Jack

Dempsey fought Argentine boxer Luis Angel Firpo in front of eighty-eight thousand people at the Polo Grounds in Manhattan, and Lucky Luciano moved heaven and earth—and paid $2,500—for two hundred ringside seats. It was all part of a deliberate campaign to rehabilitate his tarnished reputation after a drug bust that brought a storm of bad press and turned him into a pariah, even among underworld figures. Selling drugs—especially heroin—was considered the dirtiest business of all to the Mob. Luciano figured if he could invite cops, politicians, and society muckety-mucks to a fight that was impossible to get tickets for, he would have everyone eating out of the palm of his hand again—and it worked.

Luciano, Costello, Lansky, and Siegel leaked the word out that Luciano was going to invite one hundred people and their dates as his guests to the fight. Within twenty-four hours, people from all over the country were calling for tickets. His guests that night included Al Capone with twelve friends; Florenz Ziegfeld and Earl Carroll, rival Broadway producers who met that very night; Bernard Gimbel of Gimbel's department store; Jimmy Hines and Al Marinelli from Tammany Hall; Boss Jim Pendergast from Kansas City; and Charles "King" Solomon from Boston. One pair of those tickets went to none other than Nucky Johnson.

A couple of days after the fight, several of Luciano's shipments of whiskey were hijacked in the woods near Atlantic City, and two of his warehouses in upper Manhattan were raided by federal Prohibition agents. Suddenly, Luciano was having a serious supply problem, and he was desperate. Nucky Johnson, who heard about his troubles, called him to return the favor for the fight tickets. Nucky suggested that Luciano come to Atlantic City with Joe Adonis for a meeting. Though Luciano had only just met Nucky at the fight, he knew all about his formidable reputation—and that he virtually ran the state of New Jersey. He also knew that Nucky always remained neutral where the Mafia was concerned, holding himself above the fray of rival underworld gangs. All that Nucky required was a piece of everything that happened in his resort—not just from the distribution and sale of liquor, but from other ventures as well, such as the trendy slot machines that Frank Costello had introduced to the gambling halls around town.

Luciano and Adonis drove the 130 miles from Manhattan to Atlantic City and met with Johnson at his bungalow on Iowa Avenue. "I knew Nucky would do practically anything for a buck," Luciano once said. "For a lotta money, I figured he could be tempted to accept an offer the boys and I had decided was a good idea. So I said to him, 'Look, Nucky, I don't want to beat around the bush, and I'm not trying to chisel a sharp deal. I need all the Scotch I can lay my hands on, and you know everythin' that's comin' in and out. Now I want a better deal than the fair shake you've been givin' everybody. I'll make you a partner.'"

"I'll give you an exclusive on my beach," said Nucky. "Nobody else can land any stuff here. I'll give you protection all the way to the Camden ferry across from Philly. I'll let Costello bring in all the slots he can handle. You can run gambling spots that we'll decide on, near the big hotels. Now, Charlie, what do I get?"

Right on the spot, Luciano gave Johnson 10 percent of everything—not just the sale of liquor, but a tenth of the profits from *all* his rackets—for as long as Prohibition remained in effect. To take the sting out of the overly generous deal their boss promised, Luciano's gang, including Costello, Lansky, Siegel, and Adonis, all pitched into the 10 percent so that no one person had to shoulder the whole burden. "That's the smartest move you ever made," Adonis said to Luciano as they left Nucky's house. "It's worth millions."

And indeed it was. But just before they left, Luciano asked for one more favor. "I need Scotch now, Nucky, so who's making the next shipment?" Johnson told Luciano that a boatload of uncut Scotch would be coming ashore in Ventnor in two days and that a rival New York gang was going to pick it up with a couple of trucks and drive it to Waxey Gordon's in Philadelphia. He took out a map and pointed to the route they would be taking through Egg Harbor, a sleepy little backwoods town on the mainland.

Two nights later, Luciano drove back to south Jersey from New York, but this time he was in a caravan of three cars filled with ten other men armed to the teeth—including Siegel, Adonis, and Lansky. At two A.M., they cut down a tree and let it fall across a dark, lonely stretch of road in Egg Harbor. And then they waited. When the two trucks finally appeared, the drivers stopped and got out to remove the tree. Lansky and Siegel opened fire, killing one guy and wounding another. When the rest of the gang surrendered, they were viciously beaten and left on the side of the road. Luciano and his crew stole their guns, their trucks, and their Scotch and drove back to New York. All was right again in the supply-and-demand world of Lucky Luciano.

It is impossible to overstate the role that Prohibition played in the shaping of the character of Atlantic City—and the success of Nucky Johnson. In fact, between 1926 and 1933, nearly 40 percent of all the illegal alcohol funneled into the United States came ashore in or near the resort. The fact that Atlantic City had essentially exempted itself from many laws—including the Volstead Act—was an open secret in the Northeast.

Millions of people lived within a three-hundred-mile radius of Atlantic City, and to anyone looking to cut loose for a night or a weekend from the confines of Prohibition, Atlantic City was just a cheap train ride away. By the mid-1920s, the resort was, at least in the summer, a bustling metropolis in the midst of explosive growth. There were one thousand hotels and rooming houses that could accommodate four hundred thousand visitors, ninety-nine daily trains in the summer, and three airports. It had the world's longest boardwalk, stretching seven miles, with five piers. There were twenty-one theaters, three country clubs, and four newspapers.

✦

At the height of Nucky Johnson's career, Lucky Luciano, Al Capone, Frank Costello, and Meyer Lansky decided to use Atlantic City as the site for the first ever Mafia syndicate convention to restructure what had become an ad hoc national crime network. The four men shared an enthusiasm for organizing the rackets on a countrywide level, and this led to the confab. The date—the second week of May, 1929—was chosen because that was when Meyer Lansky was getting married to Anna Citron, a devout young Jewish woman whose father was a produce dealer from Hoboken. His pals figured Atlantic City would be the perfect honeymoon town for the newlyweds, and—because of Johnson's control over the resort (namely, the cops)—it would also be the perfect location for carrying out their business without having to worry about getting hassled or run out of town.

Big black limousines brought gangsters and bosses from all over the country: the New York delegation consisted of Lansky, Luciano, Costello, Adonis, Albert Anastasia, Dutch Schultz, Frank Scalise, and Vince Mangano, among others; from Cleveland came Morris "Moe" Dalitz and Louis Rothkopf; Charles "King" Solomon drove down from Boston; Detroit's Purple Gang was represented by several members; Johnny Lazia came from Kansas City as Jim Pendergast's surrogate; Waxey Gordon, Max "Boo-Boo" Hoff, and Harry Stromberg aka Nig Rosen traveled the fifty miles from Philadelphia; Willie Moretti and Longie Zwillman represented north Jersey; and Al Capone arrived from Chicago and brought with him Jake "Greasy Thumb" Guzik.

Johnson had intended to put them up at one of the most exclusive hotels on the Boardwalk. But it turned out to be too exclusive. The hotel had a policy of turning away non-WASPs, so Johnson made their reservations under Anglo-Saxon aliases; but that ruse did not fool the management, who took one look at the Italian and Jewish gangsters and refused to put them up. A call was made to Johnson, and the convoy of limousines began to drive over to the President Hotel. Along the route, Johnson met up with the motorcade. They stopped and got out of their limos, and Johnson and Capone had an ugly fight over the mishap right in the middle of the street. When the shelling finally stopped, Johnson shouted, "All you fuckers follow me!" and off they went to the Ritz-Carlton. Lansky and his bride were put up in the presidential suite at the Ritz, and the rest of the crew were housed in the President Hotel and the Ambassador nearby.

Despite the fact that some of the gangsters brought their wives and girlfriends—for whom there were fur capes as gifts from Nucky—the first few days were filled with parties, girls, and booze—parties that Skinny D'Amato attended. Every morning, the delegates would take to the rolling chairs on the Boardwalk. One morning, the *Atlantic City Press* reported a Capone sighting: "Seated in a rolling chair at Kentucky Avenue and the Boardwalk yesterday afternoon, puffing on a big black cigar and surrounded by half a dozen henchmen, Al took in the sights of the famous strand and breathed deeply and freely of the ozone with apparently not a care in the world." One brave photographer supposedly took a photograph of Nucky Johnson and Al Capone strolling down the Boardwalk together; Johnson always claimed that the *New York Evening Journal* superimposed his picture into the shot with Capone, and his evidence was that he was wearing a white summer suit while Capone was wearing a dark winter suit. Impossible!

Damon Runyon covered the conference, and it is widely believed today that he made up the story that has become legend and recycled many times over the years. The apocryphal tale includes one memorable vision of the gangsters being pushed in rolling chairs to the end of the Boardwalk in Chelsea, at which point they would take off their shoes and socks, walk down the beach toward the ocean, roll up their pants, and then wade into the surf and discuss business with the waves lapping at their shins.

Capone brought Moses Annenberg to Atlantic City, and the meetings between Annenberg and Luciano's gang were the conference's raison d'être. Annenberg owned the *Daily Racing Form*, which was read nationwide by gamblers and bookies. Before the Atlantic City conference, Capone and Annenberg conceived of a way for the crime syndicate to control horse-betting results throughout the nation, but the idea had to be approved by all the crime bosses. Through a series of meetings at their hotels on the Boardwalk, the plan was universally adopted—establishing gambling as the first vice to be controlled utterly by the Mafia. All the big-city bosses subscribed to the wire service and made sure that only their gambling dens and bookie joints received it as well, creating a sprawling, illegal, and awesome monopoly. In the underworld, Annenberg and his wire became known as "the Trust" as it spread beyond the States to Canada, Mexico, and Cuba and made Annenberg—and the Mob—a vast fortune. Indeed, at the time of his death in 1942, Annenberg was estimated to be the fifth richest man in the world, with much of his haul coming from the race wire.

✦

Just a few weeks after the underworld conference of 1929, Atlantic City Convention Hall was dedicated, on May 31. It was the largest unobstructed room in the world—built with no roof posts or pillars—and had taken six years and cost $15 million to complete. In its day, it was a modern marvel and a feat of engineering. The building's trusses have a span of 350 feet, the largest ever used, and it was constructed from twelve million tons of steel and forty-two thousand cubic yards of concrete. Its sub-basement is more than twenty-six feet below high tide and is anchored with twelve thousand thirty-foot-long pilings. Even today, Convention Hall takes your breath away. Depending on whose version of history one is inclined to believe, it was either the idea of Nucky Johnson or Mayor Edward Bader. Either way, Johnson was more than happy to take credit for the extravagant, outsize auditorium, a testament to his commitment to a twelve-month convention economy. And while the hall has become synonymous with the Miss America Pageant, which began in 1921, the first promenade of pretty ladies was not actually held in the hall until 1940. This has partially to do with the fact that just a few months after the hall was dedicated, the nation's economy collapsed into the Great Depression and the pageant was suspended until 1933.

The Depression, followed by the repeal of Prohibition in 1933, delivered a huge blow financially to Atlantic City, largely because of a situation Nucky had created. Toward the end of his reign in the late 1930s, Atlantic City had the highest per capita debt—$389.07—of any city in the country. The second highest, at $178.88, was sustained by Jersey City. Beneath the gay exterior all those years was a city in hock. As the real estate assessment shrank to one-third of its 1930 high, the tax rate nearly tripled. The sickly condition of municipal finances in the late thirties and early forties set the stage for the resort's slide into hell, culminating in the crushing blow Atlantic City would suffer in the early 1970s. In fact, the rotten-to-the-core neighborhoods that still exist in Atlantic City are the ugliest and saddest part of Nucky's legacy. He literally drove Atlantic City into the ground.

Unable to pay government and city employees, the resort began issuing scrip—a practice that lasted well into the late 1930s. In 1929, Atlantic City had fourteen banks; by the late 1930s, only two remained—and several of the ones that closed became saloons. Meanwhile, Johnson, who was still popular in certain quarters of the city, was becoming increasingly vulnerable to challengers. He responded by trying to sell the state of New Jersey on an ambitious and, in many ways, prescient twenty-five-year plan to turn Atlantic City into the "Monte Carlo of the United States." Mayor Charles D. White took Nucky's idea for a "superresort" to *The New York Times:* "Segregation is not a fair description of our plans," said White, "but we feel that when groups come here, some seeking rest and quiet, others hilariously celebrating a hurried holiday, it is absurd to have them trampling on each other's toes and spoiling each other's fun. There should be facilities for every person—and every desire—in Atlantic City. And if visitors want merry-go-rounds or a gambling casino, Atlantic City should give them what they want."

✦

But back in the early days of Prohibition, the Atlantic City Fall Pageant, as it was originally called, was actually just one small part of a larger parade that was conceived either by Nucky Johnson and Mayor Bader or the hotel owners on the Boardwalk—or, most likely, all of them in tandem. The goal of the parade was something everyone agreed on—to extend the summer season past Labor Day, a problem that Northeast shore town fathers are still struggling with today. The pageant had a week-long buildup, with most of the festivities taking place over a weekend. They included the following: Bathers Revue, Rolling Chair Parade, Night Spectacle with the Frolic of Neptune, and the Inter-City Beauty Contest—the final event being the featured one and the embryo of the Miss America Pageant. It was limited originally to only eight contestants, one each from Washington, Pittsburgh, Harrisburg, Philadelphia, Newark, New York, Ocean City, and Atlantic City itself. The pageant was such a huge success—drawing thousands to the Boardwalk—that the next year fifty-eight contestants turned up, ten from New York State alone, and *The New York Times* devoted several consecutive days to coverage.

In those first heady years of the pageant, the girls were judged on a scale that included fifteen points for "construction of the head"; ten points each for eyes, facial expression, torso, legs, arms, hands, and "grace of bearing"; and five each for hair, nose, and mouth. In its third year, the judges calibrating these precise numerical distinctions included Norman Rockwell, Flo Ziegfeld, and Lee Shubert of Shubert Theater fame. In 1926, the pageant laid claim to its first contestant who would one day become a household name—the then fifteen-year-old Joan Blondell, who once described herself as a girl with "a good, big chest, the kind garbage men whistle at."

Back in 1921, on the evening after that first Inter-City Beauty Contest, Nucky Johnson inadvertently planted the seeds of his own destruction. He had arranged for showgirls from *Folies Bergère*, *George White's Scandals*, and *Earl Carroll's Vanities* to parade down the Boardwalk. He also paid for a fancy costume for the "Girl in the Red Velvet Swing," Evelyn Nesbit, to wear in the parade, but she got drunk on gin and fell off her float, right into a pile of horse dung. Nucky kicked her out of Atlantic City that very day. Later that night, he invited the girls—minus Nesbit—back to a party at his suite at the Ritz to entertain visiting dignitaries and local bigwigs. There are several versions of what happened next, but they all end the same. Nucky Johnson insulted actress Marion Davies, who was the mistress of William Randolph Hearst, by calling her a "tramp" among other "vicious" things. Some versions of the story have it that it happened at the Ritz, where Marion was in a suite just down the hall, having a party of her own that same night. Other versions maintain that Hearst was *with* Davies in Atlantic City and that words were exchanged among the three of them at Babette's Yacht Bar, one of Nucky's favorite hangouts famous for its ship-shaped bar.

In any event, Nucky made a powerful and vindictive enemy out of someone who under any other circumstances would have been happy to be his crony. Nucky later said of Hearst and Davies: "He's a windbag who a dumb broad has played for a sucker." Hearst was not the kind of man you wanted to upset, as he was not above using his newspapers to destroy perceived enemies. At Hearst's behest, the *New York Evening Journal* began a campaign against Johnson that reached a crescendo in 1929, shortly after the underworld conference. On New Year's Day 1930, Johnson was woken up at eight A.M. by Louie to a twenty-five-point headline: ATLANTIC CITY VICE EXPOSED: RUM, DOPE, GAM-

BLING RINGS IN CONTROL; PROBE REVEALS WHITE SLAVE GANG KIDNAP-
PING SCHOOL GIRLS.

"My God, Hearst is using the type they save for the end of the
world!" bellowed Nucky. In typical tabloid hyperbole of the time, the
story began: "Atlantic City's playground of millionaires has been taken
over, lock, stock and barrel. Al Capone is one of its ring leaders. Gangsters roam the streets unmolested, assaulting, ravishing and murdering
at will with no fear of punishment. . . . In manpower, guile, ruthlessness,
a wealthy rum-gambling underworld constitutes the largest enemy
ever pitted against the United States. . . ."

Nucky knew this wasn't about Atlantic City. It was a campaign
against *him*. Three days later, his instincts were confirmed with
another gigantic headline: VICE LORD RULES ATLANTIC CITY!
FEAR KEEPS UP FLOW OF GRAFT MONEY. The story reported—in breath-
less language—that Nucky Johnson "has entertained ambassadors,
governors, senators, 'Scarface' Capone with such magic powers by his
lavish spending, and with his 'Hatchet Man' Cappy Hoffman who puffs
on his opium pipe and 'soars' into the night, with shots heard on dark
streets, and bodies in a distant ditch. The hatchet man grins, it's not a
pleasant sight. Soon he's freed on bail, being a hatchet man is fun and
has little danger."

Samuel "Cappy" Hoffman was the scariest kind of human monster.
He was a member of Max "Boo-Boo" Hoff's gang in Philadelphia, and
he had been loaned out to Nucky to do his extradirty work. Cappy had
pockmarked skin and two scars on his forehead, one from a deep bullet
hole wound and the other the result of a long, ugly slice from a knife.
Cappy's apartment had been raided back in November 1929, and he and
his wife were arraigned on narcotics charges and released on bail.
When the Hearst headlines hit the newsstands, Nucky, in an effort to
quell the controversy and to appear as if he were actually concerned
about crime, shut down a few whorehouses and gambling joints and
bent the legal machinery of Atlantic County to ensure that Cappy was
punished. In addition to the narcotics charges, Cappy was sentenced
for gambling and bookmaking and tossed in prison for five years.

But it was too late: the genie was out of the bottle. And Hearst was
on a mission. The publishing titan had been a big supporter of the polit-

ical campaign of Franklin D. Roosevelt, and he persuaded the president to bring the power of the federal government to bear on the rampant corruption in Atlantic City and to finally break the back of the Republican political machine in Atlantic County. There were rumors that J. Edgar Hoover, the head of the FBI, had come to Atlantic City with his friend columnist Walter Winchell and that the two men had donned disguises and visited a casino in one of the clubs. It was also reported that a letter to Nucky that was left behind at the Danmore Hotel by Ma Barker gangster Alvin Karpis was the straw that broke the camel's back. The newly appointed attorney general, Frank Murphy, was so disturbed by the letter that he consulted with Hoover, who was all for an investigation of Nucky's regime.

In October 1936, treasury secretary Henry Morgenthau ordered a complete and thorough investigation to be conducted jointly by the Treasury Department and the Department of Justice. On November 5, Special Agents William Frank and Edward Hill were dispatched to Atlantic City, where they promptly set up shop at the Traymore Hotel and began the slow, sneaky business of bringing down Nucky Johnson. The investigation lasted four and a half years and led to sixty-six criminal proceedings—including twenty-one actual trials and twelve contempt-of-court hearings—and forty-eight indictments. The investigation also produced thirty-three grand jury sessions during which 249 witnesses were interrogated.

The federal government eventually published a 160-page report entitled "The Case of Enoch L. Johnson." It is an extraordinary document, written in an eclectic style that interweaves the arcana of legal-investigative work with novelistic, vivid, detailed descriptions of the Atlantic City underworld of the late 1930s—in other words, the world of Skinny D'Amato. Skinny was not yet a legend, and nearly everyone who knew him in the 1920s and 1930s is dead. Consequently there is scant information about his life before he became famous. By the time Skinny became well-known, he had reinvented himself so completely that he rarely talked about his pre–500 Club life, which included some rather unsavory transgressions.

A few things slipped out over the years, though. Skinny liked to tell a story about the time he took care of Lucky Luciano when he was hiding out in Atlantic City. Luciano, said Skinny, tried to show him how to carry a gun in his waistband, letting it peek out a little so that no one would mess with him. "I couldn't even kill a fly with a fly swatter," Skinny said. The closest he ever came to a murder was on September 2, 1934, as his FBI rap sheet shows: "Material Witness on a murder case" in Camden, New Jersey.

✳

Because Nucky Johnson had been investigated repeatedly by Prohibition agents and the Bureau of Internal Revenue between 1928 and 1934, and because no criminal proceedings ever resulted, the Atlantic City boss learned all too well how not to get tripped up; he developed a foolproof technique for hiding his money. He kept no books or records, maintained no bank or brokerage accounts, and held no assets in his own name. He dealt almost exclusively in cash. Furthermore, he filed timely tax returns each year, in which he reported an annual income of $30,000 from "commissions." This was in addition to the $6,000 nontaxable government salary that he received as Atlantic County treasurer. Meanwhile, Johnson lived like a king and bragged about making $500,000 a year on vice alone. Thus, in order to bring him down, Agents Hill and Frank had to go undercover and investigate every racket in the city.

"Operating out of a furnished apartment," reads the Johnson report, "and keeping their identities concealed, [the agents] located all gambling casinos, horse race betting rooms, 'numbers' headquarters, houses of prostitution, and ascertained the names of their proprietors. By observation they determined the approximate number of employees engaged in these rackets, their methods of operation and estimated the probable gross receipts of the various establishments. By making bets in the horse rooms and by purchasing 'numbers' slips they determined the odds paid and other technical details of the gambling games. Through informants and by contacting underworld characters, the agents learned the names of the 'strong arm' men, the 'contact' men and 'head' men who were connected with each criminal group."

From their initial undercover investigation, which lasted five months, they determined that there were approximately twenty-five horse race–betting rooms and gambling casinos in Atlantic City employing five hundred to seven hundred people, and they were raking in about $8 million a year. There were eight houses of prostitution with one hundred to three hundred employees bringing in $500,000, and nine numbers banks employing eight hundred to one thousand people a year with receipts totaling $1.5 million. The agents were dumbfounded to find these rackets operating "absolutely wide open." The report went on: The proprietors made "no attempt whatever to conceal their activities—horse rooms were located on the principal business avenue of Atlantic City and their doors were open to everyone; the houses of prostitution were segregated mainly in one ward of the city but they made no pretense of hiding the nature of their business; the 'numbers' game was played everywhere as though it were not in violation of the New Jersey gambling statutes. It was difficult to find a store in which numbers were not 'written.'"

The Treasury agents quickly realized that local law enforcement "not only were well aware of these conditions but actively regulated, protected and at times even assisted these rackets" and that this fact was "well known" to the public, who "understood" that the racketeers were paying for protection. Based on hearsay, they determined that the horse rooms had to cough up $160 a week, while numbers banks paid $100 a week and brothels paid $50 a week in the winter, $100 in the summer. "It was also 'understood' by the public," reported the agents, "that none of this graft went to the police officials themselves. Everyone 'knew' it went to 'Nuck' Johnson."

But it is through the descriptions of how the rackets actually worked and what the betting rooms looked like that one is able to divine the most vivid picture of the world Skinny D'Amato inhabited— and get a glimpse into Atlantic City's future. Many of the practices and customs of the gambling underworld of the 1930s are still employed to this day, though now they're all aboveboard and spelled out in corporate handbooks. In a section of the Johnson report entitled "Investigation of Horse-Race Betting Rooms and Gambling Casinos," one can practically smell the sawdust and tobacco:

Most of the [betting rooms] had bars or cigar stores in front of the horse-room proper, but admittance could be gained by anyone who cared to walk in. The rooms themselves varied from a few barn-like places with rows of crude benches to very luxuriously furnished establishments that resembled Wall Street brokerage offices. A number of the places operated on two floors—the street floor being cheaply furnished for use of the fifty-cent and dollar bettors, while the upstairs floor was lavishly equipped and usually reserved for women clients and for the 2, 5, and 10 dollar bettors. In some of these higher class rooms, during the course of an afternoon, the patrons were served with sandwiches and tea or coffee, without expense to them. The rooms had anywhere from 100 to 750 customers and spectators; they had blackboards to record the odds and the results of the races, and were equipped with loud speaker systems over which was given a description of the race as it was being run at the track. Part of each room was partitioned off for the employees and they dealt with the customers through betting windows and a cashier's window. . . .

Practically all the horse-rooms had a large crap table somewhere in the room, where after the races were over the patrons would stop and "lose" whatever money they had "won" on the horses. Most of the rooms catered to bettors from Philadelphia, and it was understood that the management of the rooms would pay railroad fare from and to that city. . . . Some of the rooms employed automobiles to bring the patrons over to their places . . . and in the railroad stations in Philadelphia the police . . . regularly arrested "touts" who were advertising various Atlantic City horse-rooms. All of the horse-rooms employed men to stand out in front of their establishments and these men were known as "doormen." Doubtless, at some time or other, their duties as doormen had been to see that no one gained entrance to the room except bettors and they had been charged with the responsibility of keeping out any detectives or plain clothes police who might raid the room; however . . . these doormen had become nothing

more than touts whose principal duty was to induce
prospective clients to come into the room. . . .

The report went on to distinguish the "horse-rooms" from the "gambling casinos." The casinos were "generally connected with night-clubs
which acted as 'feeders' for the gambling rooms. For example, the Paradise Club, the Club Harlem, Babette's, Grace's Little Belmont, the
Bath & Turf Club, the Clicquot Club, were all typical night-clubs with
bar, restaurant and cabaret entertainment, but in the back of each was
a gambling room containing all forms of games, such as roulette wheels,
crap tables, poker, black-jack games, 'bird cage,' and in most instances
horse-race betting as well. The nightclubs were well known and widely
advertised establishments which employed high-priced orchestras and
Broadway or Hollywood stars as entertainers. The proprietors of these
places apparently cared little whether they made any profit on the
'clubs' for they were primarily gamblers and relied on the cabarets
solely to bring business to their gambling casinos. The Treasury
Agents, on a number of occasions, used these employees (much to the
doormen's embarrassment) to locate the proprietors of the room and
then serve a revenue agent's summons or a Grand Jury subpoena on
the proprietor. The doormen never once questioned who the agents
were, but eagerly endeavored to establish the contact. . . . The proprietors of the horse-rooms and gambling casinos were all under-world
characters, many of them with police and prison records."

But the real revelation of the report comes in a section subtitled
"Investigation of the Vice Racket," which is a dissection of the
Depression-era prostitution business in Atlantic City. Skinny had gone
to jail in the late 1930s for a violation of the unfortunately named White
Slave Traffic Act, passed by Congress in 1910, for transporting prosti-
tutes across state lines. No one seemed to know anything about
Skinny's time in jail, why it happened, or the circumstances surround-
ing his arrest and conviction. The Lewisburg Federal Penitentiary in
Lewisburg, Pennsylvania—where he had served his time—did not
keep records from that far back, but they directed me to the U.S.
National Archives, Northeast Division, which are warehoused in
Manhattan.

The file entitled *"The United States* vs. *Paul D'Amato"* contained mostly indictments and subpoenas. On November 15, 1937, Skinny was indicted on thirteen felony counts for violation of the White Slave Traffic Act involving two women. One indictment documented nine separate occasions—between November 1934 and February 1936—when Skinny "did knowingly persuade, induce, entice and coerce" one Betty "Boots" Kelly "to go from one place to another in interstate commerce ... for the purpose of prostitution." The second indictment included four counts of the same, but with a woman named Anna Rosenblum, aka "Maxine D'Amato," all counts occurring in the spring and summer of 1937. It appears that both women were being sent back and forth between Atlantic City and Philadelphia to render their services. On one occasion, Boots Kelly was sent to New York City; on another, to Waterbury, Connecticut. In one of the indictments, a co-defendant is named—Margie Davis, aka Margie Blum—a madam Skinny was in cahoots with.

It is unclear whether Skinny—who sometimes traveled under the name Paul DeMoore—was with Boots and Anna/Maxine on all of these sojourns, but he did travel with Anna/Maxine on at least one occasion. Of the few dozen people who were served subpoenas to testify at his trial, one was the manager of the Terminal Hotel at Twelfth and Market Streets in Philadelphia. His subpoena commands him to "produce records showing registration of Maxine D'Amato and Paul D'Amato as man and wife at your hotel."

Paulajane had known since she was a teenager that her father had been married to someone before Bettyjane. "I was in high school and I had taken the bus and gotten off at the 500 Club," she said. "I was walking towards the club when this wacky-looking woman came up to me and said, 'Are you Skinny's daughter?' and I said, 'Yes,' and she said, 'From the first marriage or the second?' and I said, 'What?' and she said, 'Oh, your father was married before.' That's the first time I ever heard about it."

"Maxine was Jewish," Anna Bunting said of Skinny's first marriage. "Skinny went to prison for something that had to do with a bordello. Something happened there and Skinny was blamed for it and she was the witness and he married her so she couldn't testify against him. Her and I were very good friends. She used to come to my house all the time. Beautiful girl. Very pretty. I know she and Skinny never lived together. She was brokenhearted because she was crazy about him. She really loved him."

Skinny's niece Antoinette Malone remembers both women, though her version is slightly different. "Maxine and Betty were two of Skinny's girlfriends, at two different times," she said. "They were gorgeous—absolutely *gorgeous*. Skinny lived in an apartment above the Venice Restaurant on Mississippi Avenue, and Maxine lived with him there for a while. I do remember my mom going to court because of Skinny, but don't ask me why."

Several people were called to testify at Skinny's trial. Skinny's sisters Marie (Malone's mother) and Pat were both summoned by the U.S. Attorney's Office. Pat's subpoena was delivered to the Ritz-Carlton, where she worked as a hatcheck girl. Also subpoenaed were a banker from Philadelphia, a Western Union Telegraph Company representative, and two men already in prison. An Atlantic City physician, Dr. Christian Arleth, was ordered to "produce records showing the examination of one Betty Kelly during 1934 while the said Betty Kelly was employed as a prostitute at Poppy Gordon's House of prostitution at No. 15 No. Michigan Ave.," as well as "records of smears of Betty Kelly taken while she was employed as a prostitute at No. 17 No. Illinois Ave. Atlantic City, N.J., at a house operated by Marie Kenny, during the year 1935."

On November 18, 1937, Skinny pleaded not guilty, but a few months later, he switched his plea to guilty. On January 17, 1938, he was sentenced by Judge John Boyd Avis of the United States District Court in Camden, New Jersey, to one year and one day on each of nine counts, to run concurrently. He was committed immediately to the Camden County Jail to await a move to the Lewisburg Federal Penitentiary.

Skinny obviously got caught in the Nucky net. In an effort to bring down Nucky Johnson, the Treasury agents realized they were going to have to drag every last whore, pimp, bookie, madam, numbers man, and gambling den troll before a grand jury and try to get them to admit that they were paying graft to Johnson. This was their only chance to prove that he was not paying his income taxes. The Nucky Johnson report states that the agents' "preliminary survey" of the vice racket "revealed eight large houses of prostitution in operation in Atlantic City and doing a flourishing business. . . . When the agents first contacted the 'madames,' with a view to checking their income tax liabilities, they found that none of them had kept any books or records reflecting their business income and few, if any, had maintained any bank accounts. Because of these circumstances, no further attempt was made to investigate them until the month of September, 1937. The occasion which enabled the Treasury Agents to again take up their inquiry into this racket was the raiding of all the houses on August 30, 1937 by special agents of the F.B.I."

Skinny's indictments were filed in Camden just three months after the vice raids. The report goes on:

> At about the same time the Treasury Agents had come to
> Atlantic City to start their income tax investigation of
> Johnson, the F.B.I. agents had likewise appeared on the scene
> because of complaints received by them to the effect that vice
> was rampant in Atlantic City, under the protection of
> Johnson, and that women from New York, Pennsylvania and
> other states were being transported there for the purpose of
> prostitution. The F.B.I. agents simultaneously raided all of
> the houses, arrested the proprietors, inmates and customers;
> the total number of arrests was approximately 200. About 140
> of the prostitutes were held as material witnesses and
> imprisoned in various county prisons. . . . They were taken
> from these prisons from time to time for appearance before the
> United States Grand Jury and, as a result of their testimony,
> all the madames and about 30 procurers were indicted for
> violations of the White Slave Act.

Finally, after a four-and-a-half-year investigation, the trial of Enoch L. Johnson began on Monday, July 14, 1941, in the United States District Court in Camden, New Jersey, before Judge Albert Maris. The case had received so much attention from the press that special tables had to be set up in the courtroom to accommodate the dozens of extra reporters. Because all of the jurors were drawn from the Republican stronghold that was south Jersey, the government did not have high hopes of getting a conviction. Despite his wicked ways, the people of Jersey loved their Nucky. But on August 1, just two weeks later, he was convicted of income tax evasion, and Judge Maris sentenced him to the maximum: ten years' imprisonment. He was also fined $20,000 and ordered to pay the entire cost of the prosecution.

On July 31, the evening before he was sentenced and twelve days before he was put behind bars, Nucky married his showgirl, Flossie, at the Presbyterian church on Pennsylvania and Pacific Avenues. He wore a cream-colored mohair suit, yellow tie, and white shoes. The ceremony received almost as much press as his trial. (Hearst's *Sunday Mirror* ran an eight-part series on Nucky entitled the *The Czar of the Boardwalk*, based on the "veteran *Mirror* reporter Arthur Mefford's 16 years of digging.") After the services, a party was held at Nucky's bungalow on Iowa Avenue, where many champagne corks popped and a dozen tabloid photographers had been invited in to document the event for posterity. "Eat, drink, and be merry, my friends," Nucky said as he raised his glass in a toast, "for tomorrow we may go to jail." After the reception, the couple went to the Drake Hotel in Philadelphia for an eight-hour honeymoon. The next morning, he was brought before Judge Maris, who "threw the book at him," as Nucky later complained.

Flamboyant to the bitter end, Nucky went out in high style. On August 11, Nucky's ever loyal bodyguard, Roly-Poly Louie Kessel, drove his boss, accompanied by his bride, in one of Nucky's limousines, through the mountains of Pennsylvania to the Lewisburg Penitentiary in the Susquehanna Valley. For the next four years, Louie and Flossie visited Nucky every week at "college." On October 4, 1944, Louie Kessel was driving Flossie in the limo. They were on their way back from Philadelphia, where Flossie had gone to plead with Judge Maris to approve Nucky's parole application. Just outside Atlantic City, they were broadsided by another car and Louie died in Flossie's arms.

Chapter Three

When Skinny got out of jail in January 1939, he returned to an Atlantic City that was just beginning to roil from the Nucky Johnson investigations. Skinny vowed he would never wind up in prison again. He steered clear of the dirty business of prostitution for a while, but he was an incorrigible gambler who could not resist the cards and dice. And while he did manage to stay out of trouble for the next twenty-five years, there were a few close calls.

Skinny went into business with a man named Jack Berenato, who was also born and raised in Atlantic City and whom Skinny had known since they were children. Berenato—known more commonly as "Colby" after the name (Jack Colby) he had assumed in the boxing days of his youth—was a short, stout man with dark eyes, thick dark eyebrows, and a bald head. He was quiet, tough, and extremely cautious. Later in life he owned two identical Buicks, one for driving around and the other for parking in front of his nightclub so that everyone would assume he was always there. He and Skinny leased a seedy little place at 2019 Pacific Avenue and opened up a room with a big blackboard for bookmaking and taking horse-racing and sports bets. The room also had one crap table. In the front, there was the obligatory "cigar store"—the Plaza Cigar Store—but the joint was, again, wide open, meaning anyone could walk in off the street and gamble. The back room accommodated up to 150 people.

During the time that Skinny and Colby were running their joint, a new threat to Atlantic City's fragile equilibrium materialized, and this time it was contained within its own ranks. Thomas D. Taggart Jr. was a local attorney who had been elected to the New Jersey State Assembly, and then the New Jersey State Senate, from 1934 to 1940. In 1940, Taggart was elected to the Atlantic City Commission, and in May of that year he was appointed by his fellow commissioners as mayor of Atlantic City, making him the chief of police.

Taggart was never married and had strange habits. He lived with his sisters in a big house on Illinois Avenue just off Pacific, behind the city's library. A religious zealot and a loner, Taggart was short, beady eyed, and pear-shaped. Many people in Atlantic City thought he was a closet homosexual. In fact, Skinny once told a journalist, "What can I say? He liked boys, young boys. Several times I even fixed him up with good-looking young fags. But he was a hell of a politician, even though he was queer." In Taggart's first year in office, he launched a campaign against the underworld through ceaseless raids on bookies and madams. He even harassed the old folks on the Boardwalk while they enjoyed pokerino and bingo games. He took to carrying two pearl-inlaid pistols on his belt, western style, earning him the nickname "Two Guns" Taggart. People laughed behind his back, calling him the "Wyatt Earp of Atlantic City."

The biggest, most flagrant casino in town at this time was the Hialeah on Michigan and Atlantic Avenues. Run by two brothers, Sam and Frank Camarota, the Hialeah was an elaborate setup of two big rooms over two floors that held about five hundred people. The Horseshoe Bar was on the ground floor in the front and was indeed shaped like a horseshoe. Customers walked through the main room—where there was usually entertainment—and to the rear and upstairs, where there was a big casino room with blackboards, racing wire, crap table, and roulette wheel.

There were several other casinos and gambling dens around town. Some were elegant, like Babette's on Mississippi and Pacific, owned by Dan Stebbins and his wife, Babette. During Prohibition, Stebbins owned several speakeasies, and his wife, whose real name was Blanche, had once been a showgirl who performed under the stage name Blanche Babette. The two became wealthy, prominent members of Atlantic City society who entertained on their forty-foot yacht. Another fancy joint was the Bath & Turf Club on Stenton Avenue just off the Boardwalk. The Bath & Turf was in a grand old house that had been converted into a business with an elegant Chinese restaurant on the ground floor. One wall in the foyer had a mural painted on it; at the push of a button, the mural opened to reveal a secret passageway to the "guest house" next door, which was outfitted as a casino. The Bath & Turf had been a favorite of Meyer Lansky's, who at one time held an interest in the club along with Nucky Johnson and the manager, Charles Schwartz.

Several other gambling establishments were more pedestrian. The Admiral on Kentucky Avenue was perhaps the best example of the no-frills horse room. It had no "front" whatsoever, didn't even pretend to be anything other than what it was—though the windows out front were decorated with cigarette advertisements to block the view. Inside, there was a large slate blackboard. A man named Vincent Lane wore headphones, and he would chalk up the prices as they came in over the radio. At the far end of the room were two crap tables running $200-limit games. Though the Admiral held up to about two hundred people, it was considered a small-time gambling operation: it accepted fifty-cent bets, and many customers, usually on "relief," would pool their quarters to place bets.

All the casinos and gambling dens would close down voluntarily during elections or other politically sensitive times. Among the denizens of the gambling underworld, the jargon went like this: "The slough is on" or the town is "sloughed," meaning no go, close up shop. Sometimes "the slough" would last only a couple of weeks, other times a few months. But once Taggart began his raids, the Hialeah was forced to close down for two years beginning in the latter part of 1940 because it was too obviously a casino. It was just after the Hialeah closed that Skinny and Colby opened up. They managed to operate their relatively low-key den under the radar for several months—partly because Taggart's secretary, a man named Vince Manno, held an interest in the "cigar store" and had managed to shield them from Taggart's wrath for a while.

That summer, there was a lot of "war talk" around the resort, more specifically rumors circulating that the U.S. Army Air Force—as the now separate military branches were then called—was going to take over Atlantic City as a training ground for troops. With the threat of such a big spotlight being trained on the resort, Taggart could no longer ignore Skinny and Colby's "cigar store." On July 14, 1941, Skinny and Colby were running a crap game that had been going for many, many hours. By one-thirty A.M., Taggart, along with several constables and police officers whom he had deputized, raided the place; thirty-four people were brought down to city hall and held overnight in a large anteroom in the detective bureau. The next morning, the group was sent to the magistrate's court, fined $200 each for "operating a dice game," and then dismissed.

Skinny was arrested and charged with "maintaining a disreputable house [gaming]," to which he pleaded no contest and received a 364-day suspended sentence. The raid and arrest spooked Skinny, and the Plaza Cigar Store stayed closed for about six weeks, at which point Skinny left the partnership.

His instincts served him well. When things had cooled off after a bit, Colby reopened on his own. Two weeks later, in the middle of the day—with about ninety people in the room betting horses and playing craps—Taggart raided the place again. Everyone was booked and held on $1,000 bail—and eventually indicted by a grand jury for bookmaking and running a crap game. Colby was sentenced to one year in state prison and fined $1,000. He appealed his sentence and was sent instead to the county jail, served only ninety-two days, and was put on probation. His probation officer was none other than Vincent Lane, the man with the headphones who ran the tote board at the Admiral horse room on Kentucky Avenue.

Such was the intricate web of corruption that continued to thrive—post-Nucky—in Atlantic City. The gamblers ran the city, literally. Not long after the raid on Colby's cigar store, Mayor Taggart went to Florida on vacation. Everyone had grown weary of his crusade, so while he was away the other four commissioners of Atlantic City launched a coup by voting to strip him of his powers as director of public safety, which relieved him of his jurisdiction over the police and fire departments. The chief of police, Harry Saunders, and the head of the vice squad, Louis Arnheim, now reported to Frank S. "Hap" Farley, the county chairman and a state senator since 1940. Farley was the emergent new boss of Atlantic County, and everyone in the resort knew that the real power behind Farley was a man named Herman Orman, commonly referred to as "Stumpy" because of a withered finger on his right hand. He owned the Cosmopolitan Hotel among other properties; more important, however, he was the man who approved all large betting operations in Atlantic City. A guy might be able to get away with running a small cigar-store book, but anything larger required Orman's approval. Bookies would sometimes lay off big bets to the bigger bookmakers, a move that could not be made without Stumpy. But when a notice appeared in the *Atlantic City Press* that all racetracks were to be shuttered around the country till the end of the war and that the U.S. Army Air Force was going to take over Atlantic City, every crap game and bookie joint in the city closed up.

✳

After Colby got out of jail, he and Skinny went into partnership again, this time with a nightclub-restaurant called Luigi's on the corner of Arkansas and Pacific. With the gambling hall in the back under Skinny's direction, the place became a favorite with his old customers and the hottest after-hours spot in the city. The 500 Café, built by a man named Phil Barr and opened in 1936, was just around the corner—and it was not doing so well.

"It was just that I had a reputation," Skinny once recalled. "I hate to explain this, because it sounds like a brag, but people came to Luigi's—to wherever I was—because I had a name. In those days Luigi's was packed every night, and the 500 was dead. They didn't have any business."

Skinny once told a reporter that the deal initially offered to him to come to the 500 Café "had a lot of dirt to it" and that he "turned it down at first, since I was half owner of Luigi's. But they came back again, and this time I couldn't say no. At that time, there was only two casinos in town—Luigi's and the Five. There was lots of horse rooms, five or six, but only two casinos. It was one night in 1941 when I went to the 500. I worked one night at Luigi's, and it was packed. The next day, I went to the Five, and it went from being dead to having a million-odd people—overnight. They all followed me from Luigi's. Word traveled that fast." When Skinny and Colby parted ways, Skinny never even bothered to sell his half of the interest in Luigi's.

The 500 Café was Phil Barr's dream. He was a young trolley conductor and boxing promoter from Philadelphia—solidly built and blond—whom everyone thought looked a lot like Bob Hope. After his wife died in the mid-1930s, Barr entrusted his only child, Catherine, to the care of a Philadelphia couple and moved to Ventnor to chase his dream of owning a nightclub. He scrounged up the money to buy two houses on Missouri Avenue and promptly tore them down to make way for his new venture. The result was a plain, two-story yellow brick building with a shiny, stainless-steel marquee that read "500 Café." The second floor was a fairly sprawling apartment for Barr; on the ground floor was the café, by day a horse-betting room with the usual blackboard and chairs set up, by night a cabaret with a small stage and dancing showgirls.

Nucky Johnson was still ruling the roost when the 500 Café opened, and Barr was quickly inculcated into the byzantine system of checks and balances, as well as his place in the complicated drama that was corrupt Atlantic City. In fact, he began carrying on an affair with Louise Mack, the legendary owner of the Entertainer's Club, one of the first openly gay bars in the county, on Snake Alley. Louise surely educated Barr on the particular rules of survival in the resort. Barr must have listened carefully, because he operated the 500 Café peacefully for five years.

The Garibaldi Club was right next door to the 500, housed in the ground floor of a small hotel. This was the same club that Skinny's father, Emilio, had been president of for a time in the early 1920s—and now it was Skinny's job to run the casino in the very same building. The club was founded by Italians near the turn of the last century and was mostly a haven for immigrants to play card games like sette-mezza, briscolo, scopa, and pinochle. When Barr built the 500 he made a deal with the owner of the hotel that housed the social club and set up a small casino in the back of the Garibaldi. In the back of the 500 Café there was a cigar and cigarette stand, with a door right next to it. In order to gain access to the casino, you had to know the code, which is to say you had to purchase the right brand of cigarettes. One night it might be Viceroy, the next, Lucky Strike. "I remember Skinny talking about when he got the offer to go to the 500," said Joe Del Raso, a prominent Philadelphia attorney who, as a teenager, had lived next door to the D'Amatos and worked at the 500 Club. "He went over to Barr's, and the deal was that he was allowed to keep all the change from the casino, all the nonpaper money. It was a really big deal."

Skinny's casino behind the 500 Café initially held about 175 gamblers and was run in much the same way that casinos are today, though on a much less grand scale. Instead of high-tech surveillance systems with cameras recording every hand, a man stood on a ladder, up above the tables, on the lookout for cheating. Big players, much like today, were never sent away empty-handed. Skinny's version of "comps" were called *vigoreges*, or complimentary services afforded high rollers— depending on the level of play or how much they lost. In Skinny's day, *vigorege* could be a "bean," or $1; a "fin," $5; or a "sawbuck," $10. If a big player came from out of town and lost a lot of money, he was given $100 for room and board and train fare home.

Skinny hadn't been there but a few months when the 500 Café was raided by the police. Dozens of people were rounded up and questioned—including the notorious scar-faced Cappy Hoffman and a fugitive named Morris Zatlin, who was a suspect in the attempted murder of Dan Stebbins, the owner of Babette's. The night of the raid on the 500 Café, police discovered all manner of gambling devices and horseroom paraphernalia. In Barr's apartment above the club, they found a safe with $5,000 in cash and a buzzer alert system to warn of imminent raids. Barr was thrown in jail, along with some of his dealers; he suffered a heart attack behind bars, and his lawyer argued for his release based on medical necessity. Not long after he got out of jail, the IRS came after him. He owed $44,912.54 plus interest to the U.S. government, and his property and bank accounts were seized. He would eventually suffer another heart attack and die in June 1942.

One of the enduring myths in Atlantic City is that Skinny won the 500 Café in a card game. The real story is much less dramatic. The Five closed down for several months, and Skinny set about cobbling together a group of investors and front men so that he could, at long last, be in charge of a nightclub. His lifelong dream of owning the Garibaldi Club next door was finally within his reach. Skinny's uncle Charles J. DiSanti was a chef, and on May 1, 1943, DiSanti "took over" the club, renting it from the mortgage holder who had repossessed it from Barr. The 500 Café was now partly owned and managed by Irvin Wolf, who had previously operated the Hotel Senator and the Rendezvous Café in Philadelphia, as well as a café at the Breakers Hotel in Atlantic City.

Skinny and his partners, which now included Mario Di Fonzo from Wilmington, Delaware, who held the liquor license, would eventually succeed in buying the property outright. In a credit investigation on Charles DiSanti and Irvin Wolf prepared by Dun & Bradstreet in August 1944, the following information was reported: "It is the general opinion that there are others financing this enterprise, as DiSanti represents only small means of his own." According to Grace D'Amato, Skinny held a 25 percent stake and borrowed $40,000 from his sister Pat and her successful husband, Sammy Cohen, to get his piece of the club. Grace D'Amato also suggests that Wolf held 25 percent and Di Fonzo owned the other 50 percent. But Nick Tosches, in his 1992 biography of Dean Martin, reported that the gangster Marco Reginelli of Camden was "the sub-rosa owner" of the nightclub. Reginelli was the reputed head of the Mob in Philadelphia, before Angelo Bruno. It seems unlikely, and many people have sworn up and down that it's utterly false because Skinny was intent on going legit. He was about to launch himself into a future where he and he alone would decide how things were going to be—and the last thing he had in mind was to be the puppet of a mobster. In fact, on opening night, Jack Colby (Berenato) sent over several cases of liquor because Skinny was out of cash. But when Skinny discovered it was stolen, he gave it back, not wanting to be indebted to criminals or to start off on the wrong foot. To make do, his brother Willie ran to the liquor store and bought one bottle each of Scotch and rye. As money started coming in, Willie ran out to restock the shelves, a few bottles at a time, throughout the night. The next day, Skinny, temporarily solvent again, went out and bought two cases of liquor and hired a bartender.

Fred Augello started working as a busboy at the 500 in 1945, when he was seventeen. He said that Marco Reginelli dined regularly with Skinny. The 500 ran a dinner show and a late-night show. If Reginelli was coming down from Philadelphia, the waiters and busboys would be told the "little man" was coming. No matter what time Reginelli arrived, a full show went on for him. None of the workers left until it was over. Reginelli and his men were generous tippers—almost embarrassingly so. When Angelo Bruno took over after Reginelli died in 1956, he too was treated like royalty.

Reginelli's regular visits to the 500 Club—and his lavish reception there—led to years of rumors that the Mob was really in charge of the 500. But Skinny's cousin Joe DiSanti has long insisted that it was simply not true, and there are documents to back up his claim. The deed, dated June 6, 1946, was drawn up by Samuel Backer, a lawyer who had an office at the Guarantee Trust Building on North Carolina and Atlantic Avenues. The agreement spells out that Mario Di Fonzo agreed to sell his half of the 500 Café at 6 South Missouri Avenue (including Eldridge's Warehouse next door at 4 South, which eventually became an extension of the club) to Irvin and Skinny for $38,628. According to the deed, the money was to be held in escrow by Backer until the two men could form a corporation and successfully transfer the liquor license, by no later than July 1. The document also required that Skinny and Irvin agree "not to use the name '500 Café,'" which is obviously why they changed it to the 500 *Club*—a subtle variation that signaled Skinny's shift from backroom gambling boss to nightclub impresario.

A certificate of incorporation filed for the new 500 Club in June 1946 listed Irvin Wolf as the corporation's principal agent. Skinny's sister Antoinette "Pat" Cohen and John DiSanti—Joe's father—were also listed. Whoever Mario Di Fonzo was, there is no doubt that by 1946 the 500 Club was entirely legitimate and aboveboard. According to Joe DiSanti, his father and his brother, John and Charles, were the ones on the mortgage from the very beginning; not a penny of Mob money was involved. "Skinny was stepping up to do something bigger than a cigar store," Joe said. "This was the first time he was going to own something himself, but he did it on a shoestring, relatively speaking, to get an operation of that size. But a lot of friends, regular guys, guys who had businesses on the Boardwalk, helped him out because they had a little money. I know of two guys who bought liquor, brought it to the club, and gave it to the bartender to put behind the bar. So here you have a guy, earning his own way by owning his own business from when he was fourteen, getting in a couple of jams, meeting some very *strong individuals* . . . but still going it on his own with the help of friends and family and not going to the *strong individuals* and asking for money because then he wouldn't have done it himself. And that made everybody else—all the *strong individuals*—respect him. The *very, very strong individuals* he had the pleasure of meeting when they were young men—we're talking about a particular group now—since he did it on his own, they respected him even more, and that's what kept him from being an underling to somebody else. He was treated as a friend, as somebody who stood on his own two feet, and favors might have been exchanged, but they were exchanged from a point of strength."

The Dun & Bradstreet report went on: The 500 Club employed ten people; the room seated 250; net sales averaged $75,000 a year and "past operators of this club could not make it pay." Despite the high tax on meals and drinks, went the report, DiSanti (read: Skinny) "is transacting a good volume of business at the present time. . . . Operates as a nightclub which is open only during the evenings and caters to a sporting class of trade."

The backroom casino kept people coming in, as usual, and mostly, Skinny ran his club without incident in those early, heady days. But one night not long after they opened, the New Jersey State Police raided the joint, looking for the casino. The dealers all scattered, and Willie scooped all the money into a bag, ran out the back door and up the fire escape onto the roof, and hid in a chimney till the cops were gone.

✦

Atlantic City had managed to hang on through the Great Depression, thanks in part to Nucky Johnson, who kept the resort just barely solvent by, among other things, pumping a lot of his own ill-gotten fortune back into the economy. But the resort suffered nonetheless, and the paydays were nowhere near what they had been during Prohibition. However, when the United States finally entered into World War II in 1941, the aging resort suffered a serious blow and began to lose its place as the "World's Playground."

From as early as the spring of 1942, East Coast beaches were declared off-limits from sunset to sunrise—beach parties and night fishing were forbidden by the Coast Guard. Because of its location between Delaware Bay and New York Harbor, New Jersey had more commercial ships torpedoed by German U-boats off its coast than any other state along the shore. The beaches were awash in tarlike slicks of oil, and pieces of sunken ships began to wash up on the shore. The Coast Guard patrolled the Boardwalk, and armed, mounted troops with dogs covered the beaches, on the lookout for spies attempting to come ashore from the U-boats. Blimps hovered over the ocean, ready to drop depth charges on enemy subs.

Atlantic City's economy was stunted by the war in other, more devastating ways: food and gasoline were rationed, and electricity was limited. In March 1942, a dim-out was ordered for the city, which meant that all streetlights were turned off and all windows on the eastern side of every building were darkened with oilcloth or shades; the top half of automobile headlamps were painted with black "eyelids" so that the light could not be seen from the sky. The massive neon signs that hovered over the ocean at the end of the magnificent piers were turned off. Even smoking was prohibited on the Boardwalk for fear the glowing tips could be seen by the Germans.

When the U.S. Army Air Force decided to lease the Atlantic City Convention Hall as a training facility, the resort braced itself. But over the next few years, some five hundred thousand army air force personnel came and went through "Camp Boardwalk," as it was unofficially called, preparing for—or recovering from—overseas duty. It proved to be a windfall for the resort, which had faced a devastating dropoff in tourist revenue as a result of the war. It also gave Atlantic City a chance to actually work *with* the federal government for a change.

The soldiers marched and drilled on the Boardwalk. Mock "invasions" were conducted on the beach while snipers and sharpshooters were trained on the roofs of hotels. Calisthenics and briefings were conducted throughout the massive auditorium that is Convention Hall, while neighboring hotels were converted into barracks and military hospitals where servicemen came for rest and recreation. By 1943, the army had taken over the Traymore, Breakers, Brighton, Shelburne, St. Charles, and Dennis Hotels, among others. "Lobbies, mezzanines, dining rooms, halls and other parts of the hotels were stripped of rugs, carpets, draperies, and other adornments," reported *The New York Times*. "Over the concrete of the floors marched thousands of leather-heeled recruits. Most bedroom furniture has been replaced with army equipment."

To many of the business owners of Atlantic City—legitimate and otherwise—the army occupation of their ailing resort was a godsend. In fact, the proprietors were so thrilled, their overzealous generosity toward the soldiers caused the U.S. Army Air Force Basic Training Center to issue a warning: "Civilians are requested not to overdo their hospitality toward soldiers in taverns. The result of buying drinks for a soldier is usually to get the soldier into trouble. . . ."

✦

Not long after Skinny took possession of the 500 Club, he started heading up to New York on weekends in the winter when things were slow. He would run all-night poker games in fancy hotel rooms for Mob guys and big players. And he started frequenting Bernard "Toots" Shor's nightclub on West Fifty-first Street, just off Fifth Avenue in Manhattan, which was famous for being Joe DiMaggio's hangout. It wasn't much of a place, really, just two rooms: the one in front featured a big circular bar where men stood three deep; the back room was a brightly lit dining room. But it was *the* place to be among the sporting crowd, and Joe was the room's biggest star during the years when he could do no wrong. Shor—a loud, rude, fat, lovable guy—was a Philadelphian who had moved to New York in 1930 and wound up running speakeasies for Lucky Luciano at the tail end of Prohibition. After repeal, he bounced from restaurant to restaurant, usually as headwaiter, until he opened his own joint with Mob money.

Shor was an incorrigible drinker and gambler—and he would never let anyone pay for anything, least of all DiMaggio. Skinny watched Shor and learned how to keep customers coming back. Shor was also friends with Joe Adonis, the New York mobster who had dozens of whorehouses under his control. Adonis, like every other gangster and bookie in America, was making a fortune off DiMaggio during the Streak—a remarkable string of hits in fifty-six consecutive games—and in those days you could bet right down to the pitch. America, in need of a distraction from the horror of the war, became utterly obsessed with DiMaggio. When Streak fever reached a crescendo, the news of Joe's hits had moved from the sports pages to the front pages; every newspaper and radio station in the country was constantly updating with bulletins. *Life* magazine commissioned an oil painting of DiMaggio for a cover. The number one song in the country was "Joltin' Joe DiMaggio" recorded by Les Brown and His Band of Renown. The underworld guys were not immune to the fever, and they wanted to show their appreciation; they did so, not surprisingly, with free limousines and hookers.

Skinny and Shor became fast friends—and their friendship lasted a lifetime. Skinny had known about Toots both through the Philadelphia connection and via Lucky Luciano, but now they were both in the same business—running a club, making celebrities comfortable—and they had a lot more to talk about. In fact, Skinny first met Joe DiMaggio one night at Shor's while Joe was sitting at his usual table in the front right-hand corner of the dining room. But it surely was a much bigger moment for Skinny than Joe.

—✳—

By the summer of 1942, the once unstoppable Joe DiMaggio was in a slump. His marriage to Dorothy Arnold was in trouble and his batting average had slipped into the low .200s. The draft was haunting the dreams of every other person in baseball but Joe was married and the new father of Joe junior, which meant that he was classified 3-A and in no immediate danger of being called up. Still, there was a whiff of arrogance and greed hanging in the air around him. At the start of the 1942 season, he had demanded a raise on his $37,500 contract—more than anyone had ever been paid to play ball—and he had refused to sign his contract when he didn't get the money. As the legendary baseball scribe Dan Daniel wrote at the time, "People just don't like to hear a ballplayer grumbling over being asked to work for a paltry $37,500 a year when the base pay for privates is 21 clackers a month."

When rumors leaked out that DiMaggio's wife was poking around Reno, Nevada—establishing residency in preparation for a divorce— fans started to boo him at every game and send hate mail. He was called a coward, and other, anti-Italian slurs, for not enlisting. Eventually Dorothy herself told Joe that if he would just sign up, like his brother and several other ball players, the booing would stop. Finally, she leveled a threat: "Sign up, or I'll divorce you." In February of 1943, DiMaggio reported for duty at Santa Ana Air Base in California, but it did not save his marriage. Six months later, Dorothy filed for divorce in Los Angeles, and in May of 1944 the judge granted it to her.

Sergeant Joe DiMaggio was stationed with the Seventh Army Air Force in Honolulu, where he spent most of his time playing ball—or pinochle for money. Eventually Dorothy moved back to New York, while Joe, depressed and alone among his fellow soldiers, checked into an army hospital, suffering from a severely ulcerated stomach. After a few months—as the rest of his unit went on to fight on the front lines— Joe begged the air force to send him to a hospital in California, where he then begged for a transfer to "Camp Boardwalk." In February 1944, Joe DiMaggio was transferred to U.S. Special Services in Atlantic City, where the Yankees would be in spring training in a couple of weeks and where Dorothy and three-year-old Joe junior would be just a 130-mile drive away in Manhattan.

When DiMaggio got word that he was getting transferred to Camp Boardwalk, his nightclub friends in New York called Sam Camarota, the owner of the Hialeah in Atlantic City, and asked him to take care of Joe while he was in town. "What am I going to do with Joe DiMaggio?" wondered Camarota. And then a light flicked on. "I'll send him to Skinny! Skinny likes celebrities!" Sure enough, Skinny was more than happy to oblige, knowing that to have DiMaggio sitting at a corner booth at the 500 was exactly what he needed to bring in the customers. Watching Toots in Manhattan taught Skinny a thing or two about what makes a place go, and having famous people around, and never charging them a dime, was rule number one. Skinny put Joe up in his brother Willie's place while he had an apartment built for him above the 500 Club. Before long, Skinny would have DiMaggio installed nightly at his own booth in the front bar and he hired a private waitress for him. Skinny was now palling around with a living legend and it changed his station in Atlantic City. People outside of Atlantic City's tight-knit Italian community and the nightclub and gambling worlds began to treat Skinny with a new level of respect because, well, everybody wanted to meet Joe DiMaggio.

✦

Skinny was hanging out at the 500 Café one afternoon in the spring of 1943, when a couple of seventeen-year-old girls walked in. Bettyjane Creamer and her best girlfriend had played hooky, hidden their books in an alley alongside the club, gone in, and sat at the bar. Bettyjane's friend had been talking for weeks about her latest crush—on a guy named Skinny who worked at the 500. But when Skinny and his brother Willie came out from the coat check behind the bar that day, Bettyjane nearly gasped. Skinny was wearing a yellow, brown, and white plaid shirt and matching yellow pants, and he was drop-dead handsome. Reflexively, she played hard to get by grabbing Willie's arm, pulling him closer, and talking to him for the rest of the afternoon. She did not want this Skinny character to see just how smitten she really was. And from that day on, Skinny pursued Bettyjane relentlessly.

Bettyjane was sixteen years younger than Skinny and an only child. Born in Philadelphia and raised in Ventnor, her parents, Edythe and Frank, were quiet, simple Protestants; Frank drove a bread truck, Edythe was a housewife. When Bettyjane was nine years old, she contracted rheumatic fever, so her parents sold their house and moved into a ground-floor apartment on Ventnor Avenue where Bettyjane would no longer have to climb stairs. Because of her illness, she was doted on, overprotected; even after she recovered and blossomed into a beautiful teenager, she always seemed frail and delicate. Naturally, her parents disapproved of Skinny. He was thirty-three, a dashing gambler with an unwholesome lifestyle and a reputation around town as someone who had been to prison. Before long, though, they warmed up to him—as eventually everybody did.

Bettyjane had entered the Miss Atlantic City Contest just a few months after meeting Skinny, in June 1943. She placed second to a woman named Janet Garbarino. Not long after the pageant, the *Atlantic City Press* ran a photograph of Bettyjane under the headline REPORTER'S PIN-UP GIRL.

> *She's considered beautiful by many, very pretty by most and extremely attractive by everyone who meets Bettyjane Creamer, the fawn-haired hazel-eyed alluring looking lassie pictured here. Bettyjane . . . is 18 years of age, stands 5 feet, 5 inches in height and possesses more curves than the road to Pike's Peak. She can do more with a soft satin gown than a wardrobe director in Hollywood, to say nothing of the fascination she arrests when sporting a sweater. She was runner-up in the "Miss Atlantic City Contest" last year, and the gallery is still puzzled as to why she didn't take first prize. . . . Should she enter this year again, it is conceded there are few around who could defeat her. Our "Pin-up Girl" has had numerous offers to work as a model with the leading big city agencies, and has successfully worked as a manikin at various times. However, her inclinations for a profession lean to the pen.*

Bettyjane did, in fact, enter the Miss Atlantic City Contest the following June, but again she came in runner-up, this time to a woman named Barbara Jones. Bettyjane became friends with Jones and the woman who had vanquished her in the Miss Atlantic City Contest the year before—Janet Garbarino. They were bonded, at least in part, by their dream of following in the footsteps of yet another of their beautiful classmates—Jessica Wilcox, Miss Atlantic City 1941. One of the main functions of Miss Atlantic City was to serve as hostess to the Miss America Pageant every September by marching in the parade and just generally being *there* for anyone who might need her. That year, the pageant was held in the mammoth Convention Hall for the first time, and it brought a lot of media to town. Jessica drew an extraordinary amount of attention, giving interviews to radio and newsmen and having her photograph taken again and again. One person who took notice of the hubbub surrounding the long-legged, bosomy local girl was John Powers, a judge at the pageant and founder of the legendary John Powers Modeling Agency in New York. Powers said to Jessica, "You'll be hearing from me," and sure enough, a few months later she received a telegram inviting her to come to New York to do a cigarette ad.

When she arrived in New York, there was no cigarette ad; in fact, there was no work at all. In two weeks she made only $10. One day she went to see a sister of a friend who worked at the other big modeling agency in New York, Harry Conover. A photographer walked into the reception area, saw Jessica sitting there, and convinced Conover to steal her from John Powers. Just a few years earlier, Harry Conover had been a top male model working for Powers; he roomed with another Powers model—a tall blond Yale student who would one day become president of the United States, Gerald Ford. When Conover left Powers to start his own agency in 1939, Ford invested $1,000 in his new venture.

It was money well spent. By the time Jessica Wilcox met Conover, his agency was a bona fide success story. He had become famous for his coven of "Conover Cover Girls," of which Jessica Wilcox would soon be the star. He convinced Jessica to change her name to Candy Johnson, but she signed her first contract Candy Jones and it stuck. Over the next several months, Conover turned Candy Jones into the first supermodel by spending a fortune on a media campaign with a candy stripe theme. She had red-and-white-striped clothing, accessories, jewelry, matchbooks, and bicycle. He littered Manhattan with thousands of red-and-white business cards that read "Candy Jones Was Here."

His scheme worked like a charm. Candy Jones soon signed a contract with Warner Bros. and became the first model to ever get $35 an hour. In one month in 1943, she appeared on the cover of eleven magazines and was voted Model of the Year by a panel of judges that included Loretta Young, who commented that she looked like "a real girl." She was the model for a postage stamp honoring women who served in the armed forces in World War II. Two photographs of Candy Jones—one in a polka-dot bikini, the other in a dress made of transparent parachute nylon—became favorite pinups among GIs stationed around the world. That same year, she was cast by Mike Todd in the Broadway play *Mexican Hayride.*

In 1946, Conover, after only one date with his new star, proposed to Candy Jones over the telephone while she was on a promotional tour for Cover Girl cosmetics. On July Fourth, the couple flew to Canada to judge the Miss Canada Contest. They were married in a church in Hamilton, Ontario, where they had to set up speakers outside for the overflow crowd.

It's not hard to understand why Candy Jones's old classmates back in Atlantic City—Bettyjane, Barbara, and Janet—might think it was a good idea to head up to New York for an appointment at the Harry Conover Agency. With their connection to Candy Jones, both Bettyjane and Janet were accepted by the Conover Agency, and they rented an apartment together and moved to New York with Bettyjane's mother as their chaperone. In the two surviving photographs from Bettyjane's portfolio, she looks a lot like Betty Grable. In one picture, she has long lacquered red nails with a gigantic ring on her finger. Wearing a simple black dress, she looks every inch the model from the 1940s. On the back is a Harry Conover stamp with the address—"Fifty-two Vanderbilt Ave."—Bettyjane's measurements, and, at the very bottom, the words *$5 per hour.*

Eventually Barbara Jones joined her friends in New York. "I went up there with Barbara," said Bud McCall, Jones's high school sweetheart, "because she didn't want to go alone. We were kids, for crying out loud! Bettyjane and Janet were living in an apartment, and I stayed there for a couple of days while Barbara was off looking for modeling jobs. Candy Jones was around, too."

When Barbara made her first visit to the Conover Agency, she insisted that Bud come with her, but he wouldn't go inside. "When she came out of the agency she was shaking like a leaf. She went in with all of her photographs and came out and said, 'They want me to do underwear ads, and I can't do it. I know I have to start somewhere, but I'm afraid of this.' She came back to Atlantic City and did modeling jobs here."

Bettyjane didn't last long, either. She got a few jobs, but nothing too exciting and certainly no magazine covers or commercial jobs for big cosmetics companies. Besides, her heart wasn't in it. She was in love with Skinny D'Amato and could think of nothing else. Despite the fact that Skinny came up to New York frequently and took her out on the town, showed her off to the guys at Toots's place, Bettyjane missed him too much whenever he returned to Atlantic City. After a couple of months, she went home to live with her parents and hang out at the 500 Club.

"She talked about Skinny all the time," said McCall. "But he was older than we were, and he was well established in his business. I was too young to go into his club, and I didn't want to embarrass him. We went out a couple times—Barb and I and another couple and Bettyjane—and we would drop her off at the 500 Club, where we met him and talked to him. He took a shine to younger people who knew Bettyjane."

In September 1943, McCall got his orders to go into the navy and shipped off to Sampson Naval Base in Seneca, New York. Within a week of his arrival, a box arrived. "I was sitting on the upper bunk and opened it up and it was a big chocolate cake. I love chocolate, but I couldn't imagine who had sent me a cake. I opened the card and it was signed 'Skinny.' I was stunned. I barely knew him. And the card said, 'When you get home on leave be sure to stop off and see me.'" When that time came, Bud called Skinny, who was living in the apartment above the club, and told him he'd be arriving back in Atlantic City by train on a Friday night at eleven o'clock.

"Why don't you stop by the club," said Skinny.

"I'd be delighted to," said Bud.

"I want to give you an address on Mississippi Ave.," said Skinny. "It's between Arctic and Atlantic, and it will be a house on the right-hand side. Stop there first. Knock on the door and tell them I sent you. It's my present to you."

Bud got off the train and walked the two blocks to Mississippi. It was a house right next door to St. Michael's, the Catholic school and church that Skinny had attended nearly thirty years earlier. "There were three windows in the front, right on the sidewalk," said Bud. "I knocked, and this very heavyset woman came to the door, in her mid-fifties. She had a long dress on. It was a room about as big as an average living room. There was another door, but it was closed. And there was a couch in the room. And I said, 'My name is Bud McCall. Mr. D'Amato sent me.' And she said, 'Ohhh, yes. Skinny told me to expect you.' She puts her arm around me and she opens up the other door, and man, oh, man, here are these women sitting around on this Victorian, plush furniture, little couches, like chaise lounges. And the place is bathed in this reddish light. There were all these women sitting in men's laps. Some were in bathing suits, some didn't have any tops on, and some were totally naked. I thought, *Oh, my god.* What did I get into here? I was only seventeen. And she said, 'This is Skinny's treat.' I had heard about these things, but I'd never seen anything like it. I was afraid the cops were going to come, because, you know, Skinny had a reputation around town. I was sweating in my uniform. I said, 'Geez, you know, I really don't have the time. I really have to get going. My mother and dad are supposed to meet me, and I have to take a trolley down to Margate.' And she said, 'Oh, why don't you stay.' And she calls over this girl, but I just left."

Skinny was obviously still up to his old tricks; he had not completely turned his back on the sex trade in Atlantic City. McCall, a nervous wreck, walked the two blocks to the 500 Club. "I was too young to go in there," he said, "but there was a doorman, a big tall black man. He was huge. I believe he had on a top hat. I told him who I was and he said, 'Yes, Mr. D'Amato's expecting you.' And he went in and Skinny came out. 'How you doing, Bud? Gee, you're looking great. Come on in. Bettyjane isn't here, but there's somebody I want you to meet.'

"He took me into this room in the dining area. They had a table in the left-hand corner and I went in and I looked at this one man sitting there . . . and it was Joe DiMaggio! I couldn't believe it. Skinny introduced me to him. He stood up and shook my hand, and his hand was as big as a baseball glove. I was totally flabbergasted. We sat down and talked for a while, and there were some other guys at the table and Skinny was asking me all kinds of questions. I told him about getting the chocolate cake. I talked with Joe DiMaggio. After a while, Skinny walked me to the door and I went home late that evening on a trolley car. Skinny wanted to send me home in a cab, but I wanted to take the trolley."

Chapter Four

If there was one day—or a single moment—in Skinny
D'Amato's life that changed his destiny, lifted him out of the murk of
his illicit past and turned him into someone who mattered to the
world beyond Atlantic City, it was July 26, 1946. The events that led up
to that moment—when Dean Martin and Jerry Lewis struck gold on
the stage of the 500 Club—have been hashed over, parsed, told, retold,
fudged, and twisted by so many different people to serve so many different agendas that they're nearly impossible to untangle. And the
actual participants in that moment, no matter how peripheral, all feel
compelled to put themselves as close to it as possible and take a little
credit.

But Skinny is always at the center of it. Pick a book on any related
topic—Rat Pack, Dean and Jerry biographies, Atlantic City—flip to the
index, and there he is: "D'Amato, Paul 'Skinny.'" Usually there are two
or three page numbers after his name, occasionally a few more. He is
often carelessly, confidently described as a member of *this* crime syndicate or a front man for *that* gangster. But even Jerry Lewis knew better—and he was the one whom the mobbed-up club owners had to deal
with as he and Dean became must-haves for any nightclub. "Talk to the
Jew," Dean would say to the Mob guys who ran most of the East Coast
nightclubs. "Skinny, Irvin Wolf, they were partners," Jerry once said.
"Wolfie was—it was nothing for him to get on the phone and get a guy
to come over and break your legs; it was nothing. And Skinny D'Amato,

who you'd think was with the Mafia, was the sweetest, nicest man. Defended us, protected us. Fought with Wolfie about us."

What is it about Dean Martin and Jerry Lewis that so fascinates people? Perhaps it has to do with the fact that their coming together was genuinely organic and resulted in something so surprising and satisfying for people at a time when the country really needed a goof— after the Depression, followed by four long years of war. Perhaps it was simply the fact that two relatively obscure and mediocre talents could cause a sensation as a team, together sustaining a kind of human chemical reaction that was far more powerful than either performer alone. And nowhere in showbiz history can the phrase *overnight success* be more appropriately applied than to the phenomenon that was Martin & Lewis.

They had careers before they met, but once they performed as a team in front of an audience, literally the next day they were the talk of the show business world. Ed Sullivan raved about them, Walter Winchell came down from New York to see what the buzz was about. Three days later, there were lines of people waiting outside on Missouri Avenue to get into the 500 Club.

Dean Martin was born Dino Crocetti in 1917 in Steubenville, Ohio, to Angela and Gaetano. Like Skinny's father, Dino's dad was a barber. Also like Skinny, Dino grew up in a town that was "wide open." In fact, Steubenville was known as "Little Chicago" because of all the pool halls, cigar joints, and whorehouses. And also like Skinny, Dino dropped out of school after hooking up with a less than savory crowd. Dino worked for a while as a welterweight boxer under the sobriquet "Kid Crochet." Soon he was working as a professional gambler, dealing blackjack and poker in a local joint called the Rex Cigar Store. Like Frank Sinatra, who was only two years older, Dino took up singing because of his fascination with radio crooners like Bing Crosby. Dino took lessons from the mayor's wife and sang at parties and clubs and taverns. He was soon invited to join a band led by Sammy Watkins, and in 1940 he started performing in a Cleveland club called the Vogue Room under the name Dean Martin. He married Elizabeth MacDonald, an Irish girl from Swarthmore, Pennsylvania, and nine months later they had a child.

When Frank Sinatra, a singer whom he did not yet know, canceled a date at the Riobamba in New York, Dean got his chance. He moved his family to New York and proceeded to make a half-assed effort to become somebody, spending several years singing in third-string night-clubs and Chinese restaurants. He got into some serious debt by whoring himself out to any agent who looked his way, and eventually he declared bankruptcy. Things were just that bad for Dean before he was booked to play the 500 Club in July 1946.

Jerry Lewis was born Joseph Levitch in 1926 in Newark to Danny and Rachel Levitch, themselves the children of Russian immigrants who settled on the Lower East Side. Danny worked the burlesque circuit as a singer and comic while Rae played the piano, both of them becoming fixtures in the resort hotels of the Catskills during the summer months. While still in high school, Joey met a girl three years older named Lonnie Brown, and together they developed a record act in which they rendered other people's songs ridiculous through grotesque lip-synching. One night in 1939, the comic Red Buttons failed to show for his gig at the Brunswick Hotel in Newark, and Lonnie and Joey got their break.

In the summer of 1941, Joey got a job working as a bellhop at the Ambassador Hotel in the Catskills, where his father was also working as a comic. When not bellhopping, he developed an act billed as Joey Levitch and His Hollywood Friends and took it from hotel to hotel. At sixteen, while playing a gig at the Ritz Theater on Staten Island, Joey met an agent named Abner Greshler and the next day signed a management contract, changed his name to Jerry Lewis, and dropped out of high school. A year later, he was living in Manhattan and making $150 a week, playing theaters around the Northeast. In 1944, he met Patti Palmer at the Downtown Theater in Detroit, where he was working as the intermission act for Ted Fio Rito and His Orchestra. Patti, six years his senior, was the band's singer. Not long after they met, Patti joined the Tommy Dorsey Band, and in 1945 she converted to Judaism and married Jerry Lewis, as she was six months pregnant with his child.

Jerry saw Dean once in the lobby of a New York hotel, noticed that he was wearing red patent-leather shoes, and wondered aloud to the doorman: "Who was that? He looks important." Turned out they had friends in common. One of those friends is Sonny King. Sonny, an Irish tenor who was Jimmy Durante's sideman for twenty-eight years, is one of the many people for whom explaining the Moment has become a second job.

According to Sonny, he was walking near Forty-ninth Street and Broadway with Dean. "We were going past a drugstore that was famous for entertainers hanging out and I said, 'Jerry!' And he ran across the street because he idolized Dean Martin, although he never knew him. All I said was 'Dean, this is Jerry Lewis. Jerry, this is Dean Martin.' They said, 'Hi, Jerry.' 'Hi, Dean.' That was it. Jerry walked along with us, and before you know it we were sitting down having coffee and they became fast friends."

Jerry Lewis said it was the other way around, that it was Dean— walking along with his agent, Lou Perry—who was summoned across the street to meet Jerry. Either way, Jerry and Dean talked about "broads," and then off they went in their separate directions, no coffee. A few nights later, however, the three of them—Dean, Jerry, and Sonny—found themselves in Sonny's room at the Bryant Hotel, room 616, drinking and talking and listening to records until four in the morning. Dean did most of the talking, and Jerry fell under his spell.

In March 1946, Dean and Jerry were booked as separate acts into the Havana-Madrid, a club in the basement of an office building on Broadway near Fifty-first Street. By this time the two men had gotten to know each other a little better, and in the early morning hours after the scheduled performances, they began to kibitz onstage, experimenting and improvising and playing off each other. Jerry has said they had no intention of becoming a team: "We were just screwing around." Sonny King would sometimes join them onstage, and the three men would do an Ink Spots routine. One night, a reporter from *Billboard* caught their late night goofing: "Martin and Lewis do an after-piece that has all the making of a sock act. Boys play straight for each other, deliberately step on each other's lines, mug and raise general bedlam. Lewis' double takes, throw-aways, mugging and deliberate over-acting are sensational. Martin's slow takes, ad libs and under-acting make him the ideal fall guy."

✦

In the summer of 1946, the 500 Club was finally beginning to take off. It was growing so popular that it could no longer handle the crowds, and Skinny made the first of four additions to the club, expanding the capacity of the showroom to 450. While the backroom casino was still a steady draw, Skinny was now engaged in the subtle art of getting the mix right. He was discovering that there were certain entertainers who brought in gamblers, and he began to experiment with unknowns—comics and singers—and checking the bank after every show.

In July 1946, Skinny and his partner Irvin Wolf—"Wolfie"—booked the sixty-two-year-old legend Sophie Tucker into the back room. Tucker, "the Last of the Red Hot Mamas," began appearing in Atlantic City as early as 1912, during the resort's vaudeville heyday. Skinny quickly realized that she brought in gamblers. She would become a mainstay at the nightclub and one of Skinny's dearest friends, appearing there many times until her death some twenty years later. Headlining in the main room that July was a Swedish woman named Jayne Manners, who was described in the ads for the show as "unpredictable." She was a former Ziegfeld girl turned Atlantic City nightclub hostess turned singing comedienne who had been implicated in the disappearance of New York State justice Joseph Force Crater in 1930. Since then, Manners had become a regular fixture in the gossip columns—each and every romance, marriage, and divorce breathlessly reported. In fact, just that past March she had been banned in Boston because of a lewd performance at a hotel showroom. Given second billing was the nineteen-year-old Jewish comic Jerry Lewis, who did "satirical impressions in pantomimicry." His entire show still consisted of nothing more than that tired old vaudeville shtick of lip-synching to records. Third on the bill was a singer named Jack Randall.

Abner Greshler had booked Lewis into the 500 Club and managed to squeeze $150 a week out of Wolf and Skinny, enough money for Lewis to bring his wife Patti and his son, Gary, down to the beach with him, which provided some much needed relief for his family from their stifling three-room apartment in Newark. He put them up at the Princess Hotel, one block from the Boardwalk.

What happened next has been told dozens of different ways—several of them by Lewis himself. One version has it that Skinny hated the singer Jack Randall. In Lewis's 1982 autobiography, he writes that after his performance he joined Skinny at a corner table to watch the rest of the show. "Skinny's thumbs were revolving in a definite sign of agitation as this gut-stabbing sound ripped across the room. By the second number I knew the singer was in serious trouble when Skinny almost soared out of his chair. 'I can't believe it—the guy sings as if his nuts are caught in his zipper!'"

"Maybe he'll get better," Lewis said to Skinny.

"Yeah, kid, right after they operate on his neck. I can't wait around. I gotta get somebody else in here, and quick."

Perhaps Skinny did hate the singer, but Wolf hated *Lewis*. He despised his act so much that he couldn't stand to be in the club when Lewis was onstage. After the first night, Lewis, perhaps realizing that he was about to get the hook, called Dean Martin's agent, Lou Perry, and asked for his help. Skinny and Wolf had previously expressed interest in booking Dean, so when Perry called Wolf, he offered Dean at the price of $500 a week—but with the stipulation that they had to keep Jerry on. "That's how the whole thing came about," Perry once told a writer. "If I hadn't made the phone call, it would've never happened."

Lewis claims that he told Skinny about Dean and that Skinny called Lou Perry. "You'll see, Mr. D'Amato," said Jerry. "Dean is not only terrific, but we've worked together."

"You have?" said Skinny.

"Sure. We do a lot of funny stuff."

Dean arrived on July 25, and that night he did his five songs, Jerry did his record act, and Jayne Manners went on last. After the show, Skinny called the two men into his office. "Where's the funny shit you guys were going to do together?" he said. Jerry has claimed that their "job was at stake," so that night he wrote the whole act—on a brown paper bag, claims Sonny King—that the two of them would perform together the next night, bits not unlike what they had been doing at the Havana-Madrid four months earlier.

Sonny King tells a very different story. He claims that Jerry had been fired and "was backstage packing his things and going mad. Dean was the new star, and all of a sudden a waiter dropped a tray of dishes and everyone heard the crash of the platters and Dean Martin said, 'I guess Jerry's packing his records up.' Jerry heard it, and he heard the people scream laughing. He ran out and, I think, out of frustration— maybe part of it was true and part of it was comedy, but whatever happened when he walked out on that stage and told Dean off in that little childish way . . . through anger, he became funny, and people started to laugh. And who was in the audience but the old-timer Sophie Tucker. She called Skinny over and said, 'Skinny, do yourself a favor, keep these guys, and let them do what they're doing tonight.' No matter what you heard otherwise, that's how it started."

"Jerry is so full of shit," said Rita Marzullo, a waitress at the 500 Club on and off for twenty years. "I know the true story because Skinny told me, as did many other people who worked at the club, which is that Jerry Lewis was on his way out. He never filled the front room and he never filled the back room. When Dean Martin came, he saved him. Jerry didn't get Dean Martin a job. The *agent* got Dean Martin there."

For years afterward, Jerry would claim again and again that he and Dean performed that night "literally for an audience of four" and that the show lasted three hours, which sounds like typical Lewis hyperbole. But the one fact that is uncontested is that it changed the lives of several people, not least of all Skinny. In the days following that first performance, Martin and Lewis would go to the beach, crowded with sunbathers, and pull the "drowning" gag that W. C. Fields made famous in Atlantic City thirty years earlier. Jerry would wade into the surf, pretend to be drowning, and Dean would rush out to "rescue" him. Once on the sand, with a crowd gathering, Dean would prepare to give Jerry mouth-to-mouth, and Jerry would suddenly come to life and say, "I'd rather have a malted, sir!"

"Vanilla or chocolate?" Dean would say, not missing a beat. And then, "Hey, don't I know you?"

"I'm Jerry Lewis!"

"Well, I'm Dean Martin."

"I know that: I'm playing at the 500 Club with you, first show is eight o'clock!"

And then they'd run like hell, all the way back to their hotel. Impossibly corny, even for the 1940s, these "publicity stunts" had to have been Jerry's idea. They were also mostly unnecessary, as the crowds poured in every night, selling out all three performances, including the four A.M. show. "In less than three nights, you couldn't get near the club," Jerry said years later. "It was unbelievable. They never packed that joint like when we were there." Skinny and Wolfie held Dean over, replacing Jayne Manners as the headliner, and gave Jerry second billing as the "extra added attraction."

Down the street from the 500 Club there was a little park. Dean and Jerry often hung out there during that first summer, always on the same bench, to relax before and after the shows. The day that Skinny and Wolfie decided to hold them over for the rest of the summer and raise their salaries to $750 a week each, Skinny went looking for his new stars, eventually finding the duo on their usual bench.

"I got a surprise for you," said Skinny. "I'm going to give you four more weeks."

They went berserk, jumped up and down, kissed the bench, kissed each other, kissed Skinny. When they officially became a team a few months later, Skinny had the bench removed from Columbus Park and installed it in the 500 Club, bolted to the floor. He hung framed photographs—huge head shots—of the two men over it with a plaque that read: "Here, on the stage of the 500 Club, Dean Martin and Jerry Lewis became a team in the summer of 1946."

(Recently, an old friend of Skinny's, Mary Korey, who was once a Miss America chaperone, and Vicki Gold Levi, the daughter of the 500 Club photographer Al Gold, went to dinner at the Gourmet Italian Cuisine Restaurant, not far from Atlantic City, and—lo and behold!—there was the bench. The restaurant owner's grandfather, Mike Marshall or, as Skinny would have known him, "Hobo," was friends with Skinny, and somehow *he* ended up with the bench. The plaque on it, which includes a picture of both Dean and Jerry, reads: "America's Greatest Comedy Team. 8th Anniversary Appearance. July 15, 1954. The world premiere of *Living it Up*.")

Skinny knew this was the best thing that had ever happened to him. The instant success of Martin & Lewis brought national publicity to the 500 Club and turned him into one of the most important nightclub owners in the country. Martin & Lewis put the 500 Club on the map—and then they launched themselves into the treacherous world of big nightclub gigs. In the fall of 1947, they got booked at the Riviera, a sprawling joint with a glass roof in Fort Lee, New Jersey, overlooking the Hudson. The Riviera was the crown jewel of the Bergen County Mob's holdings. Next stop, the Chez Paree in Chicago, where they were paid a fortune and where a young and naive Jerry finally realized he was working for mobsters—more specifically Charles Fischetti, Al Capone's cousin.

On April 8, 1948, the unstoppable Martin & Lewis made their debut at the Copacabana, considered by everyone to be the nightclub summit. The Copa had no backroom gambling, but it was mobbed up nonetheless. Frank Costello was the money man. There's a legendary story about Jerry, having no idea whom he was dealing with, making fun of Albert Anastasia, the head of the New York Mob after Lucky Luciano was deported. Dean, knowing a thing or two about a thing or two, had to step in to save his partner from being pulverized. Years later, Jerry talked about being onstage that night: "I couldn't see them in the darkness, but I swear I could feel Anastasia's cold steel eyes hitting me like bullets through the performance."

There is a famous photograph—taken that very evening at the Copa—in which Lewis, looking like a kid at the end of a long prom night, is wearing a tux with his tie undone. He's all sweaty and joyful and has that signature wide-mouth crazy face working. His arm is around Frank Sinatra. Dean Martin is in the background, pretending not to give a shit. It is a very engaging picture, especially given the fact that it was taken the very night Frank met Dean and Jerry. Skinny, eager to show off his success story, brought Frank, who he had met ten years earlier, to the Copa to see the show and meet his protégés. Frank's career was just beginning to take a nosedive, and he had performed for the first time at the 500 Club the summer before. His acquaintance with Skinny had turned a corner into something more intimate. At the end of the last show that night, Frank joined the comedians Jackie Gleason and "Fat" Jack E. Leonard onstage and, along with Martin & Lewis, proceeded to bring down the house. It was, in a way, a proto–Rat Pack moment. Skinny, meanwhile, was happy to sit back and watch it unfold. He was among his people: the gangsters he had first encountered in the late 1920s and the stars onstage whose phenomenal success he had had a hand in creating. Skinny D'Amato had found his métier. It is a role that he would play for the next thirty years—ambassador to the Mob, diplomat to the stars.

Dean and Jerry showed their loyalty to Skinny just a few months later in July, when they made their triumphant return to the 500 Club for the second anniversary of their explosive beginning. Apparently, this took some courage on their part. The Bergen County Mob was pressuring the duo to appear at the Riviera, but Dean and Jerry wanted to celebrate with Skinny—whom they loved, not feared. "I called a certain friend of mine," Jerry said years later, "and within twenty-four hours the squeeze was off." On July 21, they began a two-week engagement at the 500 Club.

By this point, Skinny, almost forty years old, had reached a level of success and fame that few in Atlantic City had ever seen—except, perhaps, Nucky Johnson. He had managed to put his time in prison behind him. Skinny made his near yearly sojourn to the World Series in New York as a guest of his pal Joe DiMaggio; he was a regular at "21" and the Stork Club and Toots Shor. He was getting rich and going legit. Suddenly, every night in the summer he was playing host to celebrities, politicians, athletes, and captains of industry. To top it all off, he had a gorgeous young blond girlfriend, Bettyjane, to share it with.

Life was good, and it was getting better.

✦

In the summer of 1946, Lucky Luciano, who had been imprisoned in Dannemora in 1936 and then deported, was sneaking around Italy—from Genoa to Sicily to Naples—in preparation for an escape out of the country and back to the United States—or, at the very least, as close as he could get. In early fall, word came from Meyer Lansky in the form of an envelope containing a slip of paper on which three words were written: "December—Hotel Nacional." The Nacional was, in pre-Castro Cuba, the most fabulous hotel in the Caribbean, and it was controlled by the island's dictator, Fulgencio Batista, and his friend Meyer Lansky.

Soon enough, Lucky would be just ninety miles from Miami, where his Mob pals and their friends, including Skinny, were beginning to spend more and more time partying and gambling. For a brief time in the late 1920s, Skinny had worked at an illegal gambling den in Palm Beach called O'Brien's. Now that he was a big shot, he returned to an earlier stomping ground with money and cachet all his own. In fact, the whole region—Miami and the Caribbean—was in one respect becoming the new Atlantic City, with nicer beaches and palm trees and an endless summer. No longer dependent on trains, travelers took to the skies as jets made flying more affordable and more comfortable. Havana was the perfect place for Lucky to join his fellow hoodlums for another big confab, much like the one held in Atlantic City in 1929.

Luciano, after a circuitous route through Caracas and Mexico City, made his way to Havana by October 1946. After a stay at the Nacional, he settled in Miramar, a fancy suburb, making no attempt whatsoever to blend in; indeed, he began dating a publicity-hungry actress and attended high-profile parties as the guest of people who were "amused" to have a gangster in their midst. Unlike the Atlantic City conference, which many attended with their wives and girlfriends, this one was a no-broads-allowed affair. Four floors of the hotel were set aside exclusively for the arrival of the usual suspects: Joe Adonis, Albert Anastasia, Joe "Bananas" Bonanno, Frank Costello, Tommy "Three-finger Brown" Luchese, Willie Moretti, and Meyer Lansky, among many others. From Chicago came the Fischetti brothers, Charles and Rocco, cousins and heirs of Al Capone.

The main order of business at the conference was to decide what to do about Bugsy Siegel, who was supposed to be making the brand-new Flamingo Hotel & Casino in Las Vegas the flagship of what would become the *other* new Atlantic City. In 1946, Vegas was still a sleepy little desert town that was mostly for gassing up and passing through. There were a few gambling joints, but it was certainly no Reno, which was the first Nevada gambling city to spring forth in the state that had, after flip-flopping on the issue, finally legalized gambling for good in 1931. But the Flamingo, built with Mob money, was set to change Las Vegas into a true gambling mecca 270 miles east of Los Angeles. The project was Bugsy Siegel's obsession and folly. He had promised his boys that he could build it for $1 million. But the construction ran way over schedule and more than $5 million over budget—some of which he borrowed from legitimate investors in Hollywood. When Luciano and Lansky discovered Siegel was skimming off the top of both funds and stashing the money in a Swiss bank account, they were left with no choice. The vote in Havana was unanimous, and Charles Fischetti was charged with handling his assassination. In June 1947, Bugsy Siegel was relaxing at the Beverly Hills mansion of his mistress, Virginia Hill, when a fusillade of gunfire crashed through the windows, killing him instantly.

Luciano maintained in his autobiography that Frank Sinatra was invited to Havana as a cover. If anyone asked what they were all doing in Havana together, they had a quick, if not believable, answer: to honor the Italian boy from New Jersey who had made it to the top. "Frank was a good kid, and we was all proud of him," Luciano said. "When I was in Dannemora, the fellas who come to see me told me about him. They said he was a skinny kid from around Hoboken with a terrific voice and one hundred percent Italian. He used to sing around the joints there, and all the guys liked him." Luciano claimed the Mob put up $50,000 to help Frank out while he was with the Tommy Dorsey Band in the early 1940s. Because he was making only $150 a week, they chipped in to pay for publicity, head shots, wardrobe, and so on. It was not uncommon for the Mob to sponsor young hopefuls—as the Fischettis did for Dean Martin—but many people over the years have raised doubts about Luciano's claim and suggested that he just wanted retroactively to take credit for Frank's success. "It all helped him become a big star," said Luciano of the supposed financial support, "and he was just showin' his appreciation by comin' down to Havana to say hello to me."

Sinatra flew to Havana with the Fischetti brothers, checked into the Hotel Nacional, and proceeded to indulge his ego in "tribute," blinded to the fact that he was being used. Unfortunately—for both Frank and Lucky—journalists and photographers were creeping around Havana looking for a story, and both men were exposed. A freelance journalist named Henry Wallace spotted Luciano one night, and before long the New York headlines were blaring: LUCKY LUCIANO ON U.S. DOORSTEP! Just a few weeks later, he was arrested by the Havana police and shipped back to Italy on the Turkish cargo steamer *Bakir*, never to return to the Americas again.

When Frank's press agent, George Evans, found out what his biggest client was up to, he "hyperventilated." And then he flew to Havana.

"Where's your common sense?" he screamed. "Why would you come here? Are you *crazy*?"

"Don't ruin it for me!" Frank screamed back. "These guys are great!"

When Evans got back to New York, he told a friend: "That's it. His career is ruined. And it's his own fucking fault."

Evans was right. Sinatra's whistle-blower was a Scripps Howard newspaper columnist named Robert Ruark, who had been gunning for the singer for some time. After a week in Havana, Frank flew to Mexico to join Nancy and the kids for a vacation, and on February 20, 1948, while he was lolling by the pool, Ruark's first column hit the stands. He blasted Sinatra, calling him a hypocrite for wanting to be the "self-confessed savior of the country's small fry" as well as mobbed up with "the likes of Lucky Luciano." In another column he referred to Luciano as "Frankie's boyfriend."

It's easy to imagine that for Frank, there was no conflict between standing up for the little guy and hanging out with the Mob. To him, *they were the same thing.* The fact that his own mother ran a speakeasy—a criminal enterprise—surely had an effect on his value system. Frank had an innate disdain for authority and rules, and the Mob was an American institution built on thumbing its nose at an uptight society.

Over the next several years, Frank tried to defend his trip to Havana by saying, essentially, that he just happened to bump into

Lucky and his gang while he was on his way there for a vacation. But Luciano said that during Frank's visit to Cuba, he gave out "a few presents to different guys, like a gold cigarette case, a watch, that kind of thing, but that was it." In 1962, just before Luciano died of a heart attack, the police raided his penthouse in Rome. Among the things seized was a gold cigarette case. It was engraved: "To my dear pal, Charlie, from his friend, Frank Sinatra."

For five tumultuous years, Frank Sinatra had been the biggest star America had ever seen. No entertainer had ever been famous in quite the way that Frank was famous. But when the press revealed his relationship to the Mob, it set in motion a downslide that was astonishing, verging on the sublime for its completeness. There had never been before, and there has never been since, a public figure who flamed out quite so spectacularly. Not long after the Havana episode, Frank started carrying on an affair with Ava Gardner. She was in her early twenties and, like Frank, difficult, insecure, mouthy, a big drinker, and oversexed. Both had contracts at MGM, and they had met at a nightclub on Sunset Boulevard when Ava was still married to Mickey Rooney. When the press caught wind of their affair, a wolf pack of reporters and photographers followed the couple everywhere they went, while an outraged public sent thousands of disapproving letters to MGM. In a way, the whole ridiculous overreaction set the tone for what would become the modern condition of fame: a kind of dysfunctional love-hate relationship between stars and their public, with the press functioning as troublemaking tattletales.

Louis B. Mayer, the head of MGM, could think only of protecting his sizable investment in Ava, whom he had been grooming for stardom since 1942. He demanded that Frank end their relationship. Frank refused, and Mayer retaliated by buying out Frank's contract a year early and sending the check to Nancy Sinatra, who swore she would never give her husband a divorce. She obtained a legal separation, and Frank's assets were frozen and his property seized. In April 1950, at a performance at the Copa in New York, Frank suffered a throat hemorrhage and then flew to Spain to spend time with Ava, who was shooting a film there.

Frank Sinatra had become radioactive.

✦

In the summer of 1939, the year Skinny was released from prison, Frank Sinatra, then twenty-four, came to Atlantic City for the first time for a July Fourth gig with the Harry James Band on Steel Pier. Sinatra was seven years younger than Skinny, almost to the day. Born in Hoboken on December 12, 1915, the only child of Dolly and Marty, Francis Albert had longed since adolescence to be a famous singer.

His dreams were stoked by the birth of radio. With the founding of NBC and CBS in 1926, it became possible for the first time to achieve fame on a national scale. Singers like Gene Austin and Rudy Vallee were early breakthroughs, but the nascent technology required singers to use megaphones in the studio, and the sound quality left a lot to be desired. It wasn't until the early 1930s—with the advent of low-fidelity radios and Victrolas—that popular music became a true craze. Bing Crosby was the first of the crooners to capture the imagination of an entire nation—including a young Frank Sinatra. When he saw Crosby perform in the summer of 1935 at the Loew's Journal Square, an old vaudeville theater in Jersey City, Frank knew exactly who and what he wanted to be.

His first break came just a few months after that revelatory evening when he auditioned for an NBC radio show and was teamed with a trio called the Three Flashes, which was subsequently renamed the Hoboken Four. They toured the country, and Sinatra quickly worked his way up the show business ladder. He sent publicity photos to Harry James, who had just left Benny Goodman to start his own band. James went to see Sinatra perform during his now legendary stint as a singing waiter at the Rustic Cabin, a roadhouse on Route 9W near Alpine, New Jersey. "In those days," Sinatra later said, "working with a big band was the end of the rainbow for any singer." He had just recently married Nancy Barbato, whom he had met in the Jersey shore town of Long Branch four years earlier, and in February 1939, he joined the James band as the male vocalist for $75 a week.

There are a couple of different stories about how and when Skinny and Frank met. One version has it that Skinny knew a young crippled girl in Atlantic City who wanted to meet Sinatra. Skinny called Harry James, whom he had befriended shortly before he was sent to prison, and arranged for Frank to spend some time with the girl. When Sinatra was much older, he once recalled that Skinny was "the most famous man in Atlantic City since I can remember, 1934 or '35." There are a lot of Sinatra-obsessed fans still creeping about, many of them with Web sites, but no one could be certain of the exact moment Frank met Skinny. But there did seem to be consensus on a best guess—the summer of 1939, when Frank first played Steel Pier with the Harry James Band.

Sinatra, like so many others before and after him, could not help but be in awe of Skinny, a man so singularly self-possessed, suave, and unflappable—not to mention soft-spoken and trustworthy. "Right from the beginning, Frank had this fascination with Skinny's lifestyle," said Joe Del Raso. "He wanted to be with the cool guys, the Mob guys. He was fascinated by Skinny's ways: his gambling prowess, having the club, the whole bit. They started hanging out and partying together." According to Grace D'Amato, "Sinatra used to perform at the Steel Pier, and then he'd come in the clubs with Harry James and Betty Grable. . . . Sinatra was very nice, well mannered, pleasant to everyone. Skinny said, 'I have something to tell you—important men do not ask, they order.' Skinny sort of molded Sinatra's character." While it is not hard to believe that Skinny had a hand in shaping the young Sinatra's persona, the quote rings false. Skinny was not the type to order people around. In fact, he instructed his own children to treat the bathroom attendants at the 500 Club the same way they would treat Frank Sinatra.

The real bond between the two men sprang from the fact that Skinny offered Frank Sinatra something that he found almost nowhere else in his life: respect and loyalty, minus the fearful awe. Skinny was one of the only people alive who could say no to Frank. Plus, Skinny and Frank had a lot in common: They were both New Jersey Italians who hated school and dropped out early. They both despised the idea of having a "real" job and were possessed by the world of show business and the late night world of clubs. They both went to bed at dawn nearly every night of their lives, and they both smoked like fiends. During

Paul E. "Skinny" D'Amato (lying down in front, black tank top) on the beach with friends in 1922, just before both of his parents died. In the background (from left to right) the Ritz, Marlborough-Blenheim, and Traymore Hotels.

Skinny, left, and a friend in front of Skinny's first gambling joint on Arctic Avenue, which he opened with $40 when he was only fourteen.

Skinny and a friend stroll the Boardwalk in the late twenties.

Bettyjane Creamer and Skinny on their first date, at Babette's Yacht Bar in June 1943.

Sophie Tucker ("Last of the Red Hot Mamas"), Skinny, and Bettyjane at the 500 Club in the mid-forties.

From left to right: Dorothy Arnold, her soon-to-be ex-husband Joe DiMaggio, Bettyjane, a teenaged Donald O'Connor, and Skinny having dinner at the 500 Club in 1944. Note DiMaggio and O'Connor are both in uniform.

Skinny and Bettyjane out on the town in Atlantic City with Babe and Toots Shor in October 1947.

Ray "Slim" Harris, a giant and the 500 Club doorman for many years, holds the car door open for Bettyjane and Skinny as they leave their wedding reception for their honeymoon in New York in 1949.

The front room of the 500 Club with its serpentine bar, after Skinny remodeled in the early fifties.

LOOK MAY 1953

AT THE 500 CLUB

PUBLISHED MONTHLY FOR PATRONS O... ...00 CLUB
6 S. MISSOURI AVENUE, ATLANTIC C...

The May 1953, edition of the 500 Club newsletter, with Jimmy Durante, Skinny, and Donald O'Connor on the cover.

1946   1954

The Five Hundred Club
requests the pleasure of your company
at a buffet supper in celebration
of the

Eighth Anniversary

of

DEAN MARTIN and JERRY LEWIS

as the

World's Greatest Comedy Team

... of Thursday
...h of July
...leven o'clock
...lion Room
...CLUB
...y, New Jersey

An invitation in the summer of 1954.

500 CLUB
Proudly Announces
STELLAR SUMMER ATTRACTIONS

JULY 6th - 12th
TONY MARTIN
Jackie Kannon - Phyllis Penn

JULY 13th - 19th
JOHNNY RAY
Joey Bishop - Joe Maize & Chordsmen

JULY 20th - 31st
LIBERACE
and his Complete Show

AUGUST 1st - 9th
JERRY LEWIS
and his Revue

AUGUST 10th - 16th
THE McGUIRE SISTERS
Blackburn Twins

AUGUST 17th - 23rd
NAT (KING) COLE
Corbett Monica

AUGUST 24th
WILL MASTIN TRIO
featuring
SAMMY DAVIS, JR.

And in All Probability
FRANKIE SINATRA

ONLY DINNER SHOW IN TOWN
Other Shows 12 and 2

Reservations:
6-1178
6-1179

6 South Missouri Avenue

An ad that ran in the Atlantic City Press one particularly starry summer.

CLUB 500 ATLANTIC CITY

*Skinny, Bettyjane, and
Jack Benny in New York,
in 1957.*

*Rita Marzullo on her sister's wedding
day, in Philadelphia, 1948. Shortly
after, Rita moved to Atlantic City, got
a job as a hatcheck girl at the
500 Club, and became Skinny's "pet."*

*Bettyjane with the McGuire Sisters at her baby shower just before Angelo was
born, in 1957, given by Peggy Bramson at her apartment on Central Park South.*

Bettyjane, Skinny, and, at far right, Jimmy Durante at El Morocco in the late fifties.

Bettyjane, Jerry Lewis, Skinny, and Dean Martin in Hollywood on the set of one of their early films.

Dean Martin stands under the 500 Café marquee that bears his name for the first time, in the summer of 1946.

Dean and Jerry backstage at the 500 Club on their first return engagement, in the summer of 1948.

Paulajane and Cathy D'Amato visit Dean Martin at his suite at the Claridge Hotel, in Atlantic City, in the early sixties.

Joe DiMaggio, Bettyjane, and Skinny at Yankee Stadium for the World Series in the late fifties.

Joe DiMaggio, Frank Sinatra, and Skinny in New York, after a charity base-ball game, in the late fifties.

Prohibition, Sinatra's parents owned a speakeasy in Hoboken called Marty O'Brien's, through which they became acquainted with goons like Waxey Gordon. Frank, like Skinny, was always impeccably dressed and well groomed nearly to the point of being obsessive-compulsive.

Frank and Skinny didn't actually see each other much for the first several years of their acquaintance. Almost immediately after they met, Sinatra's career took off, and by the spring of 1941, he was everywhere: on the radio, on records, on film, and on tour. When his movie career heated up, he moved his family to Los Angeles in 1944, making it even less likely that he and Skinny spent much time together. Skinny, meanwhile, was focused almost entirely on getting the 500 Club off the ground. He was not yet living the jet-set lifestyle that was to come.

It wasn't until Skinny and his club were flush with success after the Martin & Lewis summer of 1946 and Frank was getting beaten up by the press and his fans for his trip to Havana that the two really began to spend time together. In fact, in the summer after the Havana debacle, Frank performed for the first time at "Skinny's Saloon," as he liked to call it. Then, in August 1950, he and his band played a theater in Atlantic City. "It was so mobbed," recalled Frank's drummer, Johnny Blowers. "They had a feature film, a short subject, and then Sinatra. It was a madhouse. So they took out the feature. They just had the short and then Sinatra. We didn't even leave the theater! God almighty, I think we must have done twenty-five shows. The crowd kept demanding 'Good Night, Irene.' I don't think Frank liked it too much, but it was a big hit for him. I used to think to myself, How in the world did [Columbia Records's] Mitch Miller ever get him to do this? But anyway, he did it and it was big. It went over."

Sinatra, whose popularity in the rest of the country was now in free fall, had discovered from that gig that the people of Atlantic City still loved him. Didn't matter what gangster he was supposedly in cahoots with or which movie star he had left his wife for. New Jersey was ever faithful. But when the world wanted nothing to do with Sinatra, he really hit bottom. The low point, career-wise, came in May 1951, when, at the urging of Columbia Records's Miller, Sinatra recorded the novelty song "Mama Will Bark," on which Frank actually barked like a dog. At one point, after a particularly nasty fight with Ava Gardner in Lake

Tahoe, Frank was so distraught about the state of his personal life and how low he had sunk professionally that he took an overdose of pills in a half-assed attempt at suicide (though he always denied it).

In the summer of 1951, when Skinny found out just how bad things had gotten for Sinatra, he called and offered him a ten-day run at the 500 Club. By this time, thanks mostly to Martin & Lewis among many other top acts, like Jimmy Durante, Milton Berle, Liberace, and the Will Mastin Trio with a young Sammy Davis Jr., the 500 Club had become one of the hottest nightclubs in the country. Skinny paid Frank his top rate, the amount he'd commanded before the downfall, and perhaps more important, he offered his friend a chance to return to his roots—New Jersey—to a city that had a congenital weakness for outcasts, troublemakers, and antiheroes, especially if they were Italian. When Frank got to town, Skinny took him around to all his favorite joints, showed him off, and boosted his ego. A couple of days before his first performance at the 500, Skinny went to a local jewelry store and bought Frank a gold watch. When he gave it to him, he said, "Don't ever think you're down-and-out, pal. This is to remind you that when you come back you're going to be bigger than ever."

The night of Frank's first show that August, there were so many people on the street in front of the club that, for the rest of Frank's run, Skinny had to hire a dozen cops to control the crowds. "It was like you were seeing the Messiah come to town," said a waitress who worked down the street from the club. "That's how he was to the Italians. They went crazy." Jules Blumberg, who was a bartender at the 500 Club during that week, said, "He was God. He'd come in the place and, *my God,* you couldn't move."

"I used to stay open till five or six in the morning, and the bar would be packed," Skinny said. "When Frank played the club, he used to pack the city. There would be forty thousand or fifty thousand people who would come down here just to be in town the week he was here."

In a radio interview, broadcaster Sid Mark once asked Skinny, "What are the three most important things to Atlantic City?"

Skinny said, "The sun, the beach—"

Sid Mark cut him off and said, "Miss America?"

"Noooo. Frank Sinatra!"

While Frank was playing the 500 Club that summer of 1951, Skinny called Moe Dalitz, the former boss of the Cleveland Mob, whom Skinny had met back in 1929 at the Atlantic City conference, and asked him to give Frank a gig at the brand-new Desert Inn, one of the casino hotels he owned in Las Vegas. By this point, the Mob had shifted its base of operations to Nevada, where new casino hotels were opening as fast as they could build them: the Stardust, the Frontier, the Silver Slipper. Frank began a five-week run at the Desert Inn, and for the price of a couple of cocktails you could sit and listen to Frank Sinatra perform for hours. It was his first appearance ever in a Las Vegas casino-showroom. Skinny was also helping Frank out of his Nancy-Ava pickle.

On October 30, Nancy Sinatra finally relented and granted her tortured husband his long awaited divorce. "Regretfully, I am putting aside religious and personal considerations and agreeing to give Frank the freedom he has so earnestly requested," she said in a statement to the press. Two days later, after having established state residency with his five-week gig at the Desert Inn, Frank got a Nevada divorce and freed himself at last. Elated, he immediately made two phone calls. One was to his friend Manny Sacks, an executive at Columbia Records and Frank's right arm, who suggested that Frank and Ava get married in Philadelphia, at his brother Lester's house, to avoid the press. The other call was to Skinny, who offered to take care of all the details for the wedding, which was planned for November 7. In one public outing, during which Frank and Ava were descended upon by the media as usual, a reporter shouted, "Whatcha gonna get each other for a wedding present? Boxing gloves?"

Despite the wedding, the relationship continued to disintegrate under the weight of her growing fame and his career nosedive. His record sales were in steady decline, and Columbia Records and his talent agency both dropped him in the summer of 1952.

Frank and Skinny began making a habit of celebrating their birthdays together every December. On one of those occasions, in 1952, Frank and Joe DiMaggio were both with Skinny at the 500 Club. Frank, who was flat broke, told Skinny and Joe that he was on his way to meet Ava in Africa, where she was filming *Mogambo* with Clark Gable. As if it weren't humiliating enough that Ava had to send him airfare, Frank humbled himself even further by asking one of his friends to lend him $1,000 so that he could buy his new wife a present. He picked the wrong friend. DiMaggio—perhaps the tightest wad on two legs—refused. When Sinatra was out of earshot, Joe told Skinny that he didn't want to lend money to a "has-been." Later, Skinny asked Joe if *he* could borrow the money, and he slipped it to Frank on the sly, just to prove a point.

One night, drunk and alone in New York, Frank tried to kill himself by turning on the gas in Manny Sacks's kitchen. Sacks arrived home to his apartment on Central Park South in time to save Frank's life, though he could do nothing to stop the depression and self-loathing. His relationship with Ava, never a happy affair, had descended into hell, and eleven months into their marriage they filed for divorce. The only falling-out that Skinny and Frank ever had was when Skinny called Ava a "whore" not long after the divorce. The bad feelings didn't last long, though.

Chapter Five

When **Skinny** began managing the 500 Club with Irvin Wolf in 1942, his initial role in the venture was to run the gambling in the back room. Once the club had some success, he began to upgrade the facilities, but by the late 1940s, post–Martin & Lewis, he sank some real money into the place; the back room was expanded into a lush, deeply carpeted full-fledged casino, resplendent in reds and blacks and browns. The 500 Club did not stand alone in Atlantic City—there were other places around town that offered the same sort of ambiance—but Skinny quickly made the 500 Club into something special and exclusive. "There must have been forty different places, casinos, horse rooms, like that," he said years later. "And there was no robbery, no thievery. Nobody bothered you." Once, when a journalist asked Skinny if there were any bigger or better clubs than the Five, as people now called it, he displayed an uncharacteristic burst of self-regard. "What are you doing, insulting me? What other clubs? I don't want to brag, but the 500 Club, it was the finest, the best.

"We had everything but slot machines—Chemin de Fer, craps, roulette, blackjack. All black tie, always packed. We'd open about five in the evening and close by ten in the morning. It held 340 people when I bought it. I kept adding on until it held 1,200. We got the blackboard slate all the way from Pittsburgh. Real slate. None of the other horse parlors had slate. It was all striped with the names of the horse and the odds for all the tracks in the country. Look, everybody knew it. The state police knew about it. The FBI knew. The whole country was like that. Not just here. It was more or less like home rule. Atlantic City was Las Vegas. This town was wide open. There were crap games all over. People came here from all over the country to gamble."

During World War II, gambling became increasingly popular in cities large and small all over the country. This had mostly to do with the fact that unemployment was on the decline and incomes on the rise, which coincided with rationing and production cutbacks, which made many consumer goods less available. A lot of that extra cash flowed into leisure pursuits like going to the movies and gambling. Suddenly there were more and new kinds of customers—middle-class people! decent folk!—and the mainstreaming of gambling continued into the postwar years. Illegal casinos and off-track betting in particular enjoyed unprecedented prosperity, with the expansion of bookie operations accompanying the ever growing popularity of state-licensed racetracks on which they were dependent.

And where there was gambling, more often than not there was the Mob. Gambling was to organized crime in the 1940s what bootlegging was in the 1920s and early 1930s: their raison d'être, not to mention their bread and butter. For the most part, the Mafia was not on most Americans' radar until a few years after the war, when law enforcement experts began to scare people with warnings that a new and terrifying crime wave was on the way. One man in particular, Virgil Peterson of the Chicago Crime Commission, peered into the future and divined that an era of lawlessness not unlike the one that took place after World War I was just over the horizon. Meanwhile, J. Edgar Hoover told Americans to "build up the dikes against the coming flood." The FBI began releasing statistics: a 12.4 percent increase in crime in 1945; a 7.6 percent jump in 1946. The escalation was qualified as a sixteen-year peak in criminal activity. Hoover announced that between 1939 and 1946 there was a 198 percent increase in the arrest of girls under eighteen. This all fell into the category of "juvenile delinquency," a condition that was blamed on a breakdown in parental authority, which in turn was chalked up to the fractured home lives of many families whose men were serving in the war.

In Frank Sinatra's voluminous FBI files, which the agency began keeping in 1943 because of reports that the singer was a draft dodger, there is a missive from May 1946 from one of Hoover's top aides, Louis B. Nichols, who felt a moral imperative to share an "incident" with his boss as an example of "a symptom of the state of mind of many young people." The report went on to describe how Frank Sinatra arrived in Detroit around midnight, where a group of bobby soxers were waiting for him at the airfield. He eluded his fans, who by two A.M. had congregated at the stage door of the Downtown Theatre—where he was scheduled to give a performance in the morning—and camped out all night. "I have been told there was a line of mere kids, many of whom carried their lunches, and they remained in line until the theater opened. Truant Officers started checking the lines early in the morning and were berated by the girls. There was widespread indignation on the part of numerous individuals . . . and a severe indictment of parents of the girls. One individual went so far as to state that Frank Sinatra should be lynched." After reading this report, Hoover wrote in the margin: "Sinatra is as much to blame as the moronic bobby-soxers. H."

Something *evil* was happening in America—and Frank Sinatra was apparently to blame. And while the FBI would remain fixated on Sinatra—and nearly every person he was ever friends with, including Skinny—juvenile delinquency did not stay on the agency's front burner for long. In 1947, shortly after the Mob confab in Havana, Hoover warned the country that "gang warfare" was the next logical step in the ever increasing crime wave that was about to sweep the nation. But while police authorities in several cities challenged Hoover by denying that gang activity was on the rise, a strange combination of antigambling forces and a few well-connected, not to say corrupt, journalists conspired to fan the flames of public fear of organized crime.

Because gambling had become so popular—J. Edgar Hoover himself was a fan of the racetrack—and law enforcement so lax where illegal betting was concerned, there was an inevitable, if unpopular, movement for legalization toward the end of the 1940s. In some ways, it was not all that different from the drug legalization movement of today. Some advocates played the class card, claiming that encouraging state-sponsored on-track pari-mutuel betting while criminalizing off-track betting through bookies was unfairly punishing the working stiff. Then there was the swell notion, touted by proponents of legalization, of all that tax revenue to be gained from legalization. Just *think* of the fees that could be levied against all that money changing hands! The proponents also touted the novel idea of legal gambling as a way to cut down on police corruption, thereby increasing public respect for the law.

The pro-gambling forces, however, were unorganized and unpopular. They were also up against a formidable opponent. Virgil Peterson had been the operating director of the Chicago Crime Commission since 1942. Though he had previously been the head of three regional FBI offices, he had no particular background in fighting organized crime or gambling. But after mastering the thousands of files at the crime commission, he became a nationally recognized expert on the subject—and was convinced that gambling and organized crime were inextricably linked, forever engaged in their socially destructive symbiotic dance. In 1945, he published a commission booklet titled *Gambling: Should It Be Legalized?* in which he argued that legalization would only lend legitimacy and respectability to the Mob. Instead of driving them out of the gambling business, he claimed, legalization would merely expand all gambling indefinitely and, worse yet, increase the profits and power of organized crime. Once the door was opened, he seemed to believe, it could never be closed again.

But the businesspeople and bookies and horse room operators in convention-oriented resorts like Atlantic City had no interest in cracking down on illegal gambling. Their whole economies depended on their towns being "wide open." For these people, Peterson had another argument, ill considered though it may have been. In 1948, he gave a speech in Miami and claimed that the "myth of the wide-open town" had been forced on a clueless citizenry through corrupt political machinery in cahoots with organized crime. Fair enough. But then he went on to say that there was no proof local economies were hurt when gambling laws were actually enforced. Besides, Peterson argued, the money didn't stay in the resort, it went to the crime syndicates in New York or Chicago. (This was a gross misunderstanding of how things actually worked in Atlantic City. It ascribes much more power and reach to the Mob than it actually had.) History has proven him wrong in the extreme on all counts. Indeed, he himself helped to establish the very proof that the economies of wide-open resorts were hurt when gambling was run out of town. Peterson was the brain trust of the Kefauver Crime Committee—an antigambling Senate road show that held hearings in several American cities beginning in the spring of 1950. And it was the Kefauver Committee that forced an end to much of the gambling in Atlantic City, cutting off its air supply. The resort went into a precipitous decline—nearly to extinction—in the 1960s and early 1970s. And the one thing that finally brought it back from the brink in the 1980s was legalized gambling.

✦

Estes Kefauver's Special Committee to Investigate Organized Crime in Interstate Commerce would eventually make its way to Atlantic City, but not until the end of its fifteen-month tour of America. Though Skinny was spared the embarrassment of being grilled before the committee, the hearings were a major turning point in his life. The Kefauver Committee began its work in the spring of 1950 in Miami, but the committee's roots went back a few years. Essentially, the hearings were a federal response to the growing hysteria over crime that was a result of sensational press coverage of the reemergence of the Capone gang in Chicago and the growing influence of Frank Costello in New York. In 1947, the Justice Department formed the "racket squad" to prepare for grand jury crime investigations in several major cities. Simultaneously, the Treasury Department began an audit of income tax returns of gamblers, slot machine operators, and racketeers.

These events and others set the stage for Kefauver, an ambitious forty-five-year-old Democrat from Tennessee who was elected to the Senate in 1948 and had his eye on the presidency. In January 1950, he introduced Senate Resolution 202, calling for the judiciary committee on which he served to direct "a full and complete study and investigation of interstate gambling and racketeering activities and of the manner in which the facilities of interstate commerce are made a vehicle of organized crime." The investigation was eventually expanded to include prostitution, narcotics, loan-sharking, organized crime, extortion, and labor racketeering as well as gambling. After several months of infighting, the resolution went to a vote on May 2 and was approved by a one-vote margin, with Vice President Alben Barkley casting the deciding vote. Four other senators were appointed to the committee: Lester Hunt of Wyoming, Herbert O'Connor of Maryland, Charles Tobey of New Hampshire, and Alexander Wiley of Wisconsin.

While the mandate of the committee had grown from an investigation of gambling and racketeering to the much broader and more ambitious task of mapping the entire landscape of organized crime, gambling remained at the core—mostly because there were no federal laws regulating betting and gaming, as there were for narcotics and prostitution. But from the very beginning, the committee relied almost exclusively on the antilegalization arguments of Virgil Peterson. He dazzled the committee with two days of testimony. Senator Hunt, who pronounced that gamblers and gangsters were essentially the same thing and that most gamblers were "scum of the earth," had become slavishly devoted to Peterson's thesis that legalization would only lend legitimacy to said scum.

The committee—whose purpose, as Kefauver reiterated several times, was to raise public awareness of organized crime—did not start with a bang. The first hearings were held in Miami behind closed doors in May 1950. It wasn't until they moved to Washington in June that they became public and the press began to cover them with growing intensity. As the senators traveled to more than a dozen major cities— Tampa, Kansas City, St. Louis, Chicago, Las Vegas, Los Angeles, New York, Philadelphia, Cleveland, and Detroit among them—the press and the public's fascination grew. As in previous congressional committee hearings, television coverage of the Kefauver Committee's work was limited to short clips that aired on the evening news, which at that time was limited to a half hour a night. But it was in late January 1951, when the committee landed in New Orleans, that the television station WNOE received permission to broadcast the entire proceedings uninterrupted, usurping all other commercial programming. The public response surprised everyone, and other stations around the country prepared for wall-to-wall coverage to build on the New Orleans spectacle.

By the time the committee opened public hearings in New York in

March, *Time* magazine was sponsoring the television coverage and the investigation had become America's first Senate soap opera. We are so accustomed to this form of "infotainment" today—from Watergate to Anita Hill to Clinton's impeachment—that it seems almost quaint to think of mesmerized Americans in front of their brand-new television sets, trying to keep all the funny names straight: Greasy Thumb, Dandy Phil, Trigger Mike, Golf Bag, the Enforcer, and Little Big Man. Nearly every man in America, it seems, had a nickname in the first half of the last century. Perhaps it was the Kefauver hearings, and the public association of nicknames with shady characters, that brought an end to that tradition.

Until the Kefauver hearings, most Americans did not believe there even was such a thing as "the Mafia." The public got most of their information about the underworld and organized crime from film or works of fiction. But now these cartoon characters had faces and names—most of them ending in vowels—and Americans could no longer dismiss the Mafia as myth. The gangsters had lost their anonymity. They had officially become *notorious*. Ironically, however, the already very famous men whom the commission were initially interested in were quickly let off the hook. At the time, the public had no idea that Frank Sinatra was being interrogated in secret, in a lawyer's office in Rockefeller Center, about his Mob ties. This, of course, was just one more hideous thing thrown into the never-ending nightmare that was Frank Sinatra's life at the time.

At four A.M. on March 1, 1951, Joseph Nellis, one of the attorneys working for Kefauver, grilled Frank for two hours about the nature of his relationship with the Mob. Frank admitted that he "knew" Adonis, the Fischettis, Costello, Siegel, Luciano, and others—but that was it. "You're not going to put me on television and ruin me just because I know a lot of people?" he asked Nellis, who told Frank that the decision was not his to make. When Nellis finally asked Frank why he associated with such unsavory characters, Frank said: "Well, hell, you go into show business, you meet a lot of people. And you don't know who they are or what they do." It was the excuse he would use for the rest of his life—and every other time over the years he was called to testify about the Mob. Nellis thought Frank was lying, but he decided that even if he could get to the truth, Frank's testimony probably wouldn't add anything earthshaking to the investigation, and he did not recommend Frank as a witness to the committee. Dean Martin and several other entertainers were also scratched off the list.

The Kefauver Committee arrived in Atlantic City in July 1951. Senators Hunt and Tobey, along with chief counsel Richard Moser and special counsel Samuel Lane, set up shop in the Traymore Hotel on the Boardwalk and spent a few weeks interrogating nearly seventy people, including Stumpy Orman, the head of the rackets; Frank S. "Hap" Farley, the state senator and Atlantic County political boss; Skinny's former partner Jack "Colby" Berenato; the chief of police and many other public officials; and several cops, including a group of renegade policemen who had become infamous as "the Four Horsemen." Skinny's name came up several times during the proceedings, but, strangely enough, he was not called to testify.

It is especially curious that Skinny, who by this point was one of the biggest fish in the pond, was not interrogated. Jack "Colby" Berenato—who owned the restaurant Luigi's, with its backroom casino that was once run by Skinny—was grilled very aggressively by Kefauver himself. In fact, he was the only witness in Atlantic City whom Kefauver questioned. Berenato testified with a lawyer by his side and pleaded the Fifth Amendment many times when asked about his current operation. He did, however, speak freely when asked about his early days and the horse room/cigar store that he ran with Skinny.

SENATOR KEFAUVER: This horse parlor you operated [in the 1940s], you say it was a large room that would hold sixty people?

MR. BERENATO: Sixty to seventy-five people.

SENATOR KEFAUVER: Could anybody go in?

MR. BERENATO: No, sir.

SENATOR KEFAUVER: How did you select the people you let in?

MR. BERENATO: There was a man in the front store.

SENATOR KEFAUVER: He knew them?

MR. BERENATO: Yes.

KEFAUVER: How did you get by with the police operating?

MR. BERENATO: At that time, the entrance I had was more of a secret entrance. Behind the cigar store was a poolroom.

SENATOR KEFAUVER: It couldn't have been very secret if sixty to seventy people went in and out.

MR. BERENATO: It still could be a secret. I operated there a pretty long time without the police knowing it.

SENATOR KEFAUVER: Did Inspector Arnheim come in while you were operating?

MR. BERENATO: He came in and inspected the place quite a few times.

SENATOR KEFAUVER: Inspected what place? The restaurant or the horse room?

MR. BERENATO: It was a cigar store, and behind the cigar store was a poolroom. There was one pool table in it. To the right there was an entrance to the next property. In other words, if they came in, the man in the front saw they were detectives or cops, he wouldn't open the door to let them in, the door to the horse room. They would walk into a bare room with just a pool table and nobody there.

At one point during the interrogation, the chief counsel on the committee, Richard Moser, questioned Colby about Skinny.

MOSER: What is the 500 Club?

MR. BERENATO: It is a cabaret.

MOSER: And who owns that?

MR. BERENATO: I don't know, but a friend of mine, Paul D'Amato, is the manager there.

MOSER: Does he have an interest in it?

MR. BERENATO: I imagine he does.

MOSER: Do you have an interest in it?

MR. BERENATO: No, sir.

MOSER: Is there gambling going on there?

MR. BERENATO: No, sir.

MOSER: Isn't it true that the 500 Club operates a gambling operation and that you have an interest in it?

MR. BERENATO: Now?

MOSER: Yes.

MR. BERENATO: Right now? No, sir.

MOSER: But did it ever?

MR. BERENATO: Yes, it did have gambling there at one time.

MOSER: Do you have an interest in it?

MR. BERENATO: What year? I do not know what year you are talking about.

MOSER: Any year.

MR. BERENATO: I refuse to answer that question.

KEFAUVER: 1947 or prior thereto?

MR. BERENATO: I had no interest in 1947 or prior thereto.

MOSER: Have you had any interest since 1947?

MR. BERENATO: I refuse to answer that question.

MOSER: Isn't it true that you do have an interest in that club and you have agreed you will keep your game closed in consideration of receiving a share of that club?

MR. BERENATO: I refuse to answer that question.

There are nearly a thousand pages of transcript from the testimony in the Kefauver hearings in Atlantic City, and they paint an ugly, sad, fascinating, comical, bizarre picture of the deep, systemic corruption of the place. There is a Keystone Kops quality to some of the police work. Anyone who dared fight the system of collusion between the lawmakers/enforcers and the racketeers was either run out of town, beaten up, harassed, threatened with his life, or shunned into irrelevance. And the one story that is most emblematic of the corruption—and seems to involve nearly every player in the resort's delicate balance of power—is that of the Four Horsemen, named in reference to the Four Horsemen of the Apocalypse in the Bible.

It all started when a young police officer named Jack Portock moved to Atlantic City and joined the force in 1948, following three years on the front lines in Europe and an honorable discharge from the military at war's end. Portock was married with five children, and after a couple of years he began a campaign through the Policemen's Benevolent Association to get a referendum on the ballot in the 1950 November elections for a raise in salary for all police officers. At that time, cops made a measly $2,500 a year—not enough to raise a family and "keep straight," as Portock put it. The pay itself was part of the "airtight" system of corruption, which is to say that it was *intentionally* low. It created a necessity, in that every cop needed the protection money from gamblers to augment his official salary. Plus, the low salaries helped keep taxes low, which in turn kept Republicans in office.

Portock went about obtaining the requisite sixteen thousand voter signatures endorsing the raise and then took his campaign to Hap Farley, the state senator, county treasurer, and chairman of the Republican committee—in other words, the boss of the Republican political machine. Literally every single political office in Atlantic City and Atlantic County—from the police chief to the parole officers, from the city solicitor to the leaders of the four wards in the resort—was held by Republicans. Farley, who behind closed doors promised Portock that he would not fight the referendum for the raise but couldn't endorse it for political reasons, betrayed Portock and squashed the referendum by making certain through political pressure that as few people as possible voted "yes" on election day. On November 7, the cops did not get their raise.

Portock responded by requesting a reassignment to beat cop, where he then organized a kind of mini vigilante force for the purpose of raiding the gambling joints and horse-betting rooms and cigar stores—in other words, upsetting the balance of power and generally making life difficult for the Farley machine by exposing the rackets in the press. The other two officers who became the most well-known members of what was really a threesome were Fred Warlich, secretary to the police chief, and Francis Gribbin, a darkly handsome cop in his early thirties who had been on the force for nine years. The fourth member of the Horsemen was really all the rest of the cops who agreed with the other three—which was about 90 percent of the force—but did not have the chutzpah or seniority to be so open about it.

A week before the Kefauver hearings began in Atlantic City, the chief of police dissolved much of the vice squad—twelve men who were supposed to be cracking down on gambling but were, in fact, required to do just the opposite. As the Kefauver hearings commenced at ten A.M. on July 5, 1951, in rooms 325 and 326 of the Traymore Hotel,

Samuel Lane, special counsel for the committee, questioned the very first witness: Officer Jack Portock. "Did you request to be put on the street because you were disturbed about conditions which you knew existed in Atlantic City and you wanted to be in a position to do something about it?"

"Yes, sir," said Portock.

Senator Hunt from Wyoming was present and jumped in occasionally with a question or two. Lane asked Portock about Warlich and Gribbin, his partners in fighting the system, and said, "Did you, as a group in the police force, take independent action to intervene in the bookmaking and numbers racket in the city?"

"Yes, sir," said Portock. "We made an investigation on our own time on different number runners or number droppers, pickup men, places that wrote numbers, and on November 20, 1950, we followed one Austin Johnson . . . and arrested him for possession of numbers slips and aiding and abetting a lottery. Austin worked for 'Cherry' Haggerty . . . who is the sole racket power in the third ward. If you moved into the third ward and you opened up a cigar store and you wanted to write numbers and you did not turn your numbers in to Cherry Haggerty, he would call in the vice squad and the vice squad would close you up, tell you either you turn your numbers to Cherry Haggerty or you do not open up."

Lane then asked Portock to put aside the "local people" in the numbers business for a minute. "Won't you tell us what the county, the city, and the state organization is of the numbers racket, how they function, who banks for them, where the money comes from?"

"The big man in the state is Marco Reginelli," said Portock of the mobster from Camden who had a summer home in Margate. "He in turn handed the county down to a man named 'Stumpy' Orman. . . . He is the top man in all rackets—numbers, horses, craps, anything pertaining to an illegal move being controlled by Stumpy Orman."

"Has he any connections, so far as you know, with State Senator Hap Farley?" asked Lane.

"It is known throughout the entire town that Orman is the political power behind Senator Farley. He controls Senator Farley 100 percent." He then speculated, at Lane's urging, that Orman and Reginelli answered to Joe Adonis, Frank Costello, and Longie Zwillman. But he wasn't too sure about that. Maybe one of them, maybe all of them.

Portock then described in minute detail how the numbers racket and bookmaking worked in Atlantic City and how, in November and December 1950, he and the other three officers raided joints all over town, gleefully upending the city's equilibrium. By January, he delivered a written request to Chief of Police Harry Saunders: "Due to the fact that we have inadvertently stumbled on many gambling arrests both on and off duty, we feel that a serious gambling situation exists in Atlantic City. We also feel if we were allowed to give our full time to investigate this gambling problem, we could alleviate it tremendously, if not wipe it out in its entirety. It is further respectfully requested that we be placed on special detail in plain clothes from your office so we can effectively combat the above problems."

Portock got no response. He waited a month and then submitted another request. Still nothing. Chief Saunders refused even to *meet* with Portock. But by now the newspapers had begun to write about the raids, and the three officers were becoming popularly known as the Four Horsemen, a label coined by a reporter from the *Atlantic City Press*. Letters from sympathetic citizens began appearing in the officers' home mailboxes with tips about other illegal establishments and gamblers. Their phones rang off the hook. Finally, Chief Saunders responded to Portock's request—by reassigning him to Siberia. "Well," Portock told the Kefauver Committee, "they immediately assigned me to an isolated beat, which takes in the Boardwalk here on the lower end of town, and in which there is nothing but water and boardwalk." ("It's a wonder they didn't have you out in the ocean," Senator O'Connor remarked at one point.) He walked that beat—one that no one had been assigned in twenty-five years—until the higher-ups devised an even more effective diversion for the troublemaker. They created a superfluous "traffic squad," assigned Portock to it, and set him up with very specific hours: ten-thirty in the morning until six-thirty at night, precisely the same hours that the bookmakers and the numbers rackets operated. It ensured that Portock would be stuck at a desk while the gamblers gambled.

"What happened to Gribbin and Warlich?" asked Lane.

"Warlich was assigned to the traffic squad also with me. Gribbin was left alone, figuring he couldn't work by himself, which is an impossibility, for one police officer to do anything by himself."

But Portock was not deterred. He made another raid on his lunch break one day, and when he brought the bookmaker to the station, he was called into Chief Saunders's office and told to turn in his gun and badge. He was suspended for *arresting someone who was breaking the law.* The trumped-up charge was that he had left his post on the traffic squad without permission. When the press got hold of the story, there was a public outcry, but no departmental hearing was afforded Portock. After five days, the embattled cop was reinstated, and by now, thanks to the press, he was becoming a bit of a folk hero to the antigambling contingent in Atlantic City—a small group, but a contingent nonetheless. A minicampaign was started, and people began sending him dollar bills in the mail to make up for his lost wages.

All told, the three officers conducted twenty raids in which they arrested twenty-eight people. Only one man went to jail—Austin Johnson, the very first guy they pinched—and only because Warlich and Portock confronted the county prosecutor. "We asked him how come a man who is on probation and has been arrested twice on lottery charges could be allowed to walk the streets of Atlantic City." The prosecutor relented, and a warrant for his arrest was issued. Johnson eventually pleaded no contest and received 364 days in county jail. But the sheriff let Johnson out on weekends—and had his chauffeur drive him to his home on Friday, and from his home and back to the jail on Sunday!

One by one, the players in the Four Horsemen drama were subpoenaed to testify before the committee, usually with press and lawyers present: Murry Fredericks, James Boyd, Chief Saunders, and nearly every city official and dozens of club owners and gamblers. Also in attendance was Hap Farley, who was "invited"—not subpoenaed—as a "courtesy" because he was a "high public official," and literally the first words out of his mouth raised the committee's suspicion. Farley, an Atlantic City native, had been a state senator since 1940 and the county chairman since 1945. He also had his own law practice with his brother and was general counsel for the Atlantic City Racing Association, the organization that ran the Atlantic City Racetrack, which opened in 1945.

One would assume that a lawyer would make a decent witness. Not Farley. He made the amateur's mistake of answering—very defensively—questions that weren't even asked of him. When Moser, inevitably, asked Farley whether or not he was an "intimate friend" of Stumpy Orman's, Farley replied that they were friends, but not "intimate" friends. Then Moser asked if he had ever represented Stumpy in a legal matter, and Farley said, ridiculously, that he couldn't recall. Then, suddenly and unbidden, he burst out with this: "I never represented any gamblers. I never represented anyone along that line in any way, shape, or form. I never appeared in court for gamblers."

After a little more tense back-and-forth on this subject, Farley again jumped ill-advisedly to his own defense: "Since I have been county chairman, naturally, the underpeople who are disappointed in seeking public office or who have been defeated for public office or who have not been reappointed to positions have formulated a constant coalition of my enemies in this area, who have stopped at nothing for the purpose of vilifying my character, who have attempted to frame me, who have importuned governors . . . supreme court justices, superior court justices, to have investigations in Atlantic County, with the ulterior purpose and the only purpose of destroying me."

He ranted for a spell, giving specific examples of just exactly who had vilified him—the press, Democrats—and then explained why he couldn't possibly have endorsed an $850 pay raise for the cops ("The business minds and the business interests as well as the homeowner felt it was too much and it wasn't fair"), and then, finally, he went right ahead and attacked perhaps the only honest, brave people in the entire city government—the Four Horsemen. "Four men, through bitterness and everything else, have done everything humanly possible to try to create this investigation."

"*Create* this investigation?" said Moser.

"Create this investigation," Farley replied. "They bragged about it. Portock stood out and remarked to a gentleman that he brought this investigation here. . . . Every one of my enemies is taking credit for this investigation, only on the theory of getting Farley—"

"Senator," said Moser, "may I interrupt just for a second to say something? Namely that the one who recommended that we make an investigation of Atlantic City was myself. At the time . . . I had never heard of the so-called Four Horsemen. The only one responsible for this investigation was myself. Those people did not instigate it, and had nothing whatever to do with it. That is for the record."

"May I say to you," said Farley, "that there were meetings in various locations in Atlantic City, including newspapermen, who were bragging they were bringing this investigation to town . . . which is common knowledge in Atlantic City. . . . I am merely relating about my enemies who seek my utter destruction."

This was the great Hap Farley, the powerful state senator and boss of south Jersey? They named buildings and rest stops after this guy? One can start to comprehend how he could be controlled by a common hood like Stumpy Orman. But who was this Stumpy? He was, by far, the starriest of all the witnesses in the Kefauver hearings in Atlantic City.

In 1945, Stumpy had bought the Cosmopolitan Hotel on Atlantic Avenue. He seemed happy to admit that Nig Rosen, Joe Adonis, and Marco Reginelli—mobsters all—were friends who often stayed at his hotel when they were in town and that he regularly joined them for dinner at his restaurant, the Cosmopolitan Club. It didn't take a genius to read between the lines of Orman's testimony; he was, indeed, the Jersey-Philly Mob's man in Atlantic City. Several people testified that everyone in Atlantic City knew that Stumpy Orman was the head of the rackets and that he absolutely controlled Hap Farley.

On the fifth and final time Stumpy was called back to the Traymore, he was much more pugnacious than he had been in previous sessions. During the first four Stumpy inquisitions, the committee seemed to be taking their time, toying with him, forcing him to tell in excruciating detail about how he made his money and where he kept it, asking the same questions again and again. They pored over his tax returns, asked him where he'd bought his car, and went through a list of dozens of people, trying to divine the nature of his relationship to every slob in town. Finally, on the last day, they got tough. Moser asked the questions. Did he know a Joe Ryan? No. Did he know a Francis Smith? Yes. Did he know that Smith had a jewelry store on the Boardwalk? Yes. Had they talked recently? Several weeks ago. What about? Don't recall. "I dismissed it from my mind," he said after being pressured to *try* to remember. Finally Moser said: "Last night a man walked into Mr. Smith's store, a man named Joe Ryan, who is a jewelry salesman, and he said to the girl behind the counter: 'You tell Mr. Smith that if he testifies against Mr. Orman before the Senate committee, he is going to be rubbed out.'"

Stumpy claimed he knew nothing about it, and then Moser said, "Well, I would like to tell you, Mr. Orman, that if anything like that occurs, we are going to find the bottom of it, and I would also like to tell you that when a witness is going to appear before this committee, nobody is going to threaten to stop him from doing that. Do you understand?"

"I certainly do, and I am well aware of the consequences, and I had nothing to do with it," said Stumpy.

"Mr. Smith is going to testify before this committee, and he will be given full police protection; and, furthermore, the matter has been referred to the FBI, and they will get to the bottom of it, and I assure you if anything happens to Mr. Smith, the finger is pointed right at you. Do you understand that?"

"I don't care about any threats. I am not interested in Mr. Smith, and I am not concerned about the FBI. . . ."

"I know you are not concerned with the FBI," said Moser, "but I will say to you that [the FBI] is concerned with you."

"Just be sure that I am implicated," said Stumpy, "so long as you feel so sure that I had something to do with it."

"Well," said Moser, "have you had anything to do with actions of that kind?"

"I certainly have not," said Stumpy. "Are you satisfied that the newspapermen received that, like all your other inferences about me?"

"You are excused," said Moser.

✦

For a guy like Mr. Smith, Atlantic City was a kind of safe haven and a land of opportunity. He was uneducated and unskilled, and he possessed a deep love of gambling. Skinny D'Amato could have turned out to be a Mr. Smith. And the reasons he didn't probably have mostly to do with ambition. But ambition is often the result of a yearning in people that is born out of some mysterious combination of good instincts, great taste, and wisdom about human nature—all of which Skinny had in spades. For someone like Francis Smith, the most that could be hoped for was to run a bingo game on the Boardwalk and try to stay out of trouble. The Mr. Smiths of Atlantic City were exactly the kinds of guys who were most vulnerable to greedy bullies like Stumpy Orman.

Smith had been in the numbers game in Atlantic City in the late 1930s and early 1940s but got out of it after he was arrested by Mayor Taggart in 1942. During World War II, he worked at the war plant on the mainland. When the war ended, he opened up a pokerino game on the Boardwalk. In 1947, he attempted to add a bingo concession to his pokerino game. So he went to see Vincent Lane—an old friend, a probation officer, and the head of one of the wards in the city—who suggested that Smith see Hap Farley. The committee, of course, was interested to know why a state senator would have such a hands-on role in who did or did not get to run bingo on the Boardwalk. At the time, bingo games were legal and licensed by the city. When Smith went to see Farley, Farley was noncommittal, saying, "If I can help you, I will." Shortly thereafter, Smith ran into Stumpy Orman on the Boardwalk. Smith told him he was looking forward to getting the approval to open his bingo concession, to which Stumpy replied that he didn't think it was going to work out. Shortly after their chance meeting, not only was Smith turned down for a bingo license, but his existing pokerino license was not renewed. Smith went ballistic and turned up one night at the Cosmopolitan Club and confronted Stumpy and Hap, who were having dinner. "I was in an excited state of mind, because I felt that I was going to be pushed around and I wouldn't get the license," Smith told the committee.

They took Smith into Stumpy's private office. "Don't threaten me," Hap said to Smith. "Don't get excited. Keep your head. Nobody's going to hurt you."

"Well, this is my livelihood," said Smith, "and I want to get my pokerino license."

Farley relented, and then Smith asked again about getting a bingo license. Farley said to Stumpy, "Can we do anything for this fellow?"

"No," said Stumpy. "We can't do a thing for him. . . ."

After this meeting, Smith closed down his pokerino game and moved to Coney Island to see if he could run a game there. It did not work out, and he came back to Atlantic City and set about getting back into business on the Boardwalk—this time with a bumper game. He went to see Orman, who told him to go see the licensing official, who told him to go see the assistant county treasurer, Hap Farley's assistant, who told Smith that though the cost of a license was $1,000, he would have to pay $2,000 for the "privilege" of running a game. Smith paid up, and before long he was back in business.

Games of chance on the Boardwalk were supposed to use chips, not cash, but if you wanted to break the rules and pay out cash, you had to ask permission and grease Stumpy's palm. Smith was caught paying out cash and was visited by a man who told him, "If Stumpy catches you paying cash, he's going to knock your brains out." Smith switched to chips and then went to see the assistant in Hap Farley's office, who told him that if everyone else was using cash, he saw no reason why Smith couldn't. But first he had to pay up, and this time he was told to take the money directly to Hap Farley—at his home. "I gave him the money, he patted me on the back and said, 'Anytime you need anything, Smitty, come to me.' And he gave my kid a nickel for ice cream." There was no longer any pretense—it was a kickback, pure and simple.

Smith ran his game in relative peace for several months, and then in the spring of 1951, Theodore D. Parsons, the state attorney general, issued an edict through the press that all games of chance—bingo, wheels of fortune—where the skill of the player did not predominate had to be closed. Then one night at nine P.M., two Atlantic City detectives came by Smith's game and said, "The *slough* is on," and he had to close up. No gambling. But when Smith found out that not every game was closed down—bingo, for example, was allowed to continue operating—he became suspicious and went to see Farley, who told him, "If you can put skill into the game, we can probably help you to get open again."

Smith revised his game and then asked for it to be inspected so that he could reopen, but the man in charge of these inspections in Atlantic City refused to come by to see Smith's new and improved bumper game. When Smith complained, the inspector said, "Take it to court."

Smith left that meeting, called his wife, Mary, and said, "It looks like we're out. Forget about this game." Mary, whom Smith described as "highly excitable," was having none of it. She went to the county prosecutor, who "promised" Mary he'd see to it that the bingo games were closed down. Then Mary pulled herself together and drove to Trenton to blow the whistle. Not surprisingly, she could not get an audience with Attorney General Parsons. Still mad as hell, she came back to Atlantic City, marched herself down to city hall, and demanded that the police issue warrants and close down the bingo games. While she was at city hall, Stumpy called Smith and said, "You won't even be able to live in this town if you open anything up or step across the line. We will knock your brains out."

"I don't need you," said Smith.

"I will be up," said Stumpy.

"It will be a pleasure," said Smith.

Shortly thereafter, two "strange characters" turned up and stood across the Boardwalk from Smith's game. They hung around for a couple of hours, glancing at their watches occasionally. Smith had never seen them before, so he asked the guy who ran a game next door if he knew who they were, and he told Smith that one of them was Babe Marcella, Stumpy's bodyguard. If they were trying to intimidate Smith, they succeeded.

"I was upset," he said. "I was a little frightened, too. So I started to add it up . . . I am fighting a Mob. I figured there was no use calling city hall, so I picked up the phone. . . . I dialed the operator and said, 'Emergency, FBI.' They connected me with Philadelphia."

He told the agent in Philly the story, and they suggested he go see Agent Welsh, who lived in Ventnor on Sacramento Avenue. He asked for and got a police escort to Ventnor, sat in Welsh's kitchen, and told him the story.

"Well, I don't think you have too much to worry about," said Welsh. "They're just trying to scare you."

But Smith's fears were not assuaged. He did not return to the Boardwalk and did not sleep at home that night. A few days later, he got a call from Farley's assistant, Joe McBeth. "This is the first time I've ever had to talk to you this way," he said, "but you better stop talking about Farley or we are going to close you down permanently."

"I haven't been shooting off," Smith said.

"Well, you better control Mary, because we can close you and keep you closed."

Smith decided to get out of the game, liquidated all his equipment and merchandise, and went into the much less terrifying costume jewelry business on the Boardwalk. A month later, the Kefauver Committee rolled into town.

As Smith's testimony was winding up, chief counsel Moser said to Smith: "Did you know that last night after you left [work], Joe Ryan came into your store and said to the girl in charge of the jewelry concession, 'Tell Mr. Smith that if he testifies against Orman before the Senate committee, he is going to be rubbed out'? Do you know that?"

"No," said Smith. "But I don't doubt it."

Moser told Smith that they reported the matter to the FBI and that he and his family would be afforded every protection he desired. Then the chairman of the committee, Senator Herbert O'Conor of Maryland, said: "Mr. Smith, if criminal conditions in this country, such as have been exposed, are to be corrected, they can only be corrected when people like you have the courage—and I will say, the guts—like you have, to come forward and to state the facts...."

To which Smith responded: "I am no lily, but I feel cleaner than I ever felt in my life ... and I wish a few more people would come forward. We need it."

✦

"We could always deal with the authorities until the Kefauver Committee," said Skinny. "Before it was wide open. Then, all at once, gambling became dirty. Not just in Atlantic City, but all over the country. But it didn't matter to most cities, because gambling was only a small part of most cities. But it was bad here, because the casinos and the horse rooms were a big, big part of this town." After the hearings, "there was one casino left in town, and they kept it quiet, but they still got busted," he said. "The FBI meant business, so we left it alone."

The legacy of the Kefauver hearings in Atlantic City is not uncomplicated. On the one hand ... mission accomplished. The hearings shined a little sunlight into the darker corners of corruption; through the press, the public came to see just how treacherous life really was for the Mr. Smiths of this world. The exposure made life harder for guys like Stumpy Orman to operate under the radar. People in Atlantic City like to think that Stumpy wasn't so bad, but the hearings made it clear he was the worst the city had to offer.

On the other hand—and perhaps more significant—the Kefauver hearings destroyed the equilibrium that made the resort special for those not oppressed by the rackets. Sue Pollock, who was born in 1938, grew up in Margate, and went to Atlantic City High School, is convinced the Kefauver hearings, "in some strange way," destroyed the resort. "Atlantic City was so far from anybody's interest—powerful people's interest. It was a little place that had such a delicate balance of power: the Mafia, the Republican machine, the Jews, the blacks. It was all really nice. Everybody understood."

I had been told by a few people that Pollock had always wanted to write a book about Atlantic City, but that she had come to terms with the fact that it was never going to happen: "The title of my book was going to be *Only an Island.* I believed Atlantic City was a microcosm of the whole world of that time, where every aberration known to man was immediately accessible. Atlantic City was fun and hip because it was *properly seedy.* Everything was in our realm of consciousness. No judgments. Long ago, the high life and glamour was also rooted there because all the movie studios' head honchos were in New York and they went to Atlantic City like they now go to the Hamptons. You know those great old oceanfront mansions in Ventnor as you're approaching Atlantic City? They were built by movie moguls who came to Atlantic City. If I could, I'd buy one tomorrow."

In another way—and this is most applicable to Skinny—the Kefauver hearings marked the beginning of the media age, in which nightclub owners and mobsters and political bosses could no longer operate with impunity. Television brought Congress—and its business, including the McCarthy hearings, which followed right behind the Kefauver hearings—into everyone's living room, and the willful innocence of the American people, the sunny, postwar dream, slowly began to unravel.

Chapter Six

On June 4, 1949, a year before the Kefauver hearings began, Skinny D'Amato married Bettyjane Creamer in a small ceremony at the house of Joseph Altman, mayor of Atlantic City. A reception followed at the 500 Club in the newly expanded showroom that included a filet mignon dinner for six hundred. The wedding was the social event of the year—attended by an extraordinary cross section of Atlantic City and Philadelphia society—judges, gamblers, politicians, cops, and local celebrities—and featured strolling violinists and huge, swan-shaped ice sculptures. The next day, Skinny and Bettyjane went to New York for their honeymoon and stayed at the Hampshire House on Central Park South, where Manny Sacks lived and where Ava Gardner and Frank Sinatra had consummated their affair a year earlier—and where Frank would try to gas himself to death. On June 24, 1950, Bettyjane gave birth to Paulajane, whose name combined those of her parents; Cathy followed two years later on January 31, 1952.

Shortly before they got married, Skinny had, at long last, become the sole owner of the 500 Club. After eight successful years in business, he was finally able to buy out his partners, pay off his investors, and expand the property. The timing of his marriage and buyout of the club was fortuitous. Now that he had a family to think about, and the Feds were making life so difficult, Skinny cleaned up his act even further. "I built the club up so we didn't have to have gambling," he said. "Even then, we could have special games, where you'd invite special guests and set up for maybe a week. But not after '54. That's when it got absolutely impossible."

Skinny was determined to run a completely legitimate business, and now that he was having such success with the entertainment he was booking into the club, he got rid of the casino completely. The Missouri Hotel, located next to the club, was demolished to make room for a third expansion, which included two new lounges within the club and more parking; the nightclub was completely redesigned, and the show-room was rechristened the Vermillion Room (though no one ever called it that) and now had a one-thousand-seat capacity. Skinny also closed up the horse room upstairs to make room for his new family; by the time the Kefauver Committee made its way to Atlantic City, Paulajane was a year old.

Life above the club was fairly grand. The apartment was huge, and Bettyjane filled her first home with conservatively modern furniture in a nearly monochromatic theme—gray carpet, gray walls, and gray sofas, with floral accents here and there. More than one person said that it was like a much bigger version of Lucy and Ricky Ricardo's TV pad. There was a master suite, dining room, bedroom for the girls, and room for the housekeeper, Lillian. Miss Goetz, the children's nanny, generally stayed next door, at the Penn Plaza Hotel. Paulajane and Cathy shared a giant playroom with a chalkboard on one wall. In the early days of the 500 Club, when Phil Barr was still the owner, part of the second floor was used as a horse room for wealthy women, who were not allowed to gamble downstairs in the casino with their hus-bands. When Skinny took over managing the casino for Barr, he brought the aforementioned monolithic piece of slate all the way from Pittsburgh and installed it as a tote board upstairs; now, his children used it to practice their ABCs.

Just off the children's playroom was an elaborate deck that looked out over the rooftops of the city. Skinny set up a swing set and wading pool in the summer, and the whole family—and whatever star was in town—would often sit outside in the sun as the smell of searing lamb-chops and steaks wafted up from the kitchen. The fact is, there were, more often than not, celebrities hanging out in their apartment or downstairs in the club most of the summer. In the daytime, the club's parking lot was Paulajane and Cathy's playground. Paulajane was something of a tomboy, and when Joe DiMaggio was around, he would play catch with her outside. The girls' other playground was the nightclub itself. Paulajane would get onstage, lower the microphone, and pretend to entertain. Then, after her "set," she would head to the bar, load up a tray with salt and pepper shakers, and serve the "audience" their "drinks." When the actual entertainers showed up in the late afternoons to rehearse—Liberace, Sophie Tucker, Milton Berle—Paulajane would sit on the piano while they sang and talked and drank, preparing for another long night of three or four shows. "I learned how to play catch with Joe DiMaggio," said Paulajane, "I learned how to curse from Sophie Tucker, and Liberace taught me how to play 'Chopsticks.'"

✦

From the day they were married, Skinny would not allow Bettyjane to work. "I don't want people thinking I need the money," he told her. She was, however, allowed to model in charity fashion shows for her friend Marie McCullough, who had started a modeling agency in 1946 to provide pretty hostesses to work the booths at the events at Convention Hall. Skinny also allowed his wife to oversee the hiring of women's bathroom attendants, whose tips she shared for spending money. It hardly mattered that Bettyjane couldn't work; she had a full-time job playing hostess to a constant stream of celebrities passing through the club. Skinny, much like Nucky Johnson years earlier, had elected himself host to the famous in the resort, and whenever anyone of significance came to town, the D'Amatos were there to show them a good time. If Bettyjane had been living in Hollywood, perhaps she might have been just another pretty, stylish wife of a studio head who knew a thing or two about entertaining; but in Atlantic City, her life was extraordinary—especially for a woman who had been raised in such humble circumstances. Now, Bettyjane enjoyed the money that Skinny threw around, live-in help, expensive cars, a driver, exotic vacations, fabulous clothes, and the company of stars, politicians, and mobsters. Her friends Mary Korey and Chris Owen used to say that Bettyjane—a perfectionist who had memorized etiquette books—"could shame Perle Mesta," Washington's legendary "Hostess with the Mostest."

Bettyjane shared stories with her friends about entertaining celebrities by taking them shopping. She often took them to Needlecraft, the most exclusive dress shop on the Boardwalk, where clothes were brought to women in private suites for fittings and where tea and sandwiches and cocktails were served. Bettyjane, who was modest to the point of being a prude, once took Marilyn Monroe to Needlecraft. A saleswoman brought Marilyn a glass of champagne and some dresses, and without warning, Marilyn unzipped her slip dress and let it fall to the floor; she stood there, heels on and champagne glass in hand, stark naked in front of Bettyjane, who was so stunned that she could do nothing but look straight into her eyes. Another time she told Chris and Mary about a shopping trip with Elizabeth Taylor, during which she noticed that Taylor had a big ugly safety pin holding her bra together. "Couldn't she get a needle and thread?" said Bettyjane, incredulous. "Or throw it out and buy a new bra?"

✦

While Bettyjane kept the ladies occupied and entertained during the day, Skinny and the boys played, drank, and gambled all night long. Grace D'Amato's comment about Skinny shaping Sinatra's character has at least a whiff of truth to it. The whole Rat Pack sensibility, which reached a crescendo in the early 1960s, was technically born in Hollywood in the early 1950s among a group of actors and performers who hung out at Humphrey Bogart's house in Holmby Hills, California. Sinatra and Bogart met in 1945 and quickly took a shine to each other. In 1949, Frank moved his family into a house in Bogart's neighborhood. Shortly thereafter, he left his wife, Nancy, and began to spend a lot of time with Bogart and his wife, Lauren Bacall. "He's always here," Bogart told a reporter. "I think we're parent substitutes."

What Bogart and Sinatra (and Skinny) had in common was a disdain for the phoniness and the rules of Hollywood, as well as a genuine love of and identification with the underdog and the average guy. They gathered around them a group that included Judy Garland and her husband, Sid Luft; superagent Swifty Lazar; restaurateur Mike Romanoff; and humorist Nathaniel Benchley. Legend has it that one night in 1955, the above group, plus David Niven, Jimmy Van Heusen, and a few others, had gathered at the showroom at the Desert Inn in Las Vegas to see Noel Coward's first performance in Vegas. When Lauren Bacall arrived at their table to find them all drunk, she said: "You look like a goddamn rat pack." A few nights later, back in Beverly Hills, the same group had gathered at Romanoff's house and she snorted, "I see the rat pack's all here."

The Holmby Hills Rat Pack was born. They jokingly assigned themselves titles—Pack Master (Sinatra), Den Mother (Bacall), Vice President (Garland), and so on—drew up a logo (a rat gnawing on a human hand), and agreed to the dictum "Never rat on a rat." It was all quite ridiculous, really, and would have remained an inside joke had Bogart not talked about it to a reporter for the *New York Herald Tribune* named Joe Hyams. The Rat Pack was dedicated, said Bogart, to the "relief of boredom and the perpetuation of independence. We admire ourselves and don't care for anyone else." Bacall expounded on the idea: "You had to be nonconformist and you had to stay up late and drink and laugh a lot and not care what anybody said about you or thought about you . . . and you had to be a little musical."

When Bogart died of throat cancer on January 14, 1957, Sinatra canceled his sold-out show at the Copacabana in New York and hid in his hotel room. Jerry Lewis and Sammy Davis Jr. filled in for him; Marlene Dietrich, Joe DiMaggio, and Skinny were in the audience that night. Devastated, Frank canceled two more shows. He did not attend the funeral, a practice that he would stick with for much of his life because he preferred to remember people alive and vital and happy.

Sinatra eventually assumed leadership (whatever that meant) of the Rat Pack, but it quickly took on a very different veneer and ethos. The new Rat Pack was no longer a snotty, coed clique of Hollywood insiders who thought they were too cool for everyone else; the idea had migrated to a group of mostly Jewish and Italian drinking, gambling, womanizing, arrogant, Mob-connected nightclub junkies. The new members of the Rat Pack were men who, in one way or another, had more connection to the New York–New Jersey Italian American culture than to Hollywood.

In a way, the popularized notion of the Rat Pack of the 1960s has its real roots in Atlantic City, if not utterly located in one man: Skinny D'Amato. Early-twentieth-century Atlantic City conjured the notion that people ought to have as much fun as possible, with a total disregard for the rules and laws. The fuck-it lifestyle of sitting by the pool or on the beach all day, drinking and gambling and smoking all night, and then, perhaps, having sex with a showgirl or prostitute was invented, really, in Atlantic City. Indeed, the resort was founded for the purpose of tending to these pastimes and vices—to the exclusion of nearly everything else. Eventually—inevitably—Atlantic City produced the ultimate purveyor of this lifestyle, a young, talented gambler named Skinny who came of age during Prohibition, Atlantic City's golden era of lawlessness.

The Rat Pack formed around Skinny's particular brand of a good time. A sense of lawlessness within certain boundaries of good taste and decorum: that's what Skinny D'Amato understood better than anyone else in Atlantic City. By midcentury, he had created an environment where anyone could temporarily jettison his conscience, thereby enabling the average guy to be in possession, if only for a night, of a sense of self-importance, specialness, power—even fame. The average guy could be . . . *cool*. Frank Sinatra, after all, started out as a pencil neck from Hoboken—a kid who wanted to be more like Skinny D'Amato than, say, Bing Crosby. In many ways, Skinny was the architect—the inventor—of white-guy, working-class cool.

Skinny's whole look and style—the way he held a cigarette in his mouth and closed one eye every time he took a drag, the custom suits, the expensive watch as the *only* piece of jewelry, the silk pocket square, the suede loafers, the light, clean scent (which was, in fact, Jean Naté, a woman's perfume), the skill with a deck of cards, his neat trick of being able to spin a matchbook on its corners, the crooked, sly smile, the twitch to his lip when he was thinking, the huge tips, the way he gracefully put his arm around everyone—his whole low-key, good-time affect, really, was the essence of cool. It was a way of life that Skinny's famous friends exaggerated, commodified, and sold to the world.

"I remember watching him go to work in the morning when I was a kid," said Joe Del Raso, whose bedroom window looked out onto the D'Amatos' front lawn. "One of his drivers, Vince Bruno, would pull up in Skinny's dark blue Fleetwood Cadillac, and Skinny would walk down the path—never with his head in the air, always looking down—cigarette hanging out of his mouth, one hand in his pocket. He always had those high vent pockets. And I would think to myself, This is the coolest guy in the world. Was it an aura? A charisma? Who knows what it was. All the other characters that hung around the club, they were mostly Damon Runyon–esque guys but they weren't people you would admire. Skinny was flying ten thousand feet above them all."

The 500 Club was ground zero for the supercool lifestyle; one of the reasons people flocked there was to get a piece of it, to be part of the action. Paulajane, even as a little kid, knew something big was happening below her bedroom. "Mostly, I remember the gaiety," she said. "My parents were always having fun. Much more fun than I think we have now. Living above the club was like living on the edge of a dormant volcano. I can remember the nights my folks would entertain their friends downstairs. Those nights usually began with my mom feeding us dinner, and then she would go to her dressing room and prepare for the evening. Often I would sit with her while she relaxed in the tub. I would follow her as she went from the bathroom to her dressing room, and we would talk the entire time. And she would smile or laugh at every little thing I said, knowing that's exactly what I needed, because soon she would go down the stairs to the club, lavishing her attention on people other than me. When she finished dressing she would spray Jungle Gardenia from head to toe. After putting a lipstick, a hankie, and a pack of cigarettes in her purse, she would turn and ask, 'Do I look okay?' She would take my hand, and together we would walk to the door. She would hug and kiss me good night, and I would watch her walk down the twenty-seven steps—I had counted them so many times—to another evening of excitement. As she opened the door to the back of the club, she would look up, blow me a kiss, wave, and say good night once more. And then she was gone. Except for her scent. That always lingered."

One morning, Paulajane was going to a friend's day-long birthday party. "It was an August morning," she said. "I really don't remember the date or the year. Lillian, our housekeeper, made me breakfast, and after I dressed I went downstairs to play in the parking lot. My parents slept late most mornings. The nightclub business plays havoc with your sleep patterns. Normally my father didn't hit the bed before six A.M., so it wasn't unusual that on this morning they were still asleep. Plus, this was a *Sinatra* week. Lord knows what time they went to bed the night before. Anyway, I remember playing outside in the parking lot that morning when I heard the sound of laughter coming from inside the club. Boisterous, hysterical laughter. I couldn't imagine who in the world was having so much fun. When I walked to the place where the sounds were coming from, I saw my dad, Frank, and Sammy having a seltzer fight. Dean must have gone back to the hotel, because he didn't party like the rest of them did. They were around the circular bar in the front room, equal distances from one another, each armed with a seltzer bottle. They would hunch below the bar, out of sight, and then jump up to spray each other to death. They were sopping wet. Three grown men in $500 suits were having the time of their lives . . . playing a little boys' game."

The 1950s for Skinny and his friends was a time of unbridled release. After all the pent-up energy from the Great Depression and then World War II—fifteen long years—America was ready to cut loose. Nowhere, perhaps, did that cork pop louder than in the East Coast nightclub world. As if to signal the beginning of a new era in Atlantic City, former mayor Tommy "Two Guns" Taggart, out of office for six years, dropped dead of a heart attack in September 1950. The middle to late 1950s was a kind of second golden era for the resort— though it was nothing like the Prohibition era of Nucky Johnson, when the city thrummed with so much action. It was the nightlife and entertainment in Atlantic City that kept things percolating. And now there were some new spots—El Capitan on the Boardwalk at St. James Place; Club Nomad on Bacharach Boulevard.; the Dude Ranch, "Way Out West on the Walk," at Connecticut Avenue. In fact, one intersection—Arkansas and Pacific—was famous for being the only one in the country with a bar on all four corners: McGettigan & McGuire, the Seashell Bar, the Bamboo Club, and the Norwood. (Today, it is the location of the entrances to Caesars and Bally's Wild Wild West.)

In the spring of 1956, Skinny predicted to the *Atlantic City Press* that this would be the resort's "best year yet." That summer, Dean Martin and Jerry Lewis came back to the Five for a ten-night engagement for the first time in a few years. On the tenth night, they "buried" their act. They had grown tired of each other, and their strange dynamic, once so surprising and still very lucrative, had become corrosive and untenable. The *Today* show came to the club to do a taping on the morning of their last show; Skinny and Bettyjane appeared on the air with Martin & Lewis as the duo said good-bye to America.

On the opening night of that week, however, one thousand people were turned away. For the most part, Skinny was right about 1956 being a good year. While the population in Atlantic City had already begun its slow, imperceptible decline—from nearly 64,094 in 1942 to 61,642 in 1950—the middle of the decade saw substantial increases in residential and commercial building. Despite the fact that business was good, Skinny had read the tea leaves. In 1954, he first proposed to the political leaders of New Jersey, most of whom were his friends, the idea of legalizing gambling in Atlantic City; he saw how Las Vegas had exploded, drawing in sixteen million visitors a year.

But the men who ran the resort—not a single visionary among them—were temporarily sated by the miniboom and rejected the idea for fear it would bring more corruption (and the Mob) to town. They had reason to be hopeful. On July Fourth weekend 1957, bank deposits totaled more than $15 million, up $400,000 from the year before. On Easter weekend of that year, 150 private planes landed at Bader Field, Atlantic City's tiny airport. Also that year, Skinny was given the Press Club's award for doing the most to "spread the name and fame" of Atlantic City.

Frank Sinatra began appearing every August at the 500 Club, beginning in 1957, along with jazz musician Red Norvo and Pete Miller and His Orchestra, the house band there for many seasons. As Ed Hurst, a radio and television personality in Atlantic City since the

1940s, told me, "There were two places that kept this town alive after the war: the Steel Pier and the 500 Club." And the stars kept coming to peform on the stage of the Vermillion Room: Vic Damone, Eartha Kitt, Jayne Mansfield, Betty Hutton, Xavier Cugat, Al Martino, Nat King Cole, Kitty Kallen, Zsa Zsa Gabor. People from all over the world were turning up in Atlantic City to spend a night at the 500 Club. Skinny sometimes had his hands full juggling celebrity guests, trying to keep them all happy. One night, Mike Todd and Elizabeth Taylor showed up—as did Taylor's first husband, Nicky Hilton. "Keep them entertained," Skinny said to his brother Willie. "I'll get rid of him." Before Jayne Mansfield died in a car accident, she was at the 500 one night. At five A.M., after the last show, she asked Willie to take her to church. He pulled his rust bucket of a car around the front and drove her to Our Lady Star of the Sea Church and waited while she knelt in a pew and prayed.

The Five seemed to be under constant construction for a while, but sometime in the mid-1950s it took on the look and style that became fixed in people's minds. The club's front lounge was dominated by a serpentine bar that snaked around the room and featured a dramatic waterfall. The bar stools and walls were upholstered in zebra skin, a pattern exaggerated by ultraviolet light. Like the Moulin Rouge in Paris, the stage in the front room moved mechanically up and down at the push of a button, depending on the occasion. "I was so amazed when I first saw it," said Rita Marzullo, who started working at the club just after Skinny remodeled it, ratcheting up the glamour. "When I first went, everyone was dancing, and then, when the show came on, I saw the stage go up, up, up for the show. I was like a little kid watching a train set. And the waterfall! Oh my God, that waterfall. The place was magnificent." The tables were raked, and dinner was served nightly— finger steak was the house specialty, sliced and served on buttered white toast. There were "setups" at every table: a bottle of Scotch, rye, vodka, and gin and a bucket of ice, glasses, and mixers. So that diners didn't have to put down their drink or cigarette to applaud the performers, there were wooden knockers at every setting that they could bang on the table in lieu of clapping.

Behind the lounge was a showroom for headliners that seemed to grow bigger every year. This is the room where Sinatra performed his legendary shows, four and five a night, until sunrise, until every person waiting in the crowd outside got in the door. In the early 1960s, Skinny added another restaurant called the Beef and Beer, where clubgoers would eat spaghetti or roast beef sandwiches at five A.M. before heading home. Off the lounge there was a telephone booth where certain well-dressed patrons could be seen going in and never coming out; this was a secret entrance to "the garage," a small back room for gamblers and cardplayers that Skinny kept going for a select few.

During the summer, Skinny ran his card games in a back room at the club. But during the winter, he would head to New York and Miami, where the serious players could get in the game. The Fontainebleau was famed architect Morris Lapidus's first commission; it was built in 1954 and quickly became the Florida playground for presidents and celebrities, including Sinatra, Elvis Presley, Bob Hope, and Lucille Ball. The graceful quarter-circle curvilinear structure housed over five hundred rooms that overlooked a sumptuous half-acre lagoon-style rock grotto pool. There was a terrarium in the lobby with live alligators and the infamous "stairway to nowhere," which allowed guests to deposit their coats at the top of the stairs and parade back down. Lapidus's obsession with detail extended to the bellboys' uniforms, done in purple with gold braid.

The Fontainebleau had its own weekly newsletter, *Entre Nous*. In the issue dated March 29, 1960, under the headline "WHO'S WHO" AT THE FONTAINEBLEAU, there's a series of photographs including one of Skinny and Bettyjane looking impossibly chic, with both Paulajane and Cathy turned out in matching white jackets and white gloves. It was a rare photograph: Skinny made most of his trips to Miami without the wife and kids, because more often than not he and his friends were up to no good.

Ed Hurst, an old friend of Skinny's who now lives in Margate, spent some time around Skinny and Frank together. Hurst's friend Herb Siegel, then chairman of the board of General Artists Corporation, which was one of the largest talent agencies in the world, called him and said, "How'd you like to do a little barnstorming with me?" Siegel had just gotten a divorce, so he sent his plane to pick up Hurst, and they flew to Miami and spent three days at the Fontainebleau. "Frank was appearing there, and Skinny was there, as was Joe DiMaggio and his good friend George Solotaire, a New York City ticket broker. Apparently Frank and Skinny had their arguments—they didn't get along at times—and we were sitting at the same table with them in the Boom-Boom Room, and I don't know what transpired, but the next thing I knew, Frank threw a glass of water on Skinny. I was drunk for three days. They used to have these belly dancers at one of the hotels down there. So Frank brought them all over to this suite and they performed in the nude, and each of the guys there went to a different suite with each of the girls. And I'll never forget this as long as I live, but I go back to my room because I was bombed and laughed out, when a knock comes to my door. 'Mr. Hurst?' 'Yeah.' 'Mr. D'Amato sent me around. Said you weren't feeling well.' It's the most gorgeous girl I ever saw in my life. She said, 'What would you like?' All I can say is, I saw Skinny the next day and he said, 'You know, Ed, you look like you're feeling much better.'"

But Skinny, who was never a big drinker, wasn't there to party. He was there to gamble. Skinny had been friends with Albert "Cubby" Broccoli, the producer of many of the James Bond films, and he told Joe Del Raso late one night after the 500 Club had burned down that the scene in *Goldfinger* where the bad guys cheat at cards at the Fontainebleau using binoculars was lifted directly from Skinny's world. "There was a guy named 'The Russian' and that's how he used to run his game in the winter in Florida," Skinny said to Joe and a few of his fraternity brothers. "He used to rig the game once in a while."

"Skinny talked about how he and Sinatra used to hang out and party together," said Del Raso. "They'd take over the penthouse at the Fontainebleau Hotel and party day and night."

One night, they went to the Playboy Club in Miami just after it opened. Sinatra told Skinny he wanted to go out with a couple of the Bunnies, so Skinny went to see the manager and said, "Look, Frank wants to take a couple of the girls out afterward."

The manager said, "Absolutely not. It's against our policy. The customers are not allowed to fraternize with the Bunnies."

"Oh no, you've misunderstood me," Skinny said. "Frank would like to invite *you* out after you close to come out with us, and we'd like to invite a couple of the girls to go along."

They all went out and had a good time together, manager, Bunnies, Skinny, Frank, and whoever else was hanging on.

"Skinny would have Sinatra and Joe DiMaggio down to Florida," said Del Raso, speculating that they were his fixtures to attract the wealthy gamblers. "He'd play gin rummy during the day, win one hundred thousand dollars, and then console the losers by inviting them to have dinner with them: Frank and Joe and all the guys. These businessmen with a lot of money, but no other pizzazz, were willing to wager big money just to gain access to that circle of people. It isn't much different than the way high rollers are attracted to the major casinos today. They hire celebrity hosts and former sports players for the exact same reason."

According to Richard Ben Cramer, author of the definitive DiMaggio biography, *The Hero's Life*, Skinny *paid* DiMaggio to hang around. "It was more or less like a big casino hiring a 'greeter'—a former heavyweight champ or an ex–major leaguer—someone the suckers could talk about: they'd met him, they shook hands, they had a laugh together. But like all of Skinny and Joe's business, this was of the private variety. That was one reason Joe liked D'Amato, for the privacy that was Skinny's rule. Joe could go into the 500, and sit in the back room all day, maybe play a little cards. . . . No one would bother him in there. And if he did talk to one of D'Amato's friends, Skinny would make it worth Joe's while. . . . If he went down to Florida with Joe for a big race, Joe might lose twenty bucks at the track. But Skinny would give him a couple of grand just for sitting with some pals. If Joe would go out for a round of golf at the Breakers with one of Skinny's big guys, that was a better payday—five grand at least.

"And Skinny took care of Joe, more or less like Toots [Shor] always did. Any subject involving the Clipper's welfare, Skinny had opinions and an interest. Joe's teeth, for example: Joe never got his buckteeth fixed until Skinny took care of it—put him with the Dentist to the Stars in New York."

Another story Skinny told on occasion was about a guy who owned a big laundry company in New York who came down to play in Skinny's game one season. "He lost $1 million over several days playing gin rummy," said Del Raso, "and Skinny said, 'We figured we'd better let him win back about three or four hundred thousand because he'd be a sorehead and it'd get us in trouble.' Well, the guy went to Meyer Lansky and said, 'I think these guys cheated me. I want you to take care of them.' Lansky said, 'Well, who are you playing with?' He told him and Lansky said, 'Oh no, those guys run a straight game. You better go away.' And what Skinny said was that what this guy didn't know was Skinny used to discount the markers for Meyer Lansky, no different than any other businessman factoring his receivables. So Lansky was holdin' the markers anyway!" Del Raso remembers Skinny lamenting the end of the big-stakes card games, blaming it on the lack of "war money" left in the economy. Del Raso said, "Skinny had expressions like that for everything. It was probably money made in the black market of World War II, all in cash, in big bills, by which he meant larger bills—older, out of circulation currency. If you go back to currency from the thirties and forties the money was physically bigger. And Skinny said these guys would take him to their safe deposit boxes to pay him."

In Atlantic City during the summers, Skinny would often rent a suite at one of the grand hotels on the Boardwalk—usually the Claridge—where he could carry on his all-night, big-stakes card games. Generally, there was little threat of a raid because he paid off the cops, who at this point were too in awe of Skinny to bother him anyway, since they all wanted to be his friend. Frank Sinatra played the 500 Club for a week or two every August throughout the decade, and he would customarily rent out an entire floor—sometimes two—at the Claridge, where he would throw all-night parties.

After Sinatra's FBI files—all 1,275 pages of them—were finally released under the Freedom of Information Act in December 1998, I read the pages pertaining to the goings-on at the Claridge in July and August 1959. Later that year, Sinatra was questioned under oath by an IRS agent in Los Angeles during an investigation into possible Mob skimming in nightclubs where Sinatra performed. In his testimony,

Sinatra flatly denied that Chicago Mob boss Sam Giancana had attended his never-ending party at the Claridge that summer.

Q. Are you acquainted with a Mr. Sam Giancana?
   A. I am.

Q. How long have you known the gentleman?
   A. A couple of years. A little under a couple of years.

Q. Approximately when did you first meet Mr. Giancana?
   A. March 11, I think, 1958.

Q. Where did this meeting take place?
   A. In the Fontainebleau Hotel.

And then, further on in the file:

Q. Mr. Sinatra, information has come to our attention that during the period of July 25, 1959, to August 2, 1959, you were staying at the Hotel Claridge, Atlantic City, New Jersey, and at that time you had rented numerous rooms at this hotel and had given a party which was attended by Mr. Giancana. Is that correct?
   A. No.

Q. Has Mr. Giancana attended any parties given by you, Mr. Sinatra?
   A. No.

Sinatra was lying, and they knew it. A few years later, the FBI considered going after him for making a false statement on an affidavit. To that end, an agent filed a report in 1960 entitled "Samuel M. Giancana" in which he stated that an informant "advised on September 16, 1959, that [Giancana] had recently been to the Claridge Hotel in Atlantic City, New Jersey, in order to see Frank Sinatra and was told Sinatra had reserved the entire first floor of the hotel. The informant stated when they got off the elevator on the first floor they were approached by two 'tough looking men' and asked for identification and the purpose of their visit. The informant stated one individual in Sinatra's suite at this hotel was identified to him as Joseph Fischetti [brother of Rocco and Charles], described as the 'well known hoodlum from Miami.'"

Another report filed in 1962 was based on an interview with a showgirl whose name was redacted from the file. The agent wrote: "She stated that at the age of approximately eighteen she became employed as a professional dancer, appearing in chorus lines at various hotels, night clubs and casinos around the country. . . . She became acquainted with Frank Sinatra during approximately 1958. During this period she traveled throughout the country and worked for some time at the Tropicana and Riviera Hotels in Las Vegas.

"In July 1959, she attended a party given by Frank Sinatra in Atlantic City, New Jersey, at the Claridge Hotel. Sinatra at that time was appearing at the 500 Club as the featured entertainer. The party referred to lasted approximately two weeks and normally started at about 8:00 P.M. and lasted until about 4:00 or 5:00 A.M. the following morning. . . . She mentioned other persons in attendance at this affair, in addition to the ones mentioned above, as actress Natalie Wood, actor Robert Wagner, then the husband of Natalie Wood, Rocco Fischetti, his brother, Joseph Fischetti, John Foreman (true name John Formosa) and Paul 'Skinny' D'Amato."

✦

Skinny has regularly been referred to in books and government documents as a "lieutenant of Sam Giancana's," which doesn't quite add up. As Joe Del Raso told me, "I asked [Skinny] how he met Sam Giancana and he said, 'Frank Sinatra.' If it was the other way around, it would be different."

Giancana was just six months older than Skinny and was a sixth-grade dropout at the age of fourteen. His rap sheet dates back to 1925 and includes more than seventy arrests, including contributing to delinquency, vagrancy, burglary, assault and battery, larceny, fugitive, assault to kill, damage by violence, conspiracy to operate a "book," gambling, bombing suspect, and murder. He was the prime suspect in dozens of murder investigations, three before the age of twenty. He started out as a thief and a killer in Chicago in the 1920s and was arrested for murder in 1926 but was not prosecuted because the state's case fell apart when Alexander Burba, a cabdriver and the main witness, was murdered. His first big job was as chauffeur and bodyguard for "Machine Gun" Jack McGurn, a syndicate killer; he quickly gained a reputation as the "fastest wheelman on the West Side." By the late 1940s, Giancana was closely associated with Anthony "Tony Batters" Accardo, an ex-bodyguard of Al Capone's, and was rumored to be the gunman in the St. Valentine's Day massacre. By 1950, he was a major hoodlum in Chicago and was in charge of illegal gambling there. Ten years later, Giancana had risen to the top, where he controlled protection, prostitution, numbers, narcotics, loan-sharking, extortion, counterfeiting, and bookmaking. In consolidating his power, he ordered the deaths of some two hundred people, which brought him to the head of an international crime empire that included interests in the Sands, Riviera, and Desert Inn in Las Vegas, estimated by the FBI to generate over $2 billion in income annually, of which $50 million went directly to Giancana.

A police official once described him as "a snarling, sarcastic, ill-mannered, ill-tempered, sadistic psychopath." At the Terre Haute Penitentiary in 1940, he was given a psychological evaluation and was determined to have a general IQ of 71 verbal and 93 nonverbal. He was rejected by the army—after being drafted in 1943—as a "constitutional psychopath" with an "inadequate personality and strong antisocial trends."

None of this stopped entertainers from wanting to be his friend, including Joe E. Brown, Jimmy Durante, Dean Martin, Keely Smith, and, most important, Phyllis McGuire, who was his girlfriend for many years. Giancana wore a sapphire friendship ring every day that had been given to him by Sinatra in the early 1960s.

Throughout Sinatra's FBI files, Skinny is referred to as a "well-known hoodlum" and a "member of La Cosa Nostra." But the file also reports that Skinny "possibly had an interest in the 500 Club," which at this point he owned outright. FBI files are notoriously messy documents, filled as they are with an occasionally riveting combination of facts, rumors, false leads, gossip, unsubstantiated claims, and down-right lies. But they can also lead to certain truths. Sinatra's files point out that Skinny "has served a penitentiary sentence as a panderer" as the only specific example of his criminal background, which, of course, was in 1938. One report stated that Sinatra was an associate of Skinny D'Amato, "a hoodlum and a member of La Cosa Nostra syndicate.... Although Sinatra was not a member of the syndicate, he was big enough and close enough to the organization to obtain any favors he desired." The point that's missing is that this, most likely, was Skinny's relationship to the Mob as well. It's one of the many things they had in common—a special relationship to the Mob. He had the equivalent of diplomatic immunity because the mobsters wanted access to the club, and, more important, the celebrities and politicians. Skinny liked to say, "Well, they're coming to town with plenty of money. Where are they gonna go? To my joint or the White Tower on the corner?" Still, it wasn't like the Ravenite Social Club where mobsters hung out every single day. Skinny was never invited to any serious confabs where real decisions were made or where secrets and criminal plans were discussed. He was not a "made man." He never killed anyone. The Mob used Frank and Skinny, and vice versa.

While the Mob was certainly organized and responsible for horrible things, it may not have been nearly as pervasive, efficient, and all-encompassing as people tend to think. For example, Frank Sinatra's FBI file goes on to report that his parties at the Claridge were actually a *"cover for clandestine meetings with La Cosa Nostra leaders"* (italics mine). This is absurd. They probably weren't a cover for anything, except perhaps Sinatra's inability to spend even one minute alone—or sleeping. That Skinny was Giancana's lieutenant is likely just a myth that confers complexity on a situation that was, in fact, much simpler. Besides, Giancana did not show up in Skinny's life, nor in anyone's recollections of his life, until after 1958—*after* Frank met him at the Fontainebleau, which is where Skinny also claimed to have met him. Several people told stories about Giancana being at the 500 Club, but when I sorted through them and compared notes, they all occurred in the same year and the same month—August 1959. There are only two photographs of Giancana and Phyllis McGuire at the club, and one was taken that summer.

Bill McCullough, who now owns and runs the modeling agency founded by his mother, Marie McCullough, remembered going to the 500 Club, also that same summer, to see Sinatra's one-thirty A.M. show. "Bettyjane asked my mother and I to go, and I asked a date. There were so many people outside, you couldn't get in through the front door—forget it—so we went in through the kitchen and up on the stage and actually came down from the stage to get to our seats, which were ringside. That was kind of a trip because they had real long tables, and they really packed 'em in. Dick Clark was at our table. I think my mother was on one side of me, and Bettyjane was right across from me, and I think her mother and father were ringside, and there was a seat vacant next to me. Bettyjane was famously polite and very good about introducing people. Well, this guy comes and sits down in the seat, and Bettyjane did not introduce him to anyone. And she said, 'Hi, Sam.' And he said 'How's Skinny?' And she said, 'Well, he played cards all night and he just got up.' My mother whispered to me, 'If the lights go out suddenly, duck under the table.' I couldn't figure out why she was saying this. Obviously, it was Sam Giancana."

There was only one other time that Giancana came to the 500 Club. After the club burned down Joe Del Raso was helping Skinny sort through the boxes of pictures that were salvaged from the fire. "Skinny pointed out pictures of Christmas dinner in, I believe, 1961," said Del Raso. "Skinny was hosting Giancana, Phyllis McGuire, and some character named Cadillac Mo. Bettyjane and the children and the McCulloughs were also there. I remember Skinny laughing because he said to me, 'Look, they were in Atlantic City for Christmas when everyone was looking all over the country for them in Palm Springs and in Florida. They never thought they'd find them in my joint on Christmas Day. Who in the world would want to go to Atlantic City on December twenty-fifth?'"

Skinny would've made the greatest Mob leader in the world if he had those kind of balls," said Rita Marzullo, whom everyone calls Momma Rita. "But he had heart. He *cared* about people." Rita was born in 1929—the eighth of ten children (five boys, five girls)—and raised on Fulton Street in South Philadelphia in an ur-Italian neighborhood now called Bella Vista (the same neighborhood, in fact, where Skinny lived with the Caputos for a brief period after his parents died in the early 1920s). Rita grew up with some local boys who became both famous and infamous: Thomas Foglietta, a congressman from Pennsylvania who became the ambassador to Italy during the Clinton administration, and his right-hand man, Anthony "Junior" Del Vecchio, lived up the block; Henry J. "Buddy" Cianfrani, who became a Pennsylvania state senator—and a legend in South Philly—lived directly across the street. But she also grew up on the same streets as Angelo Bruno, who took over the Philly-Jersey Mob when Marco Reginelli died of natural causes in 1956; she went to Bartlett Junior High with Nicky Scarfo, the notorious mobster who was banished to Atlantic City in the 1970s and eventually to prison in Marion, Illinois.

The Marzullo house was down the street from Palumbo's, the famous restaurant-nightclub where the Mob hung out nearly every night. "They didn't call them the Mob back then," said Rita, "but all those guys would park their fancy cars up and down our street, and they would get out to go to Palumbo's with their wives or girlfriends, who were always decked out with furs and diamonds. I would go up and talk to these girls and say, 'When I grow up I want to be just like you.' Then I was told, 'Don't talk to them.' I knew right then—from when I was a little girl—that I wanted to be in that kind of lifestyle."

I visited Rita several times in her old stomping grounds and spent countless hours on the phone with her. We usually went out to her favorite Italian restaurant in South Philly, the Saloon, on the corner of Seventh and Catherine, where she knew everybody and where we gorged ourselves on soup, pasta, veal, and wine and talked for hours. Rita is very short and very fat and has very swollen ankles, which makes it difficult for her to walk.

Things weren't always this way. On the day we first met, she took out a folder with the few scraps of memorabilia she had managed to hang on to over the years, including a photograph of her much younger self. It was taken in 1948, when she was nineteen, on the day of her sister Marie's wedding. "I stood for her," said Rita. "If you take a good look at me, I'm crying because I didn't want to walk down the aisle with the best man because he was too old." At nineteen, Rita was tiny and gorgeous, with long thick curly black hair, beautiful dark brown eyes, and great big full lips. In the picture, she is wearing a chartreuse silk gown with a full skirt to the floor and a white straw hat with a wide brim. She is holding a nosegay of gardenias and roses.

Rita is mischievous and funny and was once a very serious party girl who lived a life of very late nights and expensive clothes and many big, fancy meals with important men. Never married, no kids, and she curses like a sailor. I could see why Skinny D'Amato liked her so much.

In 1950, just after she was jilted by a man named Sonny—with whom she had been madly in love—and just before her twenty-first birthday, she packed two suitcases and moved to Atlantic City, a place where she, like so many of her people from South Philly, had spent quite a number of summer weekends. Before she was of age, she had managed to get into the 500 Club a few times with the help of her older sister's birth certificate. The day she arrived in Atlantic City to live, she got a job as a waitress at Bella Napoli on Pacific and Georgia Avenues, and her very first customer was Buddy Greco. That night, she and a girlfriend went to the 500 Club, and a man approached her when she was on her way out of the ladies' room and said, "Angelo wants to see you." It was Angelo Bruno, the head of the Philly Mob, whom Rita had idolized since she was a child. She would follow him around the neighborhood, hoping that a scrap of attention would be tossed her way.

"What are you doing here?" Bruno asked her when she went up to his table at the Five.

"I came down here to work," she said.

"Does your family know you're here?"

"Of course," she said.

Just then, Skinny came over to the table and said to Angelo, "Introduce me."

"This is Rita," said Angelo. "She's working at the Bella Napoli."

"Why don't you come here to work?" said Skinny.

"Here?" said Rita. "You want my brothers to kill me? I can't work at a nightclub."

That night, Skinny promised Angelo that if Rita came to work at the club, he would protect her. The very next day, she packed up her two suitcases at the rooming house above Bella Napoli and moved into the Penn Plaza Hotel, right next door to the 500. "The first job Skinny gave me was as a hat check girl. Then they made me a cigarette girl. They fitted me with a short little outfit, and I felt so embarrassed because I never had my legs exposed in front of a lot of strangers. But Skinny always used to say to the girls who worked at his club, 'Now, I don't want you girls coming to work looking like schoolteachers.' I was green when I went there. Even though I came from a big city like Philly, I learned a lot in a small town like Atlantic City.

"When I walked in the club, the first thing that amazed me was the doorman, Slim, who stood outside. He was a black man, over seven feet tall, and Skinny had him in a beautiful red captain's uniform. He could put his arm over a Jaguar and open up the passenger side. Everybody loved Slim.

"When you walked in the front door, Skinny had all the pictures of everybody who was appearing there. This is where T.T. worked. 'T.T.' was short for Trenton Tommy. His real name was Tommy Argenti. He was just over five feet tall, couldn't have weighed more than 130 pounds, and Skinny gave him the title of 'bouncer,' which made everybody laugh. The first night I worked there, I sat at the bar, I was so amazed. He had this gorgeous waterfall over the bar. I wasn't even watching the show because I was so mesmerized by this waterfall. Skinny took me all over and showed me every inch of the club. The supper club was run by Rags, who was the maître d'. He was a Damon Runyon character if there ever was one. You'd pass by, and there's Skinny's private table, and only certain people were allowed to sit with him. Over his private table was this humongous, gorgeous portrait of Sinatra with his hands out, embracing Skinny. Oh, how Sinatra loved Skinny. Next to Skinny's table was this alcove, and it was dark in there, and I seen a man move. Skinny said he was a detective, there to protect people. As you walked past this little alcove, there was the ladies' room. Inside the ladies' room was this fantastic little attendant, Agnes. After you passed the ladies' room, there was the service bar and then the doors to the supper club." The first week Rita worked at the 500, she saw Liz Taylor and Mike Todd sitting near the service bar—fighting. "I almost had a heart attack," said Rita. "Oooh, you should've heard her cursing him. They were arguing, and he's trying to kiss her and hug her and everything, but, boy, did she have a temper."

After her stint as a cigarette girl, Skinny dared Rita to get on the stage and be a chorus girl. "I said, 'Skin, *c'mon.'* I was known to have a beautiful sense of humor. A lot of the comedians used to come over and say to me, 'Zings come outta your mouth! Gems!' It wasn't unusual for there to be a Mob boss sitting on one side of you, the chief of police on the other, and Frank Sinatra or Dean Martin over there—all partying together. I'd go around saying, in jest, 'Check all your guns at the door!' All the bodyguards would laugh. Everybody loved me and my humor."

Eventually Rita did get onstage and pulled off a kind of Fanny Brice routine. "I was hysterical, and they wanted me to stay as a chorus girl. I had fun onstage, but then after I sang, I'd go out with the chorus girls. But when Skinny found out he called me into his office and hollered at me. He didn't want me to hang out with them. He said, 'I promised Angelo [Bruno] I'd protect you.' That's when I became a waitress. And one of my first customers was Edward G. Robinson. He drove me out of my mind. But that's another story."

Rita made a fortune waitressing, partly because of her winning personality, but also because she quickly became Skinny's "pet," which is to say that she routinely got all the plum assignments. For example, when Frank or Dean were in town, she was usually the only waitress allowed to bring food and drinks backstage. "The only two entertainers at the 500 Club that ever tipped, and tipped *large*, were Sinatra and Dean Martin," said Rita. "And it was all according to who you were. Like Mo, who was the headwaiter, got a couple thousand when they left after ten days. But, oh, *what they'd put us through*! I always got a thousand or fifteen hundred and a gift. This one year, a few of us got solid gold toothbrushes. If you gave Sinatra a match, he'd hand you a hundred dollars."

When Rita first came to Atlantic City, Sinatra wouldn't leave her alone. "He would chase me and chase me and chase me. But I was so in love with Sonny I couldn't see anybody. Besides, he was too old for me—I never went out with older men. Sinatra was great, I loved him to death, but I would *never* go out with him. To go out with him in a crowd, yes, but Sinatra used to send me flowers and messages. He would send Jay Rossi, an entertainer at the club, to talk to me. Jay would say to Sinatra, 'She don't want to be bothered. Leave her alone.' I said to Skinny, 'Wouldn't you *please* tell him to leave me alone? I don't want to lose the job, I don't want you to get mad at me.'"

She waited on dozens of stars and captains of industry, Mob bosses and athletes. From Joan Crawford and her husband, Alfred Steele, board chairman of Pepsi-Cola, to Janet Leigh and Tony Curtis, who flew in whenever Sinatra performed, to Jersey Joe Walcott, Yogi Berra, DiMaggio, of course, and Jack Kelly, the father of Grace Kelly, who summered in Ocean City.

"Jack Kelly had his own special table all year round," said Rita. "One time, Skinny was giving some party in the daytime, it might have been his annual Easter party after the parade on the Boardwalk, and Bettyjane was with him and a lot of the family was there—his in-laws, Paulajane, and Cathy. So Jack Kelly and Skinny were at the table, and Grace Kelly came in. She was still young and single and she was chasing Skinny all over the place. Grace Kelly! And he's hiding in that little alcove, saying, 'Did she leave yet? Did she leave yet?' And now I'm furious because his wife is sitting there with his kids. And Paulajane—oh my God, every time she got up on the stage and sang, it was 'Take Me Out to the Ball Game.' That was her song. So, I think Paulajane was singing, and Grace Kelly made herself so obvious, and I said to Skinny, 'You want me to say something?' And he said, 'No. Keep your mouth shut. Don't say nothing. She'll leave, she'll leave.' Finally she sees that her father was starting to notice, and he reprimanded her. Grace Kelly! And she finally left and Skinny came out of hiding. So many girls chased Skinny. Oh my God, so many girls.

"Skinny always dominated the room, whether there were movie stars, presidents, lords, or kings of state in the room or not. Everyone was mesmerized by his presence. *No one* filled the room like he did. All that Mob bullshit about him is nothing but all *bullshit*. I saw it with my own eyes—one time, Sinatra, Bob Hope, and Joan Crawford had everyone crowded around them, and when Skinny walked in it was like Moses had entered the room and the crowd parted like the Red Sea to let Skinny walk through. And then it closed up and everyone ran to be by Skinny's side and be greeted by him. He didn't have much education, but his IQ must have been off the charts. And Sinatra followed the crowd to be by Skinny's side, and he didn't get angry. He was very proud of how everyone loved Skinny so much. Sinatra loved Skinny the way *I* loved him."

Rita is also famous for her cooking, and after a while, she started working in the kitchen of Skinny's club, making the Italian dishes popular among the South Philly crowd. One night she was making meatballs, and Skinny said to the kitchen staff, "I'm waiting for a couple of important calls. Nobody answer the phone but Rita." When the phone rang, Rita answered it.

"Put the greaseball on the phone," came the voice on the other end.

"Who?" she said.

"You know who I mean," said the voice. "The *greaseball*."

"Who's the greaseball? We have a couple of greaseball cooks in here from Italy." But then she recognized the voice; it was Sinatra. "You talking about Skinny?" she said.

"Yeah," said Sinatra. "Put him on the phone."

Rita went out into the dining room, found Skinny sitting around smoking with a bunch of guys, and said, "*He's* on the phone." Ever after, that was their code. "'Get the greaseball,' and I'd say to Skinny, 'Hey, the greaseball's on the phone!'"

Rita was there the night Martin & Lewis "buried" their act. "They were up onstage, and they were really going crazy," she said. "They took a big bowl of salad from the waiters, and they were throwing it at everybody and acting like two kids, but everybody loved it. Then they called Skinny to come up onstage. Now Skinny was very bashful, and he didn't like to be recognized. Very reluctantly he went up, and they told the whole story about the break that he gave them and that he was the best boss. They were talking about how they were going to miss him and how humble he was—such beautiful, beautiful things about him—and they had him crying. Dean Martin wouldn't let him walk offstage, they were hugging and kissing, and they were both crying. When he finally walked offstage, Jerry Lewis said, 'There goes a gentleman personified.' Everybody's hands are burning from applauding so much, I'm crying so much. I sat down and put my feet up—they were killing me—and Skinny walks offstage and walks by, still crying, and said to me, 'Are you comfortable? Can I get you a pillow? Get your feet off the chair!' I said, 'The whole world's giving you a standing ovation and you're worried about my legs up on the chair?' So I followed him and said, 'Skin, are you mad at me?' He said, 'No, but what are you crying for?' I said, 'Because I love you so much and everything they said is true—you are the best boss in the whole world.' He said, 'Stop crying.' I said, 'Are you really mad because I had my feet on the chair?' He said, 'I had to take it out on somebody, so I took it out on you.'"

Skinny gave Rita special treatment because they had something in common—they knew how to act around stars and big shots. They weren't intimidated or impressed, and they didn't ask them for anything. Eventually Rita seemed closer to Skinny than some members of his own family. "He was somebody's father, somebody's brother, somebody's brother-in-law, somebody's son," said Rita. "And they knew him that way. I knew him because I was right there with him at work seven nights a week and we did so much together. He was like a brother to me. There was no way you could not love this man. Skinny would have loved you, and you would have loved him. He was so kind and generous. He paid so many people's hospital bills and mortgages. He would send me to so many people's houses in Atlantic City to pay for their coal, to pay their rent, buy them food. He'd give me money and send me out to buy clothes for people. They'd want to know who sent me, and I had to say, 'Santa Claus.' I couldn't say his name to nobody."

After working at the 500 Club for about a year, Rita became friendly with a woman named Marie Falgiatore, who was a waitress at Le Bistro just up the block. Rita would sit outside on the porch of the Penn Plaza and see her walking up the street; like everyone else, she was struck by how beautiful she was. One day, Rita said hello to Marie and told her she should come work at the 500. "You could triple your tips," she said. The day Marie started, Joe DiMaggio took one look at the raven-haired doll and asked Skinny to make Marie his private waitress. By this point, DiMaggio had his own special area in the club, just inside the door, right past the coat check—next to Skinny's table.

"Everybody fell in love with Marie," said Rita. "She was magnificently beautiful. She looked like a cross between Ava Gardner and Liz Taylor. But she wouldn't go out with nobody because, like me, she was suffering over her lost love, and she had three sons to raise. One night, in comes Cappy, whose real name was Anthony Coppola [and was a member of the New York Mob], and when he sees Marie, he flips. He asked everybody: 'Who is she? Who is she? I want to meet her.' But she's tough. She don't go out with nobody. 'No, no, no, I have to meet her,' he said. So he went to Skinny and asked if he would please talk on his behalf."

Cappy had recently carried on an affair with Liz Renay, the actress who famously stripped naked before the media and five thousand onlookers on Hollywood and Vine at high noon sometime in the 1950s. (Years later, Renay wrote a book called *My First 2,000 Men* and went on Geraldo Rivera's talk show to talk about Cappy and all the jewels he gave her.) Marie finally relented and agreed to go to the breakfast show at Club Harlem with Cappy—but only if Rita came along.

"So we go to the Harlem, and Cappy's saying to her at the table, 'What can I buy you? A car, furs, diamonds.' She had just bought a house in Ventnor, and she needed everything. And she said, 'I need a lawn mower.' I spit out my drink. Cappy said, 'A *lawn mower*? Whoever asks for a lawn mower?' She said, 'Well, that's what I need.' He said, 'Wait till my friends hear that you want a lawn mower.' So the next day, he not only sent her a lawn mower, but a gardener to take care of all her needs and people to fix up her house. Later, he bought her a brand-new Lincoln Continental. Then we find out who Cappy was—Albert Anastasia's bodyguard, companion, and driver. Albert Anastasia was Murder Incorporated out of New York. But she didn't care. DiMaggio said to Cappy, 'Don't mess with her. She's good people. Treat her royal,' and he did. They were together for about five years."

Marie and Rita became known as "the pets" to everyone in the club. When the television series *The Fugitive* began, all the waitresses at the Five became obsessed with the show's star, David Janssen. "Skinny used to listen to us girls talk about how much we were in love with him," said Rita, "and I could see by the look on his face that he was scheming something."

One day, Skinny invited Marie and Rita to go to New York for the day. Skinny's driver, Lefty DeJoseph, picked them up and, along with Skinny and Jimmy Ceres, a club employee who used to work for Joe DiMaggio, off they went to Manhattan one morning. "He told us when we were done shopping and getting our hair done to call him at Toots Shor or Jilly Rizzo's and Lefty would come pick us up." They eventually went to Shor's and were led to Skinny's table, where he was sitting with a bunch of "big shots," Jackie Gleason and . . . David Janssen!

"Marie's eyes were popping out of her head," said Rita. "Skinny had his famous big crooked smile on his face. I was seated between Skinny and this handsome hunk, and I screamed, *'Richard Kimble!'* Everyone turned to look at our table and got hysterical. I hugged and kissed him and Skinny. He was so generous with his love and gifts; all our clothes and our hair and the whole day was on him."

But Skinny was also overly protective. If he was willing to arrange for Rita to meet her fantasy man, she was not allowed to date any real men who were actually interested in her. One year, Skinny hired a magician—Rita can't remember his name—whose shtick was hypnotizing people onstage and making fools out of them. One night, when things were slow, Joe White, the bartender, and Rita got onstage. "Everybody in the audience was cheering us on," said Rita. "And I was watching Skinny, and he had this scowl on his face, which I read to mean: Get off the stage. So I walked off and the fun was over." She went over to Skinny and said, "What's wrong?"

"I don't like the way that son of a bitch was eyeballing you," said Skinny. "Stay away from him."

But the magician wouldn't leave Rita alone. "He sent flowers and asked me to meet him after work for a drink. I tore up all the notes, but Skinny was clocking everything. Finally the bastard begged me to join his act and become his assistant and travel all over the world with him. I told him to take a walk. If I was stupid enough to fall for his bullshit, that first night out of Atlantic City he would've tried to get me in bed. I didn't want to tell Skinny, so I just ignored him. But he was so persistent, he was stalking me, and one night, he cornered me outside the 500 Club. I gave him a tirade of my famous curse words and such a shot that I knocked his two caps out of his mouth. T.T. ran in the club and called Skinny, and the two of them and Chickie Narducci, one of the bartenders, had to pull me off of him. I was clocking him with my platform shoes. Skinny pulled him across the street to the parking lot and slapped the shit out of him and then fired him. I still can see Skinny, his hair all mussed—which he never let happen—and the look on his face as he was giving that son of a bitch a good tuning. All the guys from the club had to pull Skinny off of him, and the bastard tried to hit Skinny back. *Oh, madon!* Skinny never did that before or after—he never hit anybody. He was always so protective of me and Marie for years. But he *screamed* at me for not telling him the bastard was bothering me. A couple days later, Skinny caught some grief from the guy's agent and the union, but Frank Sinatra made a call and took care of it. He and Skinny eventually made up, and the guy apologized to me, but he never played Atlantic City again."

"The pets" were on top of the world—and having a blast. But like so many things in Atlantic City, their good time ended in tragedy. Marie lived with her youngest son, Christopher, in a brand-new apartment building called the Brighton Towers on Atlantic Avenue, just down the street from Tony's Baltimore Grille. One morning, the building caught fire and Marie ran to the elevator, where she got trapped. She was burned to death. Many of the injured were taken to the Baltimore Grille, and when Rita arrived on the scene she searched everywhere for

Marie—until she heard one of the waitresses say, "Oh God, she doesn't know." She jumped in a cab and went to the Atlantic City Medical Center, and when a doctor showed her Marie's charred body, she lost her mind. Skinny and Willie eventually made their way to the hospital to take Rita home.

"Skinny always told us he would take care of us if anything ever happened," said Rita. "And he did." He paid for an elaborate funeral and burial for Marie, to which hundreds came. It is one of those events in Atlantic City that everyone remembers. Frank and Dean sent flowers, and the Mob guys came with envelopes filled with cash for Marie's sons. Rita spent the next several days sitting on a bench in front of the Brighton Towers, virtually catatonic, staring up at the ruined building. She simply could not get over it and move on. One day, Skinny appeared and sat on the bench next to her. "You gotta get out of here," he said to her as he hugged the tiny, broken Rita. "Take a vacation and I'll pay for it. Anywhere you want to go." She went to Miami—and stayed for two years. Angelo Bruno put her in touch with friends who took care of her. When she finally decided to come home, Skinny sent her a plane ticket. But when she arrived in Atlantic City, everything had changed. The fun was over, her heart was broken, and Marie was dead. Her beloved city had lost its soul.

✳

Before Rita Marzullo became Momma Rita, her nickname was Rita Missouri, because—like Skinny and his wife and kids and the people who lived next door at the Penn Plaza—she worked, lived, and played on the same block. In the late 1950s, the Missouri Avenue between Atlantic and Pacific was a thriving, self-contained, twenty-four-hour scene, especially in the summer. On the south side of the street, on the corner of Pacific, there was a bar called the Applegate, which later became Le Bistro, where Jackie Mason, Vic Damone, and a young Lenny Bruce often performed. Next door was a small hotel and then a courtyard and then the Penn Plaza Hotel. Between the Penn Plaza and the 500 Club there was a parking lot, and on the other side of the 500 stood the Missouri Hotel, where Paulajane fell down a flight of stairs when she was nine and broke her collarbone and where showgirls, waitresses, and prostitutes who all worked in official and unofficial capacities at the 500 Club often stayed. Needless to say, there was no shortage of horny guys with money at the club; Skinny eventually washed his hands of the whore business when he no longer needed the money, but he let other people shake down the b-girls (short for bar girls), as they were sometimes called.

On the corner of Atlantic was the Escort Bar and then, across the street, the Welcome Bar; both establishments catered to the very late night bartender-waitress crowd. The Welcome Bar was also a haunt of the Mob guys as well as the detectives who were supposed to be watching them. On the other side of the street, at the other corner of Atlantic and Missouri, was Jules Men's Shop. Adjacent to that was a huge parking lot for the 500 Club, which was run by Tony and Dutchie, two longtime fixtures of the neighborhood. Behind the parking lot were a few big old houses, which were sometimes rented out to employees of the 500. Next to the lot was another small hotel, another parking lot, the Golden Gate bar, and then the legendary twenty-four-hour luncheonette Harry the Hats, which was famous for its spareribs. Finally, on the other corner of Pacific and Missouri, there was a gas station. The block was also distinguished by four of five newsstandlike food concessions that sold corn on the cob, clams on the half shell, fried egg sandwiches, and Italian sausage with peppers and onions.

When Rita was living at the Penn Plaza in the 1950s, Paulajane's and Cathy's lives were mostly idyllic—and they had lots of other adults around to shower them with love and affection, even if it was of an odd sort. "When I was living next door," said Rita, "those girls would wake up and run outside to play in the parking lot. They used to come right next door to the Penn Plaza where I lived on the first floor, and they'd be knocking on my door. Now you gotta understand, the 500 closed at five A.M. After work it was *our* time to party, and we'd come home maybe seven, eight o'clock in the morning. Now I'm dead tired and they're knocking at my door at ten A.M. Sometimes I wouldn't answer. So Paulajane would say, 'Oh, I know how to get in there,' and they'd come on the side—which was an alley—they'd come up to my bedroom window, open the screen, climb on the bed, and jump up and down on me until I had to get up and play with them. They were something, those kids."

Paulajane was always the chosen, golden child, and her parents favored her from the start. This had partly to do with the fact that she was their first, but also because Cathy was not the confident self-starter that her sister was. In fact, Cathy didn't say her first word until she was nearly five, and Paulajane learned to speak for her—a dynamic that continues to this day.

Rita picked up on it immediately. Once, after finding Cathy crying and feeling left out, Rita scooped her up and took her out for ice cream. The next day, she warned Skinny to be careful about favoring Paulajane. "You know, Skin," she said, "I can't understand this. You love everybody the same—you love me, you love your friends, your workers—but you do show more love to Paulajane than you do to Cathy."

"No, I don't," said Skinny.

"You certainly do," said Rita.

"Paulajane was always with him," Rita told me. "She was like on top of him, running after him and Cathy was more shy and got less attention. The next morning, I woke up and went into Skinny's office, and he was upset. I said, 'What's wrong?' And he said, 'I want to be the best father in the world, and I'm hurt by what you said because I love my children so much. I didn't know that I was doing this.' He was upset about that the whole day."

Skinny was shaken up because he knew in his heart that Rita was right. He was so busy with the club and everything that came with it—including his gambling jones—that he had very little time for his family. Paulajane demanded more attention than anyone else; consequently, she received more than anyone else. Later in life, Paulajane couldn't understand why her father always made such a fuss over Cathy and seemed to take *her* for granted.

The Penn Plaza also served to expand the world of Paulajane and Cathy beyond the tiny universe of the club and the apartment above it. Genevieve Norato grew up at the Penn Plaza Hotel. She is four years older than Paulajane, but they played together during the day, and she often went to the Traymore, where the D'Amatos had their own private cabana. Sometimes Boo-Boo, one of their drivers, would take them over in a limousine or in Skinny's Cadillac, and often Genevieve and her sisters would go with them.

"The doors would open and in would walk the D'Amatos, and we were like part of the family," said Genevieve. "They were treated like royalty. And Joey Bishop or Jack E. Leonard would be there with them in their cabana. I loved them and I loved being with them. There was this whole fun childhood kind of magic that happened at the shore every summer."

More often than not, Genevieve and Paulajane would have sleepovers. "When I would sleep at their apartment," said Genevieve, "Paula would have to go to bed, and then Bettyjane and I would stay up and play cards and we'd order a club sandwich from the club and we'd have ourselves a good old time."

I had gone to see Genevieve at her sister Anita's house in Ventnor, where she was visiting for the weekend. Anita is a pastry chef at the Sands, and Genevieve lives outside of Philadelphia. We sat around the dining room table with their mother, Lee, who was suffering from Alzheimer's and was heartbreakingly unaware of what was going on around her. Also at the table was Danny Colingo, a singer and protégé of Skinny's who used to perform at the 500 Club when he was a teenager.

Genevieve and Anita are the daughters of Elizabeth (Lee) and Arthur Norato, a couple who took over the Penn Plaza Hotel in the summer of 1957, just a few months before Bettyjane gave birth to Angelo. The Noratos bought the Penn Plaza for $35,000 from a man named Irving Nathanson, who had owned it for many years but had lost all of his money gambling—much of it in card games with Skinny—and had to sell. Genevieve, one of four daughters, was eleven years old when they moved into the hotel. "My mother was a very aggressive businesswoman," said Genevieve. "She came from Italy and was orphaned by the time she was twelve years old. Lee Norato's father died in Italy packing bombs away after World War One, and they never found his body." Lee's mother remarried, came to America, and died two years later in childbirth. Lee and her brother and sisters found themselves alone with a stepfather they hardly knew—and who tried to molest Lee. After a custody battle with their stepfather, Lee's mother's relatives took Lee and her siblings into their home in South Philadelphia. Lee eventually met Arthur, who lived across the street. He was the son of a musician from Providence, Rhode Island, who played in the Philadelphia Orchestra.

"One year, around 1940, my mother got this idea that she wanted to get a place for the summer, and when she told my father, he thought she meant just for their family. And she said, 'No, no, I want to rent a building to rent rooms to people.'"

Arthur worked for the Philadelphia Laundry Company, and he had a delivery route in Atlantic City, so one day, Lee met him at the Venice Hotel on Florida Avenue to talk to the owner. The owner sent them to another hotel down the street, where Lee dickered the guy down from $1,000 to $500 in rent for the season. They made a lot of money that summer, so the next year, they bought a small hotel on Missouri Avenue, which they operated for a few years. When they sold it, they rented another property—the Beachwood Hotel on Florida Avenue— where they stayed put for ten years.

"My mother wanted to buy a place again," said Genevieve. "She met a woman named Sadie Roberto in a card game. My mother was a serious cardplayer. She played like a man. Never played with Skinny, though, because women weren't allowed to play in those games. But Sadie was a loan shark. Tiny woman who drove a great big Cadillac, and she was a friend of Skinny's. Sadie used to say that Skinny was the only person who ever paid her back. So Sadie took my mother over to meet Skinny one day, and Skinny took my mother to meet Irving Nathanson, who owned the Penn Plaza. It was supposedly a 'house of ill repute,' but my parents didn't know that. The first summer, men and women would come in very late just for the night, and she caught on and said, 'No way.' By the next summer, she had turned the Penn Plaza into a nice family business."

The Noratos lived in a four-bedroom house behind the hotel, but they spent a lot of time on the Penn Plaza's front porch, where all the regulars and people from the neighborhood sat outside and talked— including Rita, who always stayed in room 44. The Penn Plaza was a fairly plain, three-story brick building with fifty-five rooms, some of them with kitchens. The style of the building was typical of Atlantic City; post–World War I summer rooming houses went up all over the resort in the twenties. Today, there are hundreds of them left in terrible shape, begging for renovation and a new life. In the late 1950s, the Penn Plaza's front porch had white railings and rocking chairs and flower boxes.

"The 500 Club was the main draw on the block," said Genevieve. "Skinny would send a lot of the entertainers over to stay with us. Of course, the big stars, like Sinatra, stayed at the Claridge. But part of the whole thing for our customers at the Penn Plaza was that they always wanted to know who was at the club the week they were staying, and they would just sit and watch all the people come and go from the club. It was like our own private show every night, just sitting on the porch."

"Especially when Sinatra was in town," said Anita. "People would hang from the billboards, stand on rooftops—anywhere to get a glimpse of Sinatra coming. During the time that he was in town, Skinny would put up a big sign that said, 'He's Here!' It was like something you'd see in the movies. The street would be packed with hundreds of people waiting for Sinatra to pull up."

Genevieve spent a lot of time in and around the club during the day because she and Paulajane were inseparable. "I remember one time," she said, "we passed the office and the door was open, and I looked in and Robert Wagner and Natalie Wood were making a phone call at Skinny's desk. God, they were beautiful." She paused for a second. "You know . . . to tell you the truth, I used to get more excited seeing Skinny than seeing Sinatra. They were both walking side by side one night, going through the kitchen and into the club, and, oh, I was so gaga over Skinny. He was *so* cool and so handsome and tall and beautifully dressed. He was a magical person. Like a Hollywood star, he just had an indescribable magnetic aura around him." She looked over at her mother, who was playing with her teaspoon, oblivious. "It was a different time," she said wistfully. And then she looked at me. "And it will never happen again."

Chapter Eight

If that July night in 1946—when Dean and Jerry first performed together on the stage of the 500 Club—was indeed the moment that changed Skinny's station in life and made people forget who he once was (a pimp with a prison record) and allowed them to see him for what he might become (a great man), his downfall began when Frank Sinatra asked him in 1960 to manage the Cal-Neva Lodge, an out-of-the-way casino-hotel perched at the northern end of Lake Tahoe. Or perhaps it began a year earlier, when Joseph P. Kennedy, the patriarch of the future political dynasty, asked Skinny to help his son John F. Kennedy get elected president of the United States.

As the fifties gave way to the sixties, Atlantic City was in free fall. This, of course, had a lot to do with why Skinny said yes to both Sinatra and Kennedy. The 500 Club was still packing them in every summer night and had managed to maintain its exalted place in the East Coast nightclub world—partly because Frank, out of gratitude to Skinny's kindness and loyalty over the years, turned up faithfully every summer to play his week-long, three-shows-a-night gigs. But Skinny could see that Atlantic City was going under, and he began to think beyond Absecon Island for the first time in his life. In fact, in the early 1960s, Skinny's and Frank's lives became more entangled than ever—and not just through the world of nightclubs, show business, and gambling, but also in the much more treacherous world of politics.

The early moments of John F. Kennedy's campaign in 1959, the days of the West Virginia primary and the Democratic convention in Los Angeles in 1960, and the years of leadership ending with Kennedy's assassination in November 1963 were without question a very strange period in American politics. It has been hashed over in book after book from every conceivable angle, but the whole surreal and sordid convergence of Hollywood starlets, the Mafia, politics, prostitutes, the FBI, and the Rat Pack can all be traced back to the fascination that Frank Sinatra—an oversexed entertainer with a taste for politics and ties to the Mob—had for JFK—an oversexed politician with a taste for show-biz and a father with ties to the Mob.

The seed of Sinatra's relationship to the Kennedys was planted in the spring of 1944, when Frank, then under contract to MGM, met a twenty-one-year-old actor named Peter Lawford at a party for Henry Ford II that was hosted by MGM chief Louis B. Mayer at his home in Los Angeles. By this point, Frank was having real success in Hollywood, while Lawford was just getting started.

Even though Lawford and Sinatra were eight years apart in age, they had enough in common—deeply insecure only children raised by domineering, somewhat loony mothers—that they became something like drinking buddies. They had also both dated Lana Turner. But in 1953, not long after Frank and Ava's tortured marriage finally came to an end, Lawford made the fatal mistake of being seen by a gossip columnist having a drink with Ava. When Frank found out, he threatened Peter with his life and then didn't speak to him until . . . he married a Kennedy.

Frank's liberal political leanings were passed on to him by his mother, Dolly, who, as a Democratic committee woman in Hoboken, was often called upon by the Irish politicians to help get out the Italian vote. Frank would later tell his own children that he was carrying placards for candidates before he could read their names. As early as 1945, Frank began speaking out against racial injustice. That same year, he made a ten-minute short film, *The House I Live In*, about religious and racial tolerance. In it, Frank gives a lecture to a bunch of street toughs: "Look, fellas, religion makes no difference except to a Nazi or somebody as stupid. My dad came from Italy, but I'm an American. Should I hate your father 'cause he came from Ireland or France or Russia?

Wouldn't that make me a first-class fathead?" The film received a great deal of critical praise and was given a special Academy Award in 1946.

In 1952, Frank stepped directly into the political fray and campaigned for Adlai Stevenson in his first effort to become the Democratic presidential nominee. Four years later, he sang the national anthem at the opening ceremonies of the Democratic National Convention in Chicago, which eventually led to the nomination of Stevenson. Oddly enough, it was JFK and Estes Kefauver who locked horns in a battle to become Stevenson's vice presidential running mate at the convention. Kefauver won, but Sinatra was impressed by what he saw during those days in Chicago—that the Kennedys had money, style, star quality, connections, and a well-oiled political machine—and he vowed to get behind them during their next fight.

Lawford, who never really had a great career as an actor, became famous as an eligible bachelor and dependable party guest by turning up at nearly every event in Hollywood throughout the late 1940s and early 1950s. He dated several famously beautiful women but seemed more interested in having fun and lying on the beach than taking his life, relationships, or career very seriously. In 1954, nine months after his father died at the age of eighty-seven, Lawford, still deeply shaken by the loss, married Patricia Kennedy, Joseph's sixth child. Pat Kennedy was no beauty—that famous Kennedy lantern jaw has always looked horsey on the ladies—and Lawford hardly seemed worthy. Thus, there was a tremendous amount of suspicion about Lawford's motives. Their relationship, in fact, appeared to the people around them more like that of siblings than husband and wife. (Lawford was hounded by rumors of homosexuality for most of his premarried life.)

In 1958, Sinatra attended a party at Gary Cooper's house, and—lo and behold!—there were Peter and Pat Lawford. Sinatra hadn't spoken to his old friend in five years, but that night they reconnected—just in time for Frank to worm his way into the Kennedy fold. Within a few months, Frank and Peter were buddies again; when Pat gave birth to a daughter in November, she named her Victoria Frances—the middle name in Frank's honor. Peter and Frank also became partners in a Beverly Hills restaurant, Puccini, which would later become infamous as, among other things, the place where Judith Campbell—the mistress to

JFK, Giancana, and Sinatra—was introduced into this creepy three-way that launched her into history.

(For the record, Skinny really liked Judith Campbell. For one, they both got sucked into the same mess by the same guy—Frank. Indeed, the moment that Judith was first introduced by Frank to Sam Giancana at the Fontainebleau, Skinny was standing right beside them. Also, Skinny thought of Judith as "one of the guys," which, in his world, was the highest compliment a woman could be paid.)

Not long after Sinatra and Lawford had become pals again, Lawford introduced him to the Kennedys and the Kennedys to the Rat Pack. On the eve of JFK's presidency, the Lawfords had settled with their three children into a huge mansion in Santa Monica that had originally been built for Louis B. Mayer. The Lawfords were both big drinkers, and it was at this house that a lot of parties took place and where JFK allegedly slept with Marilyn Monroe for the first time. When Jack Kennedy came to the West Coast, he often stayed with the Lawfords and partied with Frank and his pals. But Jack also spent weekends at Sinatra's Palm Springs home, most famously in November 1959, after which Frank mounted a plaque on the wall that read, "John F. Kennedy slept here." And he also participated in some of Frank's debauched hotel parties both before and after he became president. Tina Sinatra told the writer Seymour Hersh in 1997 that her father was attracted to Kennedy's "lifestyle. And his power. I know they had a lot of fun together. Their small circle of friends would come together to have a good time. . . . I was never, ever there. This was not a weekend you brought kids into." But, she added, Frank "was a happy bachelor-type guy. He was single. Jack Kennedy wasn't."

Jeanne Martin, Dean Martin's former wife, once told the writer Anthony Summers, "I saw Peter [Lawford] in the role of pimp for Jack Kennedy. It was a nasty business—they were just too gleeful about it, not discreet at all. . . . It was like high school time, very sophomoric. The things that went on in that beach house were just mind-boggling." Peter Lawford later admitted as much: "I was Frank's pimp, and Frank was Jack's. It sounds terrible now, but then it was really a lot of fun." When asked about the friendship between the senator and the singer,

Lawford said: "Let's just say that the Kennedys are interested in the lively arts, and that Sinatra is the liveliest art of all."

But John Fitzgerald Kennedy was born into money and privilege, so it was Joe Kennedy with whom Sinatra actually connected. This was probably partly to do with the fact that they were both self-made men. But they were also both intimately acquainted with the same bunch of unsavory underworld characters. Lawford recalled that in the summer of 1959, Sinatra and Lawford flew to Palm Beach to visit with Joseph Kennedy, who had said he wanted their assistance with Jack's presidential campaign. "Joe Kennedy ran the campaign from an outdoor enclosure next to the swimming pool," Lawford later recalled. "He called it 'the bullpen.' There was no roof on the structure. Inside were a telephone and a deck chair. Joe spent his mornings on the telephone barking orders at frightened minions and employees. What seemed off about the arrangement was that he made the calls in the nude, which was the reason for the enclosure." At first, Sinatra's role in the campaign was more like court jester: he rerecorded the song "High Hopes" with new lyrics so that it might become the Kennedy campaign theme song, and he was called upon to lend a certain Hollywood sheen to the whole enterprise—a practice that has become commonplace now but was fairly new at the time.

Old man Kennedy eventually summoned Frank and asked him to go to Sam Giancana and ask explicitly for his help in getting his son elected. "What I understood," Tina Sinatra told Hersh in 1997, "was that a meeting was called late in '59 at Hyannis Port. Dad was more than willing to go. He hadn't been to the house before. Over lunch, Joe said, 'I think that you can help me in [West Virginia and Illinois] with our friends. You understand, Frank, I can't go. They're my friends, too, but I can't approach them. But you can.' I know that it gave my dad pause. But it still wasn't anything he felt he shouldn't do. So off to Sam Giancana he went."

How Skinny got involved in all of this remains something of a mystery, but it seems likely that a combination of requests from Frank Sinatra and Joe Kennedy persuaded him to work on behalf of JFK. The first time it was reported that Skinny played a role in the Kennedy campaign was in 1986, in Ovid Demaris's book *The Boardwalk Jungle*. "During the 1960 presidential campaign," he wrote, "Giancana sent Skinny D'Amato to West Virginia to get votes for Jack Kennedy. He was to use his influence with the sheriffs who controlled the political machine of the state. Most of them had been customers at the 500 Club, and according to Skinny, love him like a brother. Whether he helped turn the tide for Kennedy in that crucial primary state is not as important as the fact that Giancana sent him there on Kennedy's behalf."

That same year, Kitty Kelley repeated Demaris's claims in her notorious unauthorized Sinatra bio, *His Way*, but she advanced the story ever so slightly by reporting that these gambling sheriffs of West Virginia "owed Skinny money" and "were more than happy to do him a favor that was rewarded with a cash supply of more than fifty thousand dollars." Then, in 1992, Dan Fleming, a political scientist who lives in Virginia, published *Kennedy vs. Humphrey, West Virginia, 1960*, an exhaustive, dry-as-dust autopsy of the West Virginia primary (which, by the way, has come to be seen in retrospect as the most significant state primary in American political history, largely because it finally broke the back of the stubborn, unwritten rule that a Catholic could never be president). As Theodore H. White wrote in his 1978 book, *In Search of History*, Kennedy "unlatched the door, and through the door marched not only Catholics, but blacks, and Jews, and ethnics, women, youth, academics, newspersons and an entirely new breed of young politicians who did not think of themselves as politicians." But more important, perhaps, the West Virginia primary ushered in the modern condition of politics that we now take so for granted, which is to say that television and huge piles of cash are vital—and poisonous—to the process.

The Northern Panhandle of West Virginia—comprising Hancock, Brooke, and Ohio Counties—is basically a suburb of Pittsburgh and in 1960 had a population dominated by Italians and Eastern Europeans, not to mention the strongest concentration of Catholics in the state. The Panhandle was also a place where, at that time, the rackets thrived through a combination of the Pittsburgh Mafia and the Wheeling crime boss, William Lias, who operated the Wheeling Downs racetrack and the numbers games and slot machines. In other words, this one small part of West Virginia was Skinny D'Amato country.

The section in Fleming's book that concerns Skinny sets out to disprove that the Mafia played a significant role in Kennedy's victory in the state. The problem with his thesis, however, is that it assumes that Skinny was actually *in* the Mafia. What makes more sense is that Skinny was acting on behalf of Frank Sinatra, a man for whom he would take a bullet. Fleming writes that he interviewed several of D'Amato's friends in Atlantic City and that none of them "could envision Skinny as any kind of a real deal maker in West Virginia. All the friends of Skinny described him as a person who cared little about his own financial gain and could not see him as a person of political intrigue. . . . No details could be unearthed about where Skinny D'Amato went in West Virginia and whom he saw there. The entire account lacks credibility as a major factor in deciding the primary."

Skinny's neighbor, Joe Del Raso, said that "it's common knowledge that Skinny was always very active in state politics. The problem with Skinny was he knew how to put it all together, but he never followed through. The devil's in the details. He had pretty good sway over the Italian American voters in New Jersey, which still, to this day, has the largest concentration of Italians in the United States." Skinny told Del Raso that Joe Kennedy called him directly to ask for his help in the primary. It was well known that Joe Kennedy had contacts of every sort in New York, New Jersey, and Pennsylvania, and Skinny knew the political leaders of New Jersey through his nightclub. One of them, Angelo Malandra, was in fact a very close friend—so close that Skinny had named his son after him (and not, as many mistakenly believe, after Angelo Bruno). Malandra had been a criminal defense lawyer, the Democratic chairman of Camden County, and, before he died in 1973, a judge on Camden's juvenile and domestic relations court. Malandra had also been a friend of Robert Kennedy's and organized a party and rally in Camden attended by JFK in the fall of 1960. In fact, there is a photograph of Skinny and Malandra with the future president at that rally. Malandra is standing off to the side. Skinny is whispering in JFK's ear.

The last reporter to try to get to the bottom of Skinny D'Amato's role in the West Virginia primary was Seymour Hersh in his 1997 book, *The Dark Side of Camelot*. Skinny agreed to Joe Kennedy's request, wrote Hersh, "with one demand: if Jack Kennedy was successful in gaining the White House, he would reverse a 1956 federal deportation order for Joey Adonis, the New Jersey gang leader. With Joe Kennedy's promise, D'Amato raised $50,000 . . . from assorted gangsters." Hersh goes on to say that Skinny had been quoted telling a business associate that the money was used not for bribes, but to buy office furniture needed by local pols in West Virginia. After Kennedy's victory, Skinny said that he tried to hold Joe to his promise but was told that, though it was okay with Jack, the president, Bobby, the new attorney general, was having none of it. "Skinny's big mouth got him in trouble," wrote Hersh. "Soon after taking office, Bobby Kennedy was informed by the FBI that D'Amato had been overheard on a wiretap bragging about his role in moving cash from Las Vegas to help Jack Kennedy win the election. A few months later, D'Amato suddenly found himself facing federal indictment on income tax charges stemming from his failure to file a corporate tax return for his nightclub."

When Frank Sinatra's lawyer, Mickey Rudin, found out about the indictment, he called Stephen Smith, Jack Kennedy's brother-in-law and the campaign's finance director, and asked to meet him for a drink at the University Club in New York.

"What can I do for you?" said Smith.

"I'm unhappy about Skinny being indicted on bullshit charges," said Rudin. "It's unfair. No taxes were paid because there was no profit. This is a political act."

"Well, you don't understand politics," said Smith, and that was the end of their meeting.

Skinny—like Sinatra and Giancana—had gotten himself mixed up with people who did not play by the same Italian American rules of the brotherhood. The Kennedys were not men of their word; they used Sinatra and his Mob friends, pure and simple, and when political expediency dictated something other than loyalty, they turned on them.

How the modest, unpretentious Cal-Neva Lodge—which was originally built in 1926 as a private, log cabin getaway for the friends of a wealthy San Francisco businessman—came to be the locus of so much celebrity drama, political intrigue, and nefarious underworld activity defies explanation. But one thing is clear: Nearly everyone who ever had a stake in it lived to regret it, including Skinny.

The Cal-Neva is famously situated on the border between California and Nevada (hence the hyphenate), with six acres of property on one side and eight on the other. In the early 1960s, the resort consisted of eleven cabins—or chalets, as they were called—and fifty-five rooms. The main building actually straddles the states' border, and there is a white line painted on the floor, bisecting the cavernous Indian Room as well as the kidney-shaped swimming pool out back. In the 1920s, one reporter wrote that card tables were actually pushed back and forth across the state line "depending on which state's police showed up to bust the place." One of Cathy D'Amato's most enduring childhood memories of the three summers she spent at the resort in the early 1960s is that she never tired of announcing to her sister, Paulajane, "I'm going to Nevada!" and then swimming to the other side of the pool. The gimmick did serve a purpose beyond allowing tourists to stand in both states at once. Casino activity could take place only on the Nevada side, so the resort—not unlike Atlantic City—had, literally, a split personality.

The Cal-Neva sits high up on a bluff on the north shore of Lake Tahoe in a town known as Crystal Bay, which, unlike the much more accessible and now overdeveloped south shore, can be reached only by one long, winding, narrow, curvaceous mountain road. This is, perhaps, the main reason that celebrities and the Mob took a shine to the Cal-Neva: both could achieve a measure of privacy unattainable at other, similar resorts.

The Cal-Neva Lodge had passed through many owners before Frank Sinatra and his friends took possession of it in 1960. Two years after it was built, local political boss Norman Blitz bought the property. Blitz, a real estate mogul who eventually became known as the "Duke of Nevada" because of his vast wealth and land holdings, as well as his proximity to powerful people, married Esther Auchincloss Nash in 1930. Nash was the aunt of Joe Kennedy's future daughter-in-law,

Jacqueline Bouvier. Blitz sold the Cal-Neva that year to Jim McKay and the fight promoter Bill Graham, both of whom were convicted in 1934 of mail fraud in a horse race swindle and sent to prison for nine years. Graham supposedly used the Cal-Neva to exchange marked or "hot" cash for famous bank robbers like "Baby Face" Nelson and "Pretty Boy" Floyd, who hid out at the lodge.

On May 17, 1937, the Cal-Neva burned to the ground. Blitz hired five hundred men to work around the clock to rebuild it in thirty-one days. Sanford "Sandy" Adler, the next owner, built the Indian Room, and the Cal-Neva gained its reputation as a place where you could see first-class entertainment in rustic surroundings. A modern hotel tower was added in the 1970s, but the rest of the buildings on the property remain almost exactly as they were built after the fire. There's a large A-framed lobby and a massive stone fireplace in the Indian Room that incorporates a huge granite boulder the room was built around. Behind the main building, overlooking the lake, are cabins and chalets, some freestanding, others in a long, motel-like strip. There is also the famous circular bar with a stained-glass dome above made from hundreds of pieces of beautifully colored Austrian crystal. Today, you can sit at the circle bar and drink for free for hours while playing video poker to your heart's content, though the whole place has a dusty, run-down penny arcade aspect.

For nearly a decade through the forties and fifties, Bugsy Siegel's San Francisco partner, Elmer M. "Bones" Remer, was at the helm. Remer, who was the only person from Lake Tahoe questioned in the Kefauver hearings, ran into serious tax problems, and in 1955, a group of partners led by a man named Bert "Wingy" Grober took control of the property. Grober, a native of Newark, New Jersey, owned two successful restaurants—Wingy's Inn in Philadelphia, through which he got to know Skinny, and the Park Avenue Steak House in Miami Beach. His supplier for liquor and steaks in Miami was none other than Joe Kennedy. In fact, a man named Charlie Block, who worked for Joe in Florida, was Wingy's partner in the Park Avenue Steak House. Wingy, like Skinny, was a serious gambler who was well connected to the Mob—especially Meyer Lansky.

When exactly the Kennedys started hanging out at Cal-Neva is unclear. Some say that it was a favorite haunt of Joe Kennedy's since

Prohibition; he came just after it opened and stayed for longer and longer stretches, turning it into a kind of western HQ for his political and business wheeling and dealing, as well as a hideaway for his affairs, including one with Gloria Swanson. Kennedy's Tahoe circle also included Bing Crosby, yeast heir Max Fleischmann, and broker Dean Witter. Others have claimed that Joe actually owned the joint for a time and that Wingy was his front man. But what is clear is that during Wingy's five-year tenure as owner—up to and including the period of JFK's presidential campaign—the Kennedys spent a lot of time on the north shore.

The Cal-Neva had always been a difficult business proposition. Like Atlantic City, Lake Tahoe thrived during Prohibition, hung in through World War II, but began to fall off in the 1950s when Las Vegas exploded. Also like Atlantic City, Lake Tahoe has a short season. The Sierra Nevadas get a huge amount of snow in the winter, making the resort town nearly inaccessible until after the thaw. But even during the summer months it can get very cold at night.

It has been reported in a few books that a New York–based federal Prohibition agent named Byron Rix reported to the FBI that a secret meeting took place at Cal-Neva in 1960. Rix, who was acquainted with the Kennedys and worked in the gambling business in Las Vegas, had been told by several people about the meeting. The FBI shared Rix's story with the attorney general, Bobby Kennedy, in a memo in 1962, noting that "this memorandum is marked 'Personal' for the Attorney General and copies are not being sent to any lower echelon officials in the Department in view of Rix's remarks concerning the Attorney General's father. . . .

"Before the last presidential election," the report went on, "Joseph P. Kennedy (the father of President John F. Kennedy) had been visited by many gangsters with gambling interests and a deal was made which resulted in Peter Lawford, Frank Sinatra, Dean Martin and others obtaining a lucrative gambling establishment, the Cal-Neva Hotel, at Lake Tahoe. These gangsters reportedly met with Joseph Kennedy at the Cal-Neva, where Kennedy was staying at the time."

Like so many others before him, Wingy Grober could not make a go of it, and in the summer of 1960, a deal was apparently brokered through Joe Kennedy in which Grober would sell the Cal-Neva for a mere $250,000. One account has it that Frank was to get 25 percent; Frank's right-hand man and business partner, Hank Sanicola, 16; Skinny D'Amato, 13; and Dean Martin, 3. On September 20, 1960, Sinatra received his license from the Nevada Gaming Control Board, and the Rat Pack now had their own clubhouse.

Skinny was ostensibly brought in to run the gambling end of the operation, much as he had in his early days at the 500, when Phil Barr still owned the joint. But because of his great instincts with entertainment, he had a hand in that as well. "I worked for Skinny at the Cal-Neva Lodge," said Sonny King, the man who introduced Martin and Lewis. "It was the start of a new kind of policy in nightclubs and gambling. The nightclub featured all the top stars like Lena Horne and Peggy Lee and Frank and Dean and Sammy. Naturally Frank was his partner in the nightclub. One of the performers, like Frank or Dean or Jimmy Durante, would deal the cards in the casino, at the blackjack table. And that would bring hordes of people around the table, because no one ever lost. Dean was a professional dealer in his youth in Ohio, and if you had a seventeen and he had nineteen in the hole, naturally, you'd lose, but he wouldn't. He would turn over his card and say, 'I have a nineteen. What do you have?' Of course, you would hit. If you got a six and you had a twenty-three, it was over. But Dean would say, 'That's twenty-one, because I can't add,' and he'd pay you. He'd do it two or three times and then make room for somebody else. It made people stay in the casino. Today, there's nothing that would make you stay unless you were an addict."

Ray Langford, the daytime bell captain at Cal-Neva during the Frank-Skinny era, said, "Skinny was the right hand of God. When Skinny walked in, everyone stood at attention. It might as well have been Frank in his shoes, you know? Because he was the one who watched the casino, and you had to respect him. But he was a casual person. He was a very nice man, best dresser I've ever seen. He was just a cool guy, and he knew what he was doing. Just from talking to people who came to Cal-Neva from Atlantic City—car dealers, restaurant and liquor store owners—I know he had the keys to that city."

According to Jimmy Mancini, the nighttime bell captain, "Skinny didn't seem to be working for anybody. He was just there to watch. He definitely had an interest, because he would ask that main question: 'How's the action?' That was always the first thing he said to me when I brought coffee down to his cabin. He drank coffee all night long and never slept, and he was really concerned about the take at the casino."

It seems fitting that Skinny's Cal-Neva Lodge business card reads, simply, "Paul (Skinny) D'Amato." He did not have an official title, which was probably intentional. He was there because Frank Sinatra trusted him, and everyone who worked there understood that. But the powers-that-be in Nevada did not. The first page of Skinny's FBI file is a memo from J. Edgar Hoover's office in Washington, D.C., to a field office in Newark, New Jersey. It is dated February 14, 1961, and firmly suggests that an investigation be conducted "to determine if D'Amato's activities justify considering him a top hoodlum." Just as Skinny's role in the West Virginia primary had come to light, Skinny began to make noises in Nevada about getting a gambling license so that he could become a part owner of the Cal-Neva. It would appear that these two things collided to make his life very complicated.

Less than six weeks later, the Newark office filed a ten-page report on Skinny with Hoover's office in Washington. The agents quickly found out—by interviewing Skinny directly—that he described himself as being "from the wrong side of the tracks" but that he now "considers himself to be one of the wealthiest men in Atlantic City who is frequently mentioned in connection with charities and social events . . . and is by reputation a heavy contributor to various charities." They learned that he had recently purchased a home "with seven bathrooms" at 12 So. Suffolk Avenue for $25,000 and "after some extensive renovating" planned to move in soon. The report noted an *Atlantic City Press* story on the fact that Skinny and Bettyjane recently celebrated their tenth wedding anniversary "to the strains of soft violins and to the congratulations of several hundred guests . . . at a lavish buffet dance at the 500 Club." Those guests included Joe DiMaggio, Mr. and Mrs. Milton Berle, Mr. and Mrs. Toots Shor, and Mrs. Jack E. Leonard.

They included in their report information gathered from another investigation that took place in 1952, in which Skinny told an agent that the Mob (the names were blacked out) "never financed or 'payrolled' the 500 Club casino or craps tables" and that he was "100% owner" of the club. "Since 1946," read the report, "when various investigations and probes were instituted in Atlantic City, D'Amato has not been able to operate his casino with any regularity, and only on rare occasions, such as holidays or special conventions, has he had permission to operate his gambling room and then only for very short intervals. He admitted an arrest for booking horses." Skinny also told the agents that "there are three girls . . . that hang out in the 500 Club. He suspects they are Lesbians or prostitutes. He has ordered that if they leave the club with a date, they are not to be allowed back in the club that night."

Eventually, Skinny's FBI file gets around to reporting that in 1959 he was "offered the opportunity to invest in the Hotel Havana-Riviera casino through a booking agent in New York City. He visited Havana in December 1958, and declined the offer to invest. He also advised that Lou Chester, a Toronto stock-broker and president of the General Development Company, is the owner of the building wherein L'Aiglon Restaurant, Miami Beach, Florida, is located. Chester also owns the Copa City, allegedly the largest nightclub in Miami Beach, and had recently offered the L'Aiglon and Copa City to D'Amato to manage." Skinny turned the offer down. Paulajane remembers that her parents went house hunting in Miami when she was a little girl but that "the deal must have fallen through" because they suddenly stopped. Clearly, Skinny was looking for other opportunities even before the Cal-Neva.

This same report noted that Dorothy Kilgallen, "the Voice of Broadway," wrote in her syndicated column of April 28, 1962, that "Broadway hears that the latest combine to put in a bid for the Copacabana consists of a famous sporting figure, Skinny D'Amato, and a crooner." Then, on May 8, the *Philadelphia News* reported that Kilgallen's recent gossip "that Frank Sinatra, Skinny D'Amato, and friends are dickering for the Copacabana is a little stale. The deal has been hanging fire for three or four years, but every time a definite proposal was made the Copa ownership cooled and jacked up the price. The Sinatra syndicate just borrowed $1,200,000 for their Cal-Neva Lodge operation on Lake Tahoe, which makes the New York bid even more unlikely."

Then, a month later, on June 4, Kilgallen wrote, "The widely publicized sale of Skinny D'Amato's 500 Club in Atlantic City was quietly cancelled a couple of days ago. Skinny still plans to spend a lot of time in Lake Tahoe but he will hold onto his controlling interest in the 500—the goose that lays those golden eggs. The inside story is interesting." The FBI was clearly titillated by this reference to the "inside story" and filed a lengthy report, all of which has been redacted from Skinny's file.

It is unclear exactly what went down, but that summer, Skinny sold a stake in the 500 Club to Herbie Freedman, an Atlantic City native and liquor distributor who took over day-to-day management of the club. At this point, it seems, Skinny had every intention of pulling up stakes altogether and getting out of Atlantic City. Partnering with Freedman—and leaving the 500 Club's business unattended—would turn out to be a huge mistake that he lived to regret.

The agents dutifully reported Skinny's comings and goings from Atlantic City as he traveled to Tahoe and Vegas. "He stated that he is presently attempting to sell the 500 Club as it is too big of a job for him to handle," while he is also "employed as the Director of Publicity and Co-Host at the Cal-Neva Lodge, which is owned by Frank Sinatra. He stated that he likes to work for Sinatra, who is a fabulous guy, and who had wanted D'Amato to move to Los Angeles, California, where he could be in close touch with Sinatra. . . . He stated that at the lodge, Sinatra refers to D'Amato as being his 'Dago Secret Service.'"

On October 26, 1961, an agent in New Jersey filed another report: "D'Amato stated that he has no financial interest in the Cal-Neva Lodge and is not aware of any undisclosed interests at this lodge." Skinny told the agent "his last arrest was about 20 years ago and that he has been clean since that time and, on this basis, is certain the application for a percentage of the Cal-Neva Lodge will be approved. He said that he intends to purchase about 'five or six points' of the Cal-Neva Lodge. . . . He added that he had withdrawn his original application as the gambling interests in Las Vegas felt he would try to then move into Las Vegas and by withdrawing his application, these interests would no longer fear him. He said that had he persisted, these same interests would have seen to it that his application would have been denied."

But there are other documents that tell another story. I unearthed a series of memos and letters that went back and forth between Virgil

Peterson, the operating director of the Chicago Crime Commission, and Charles LaFrance, chief investigator of the Nevada Gaming Control Board. They seem to tell the tale of what really happened to Skinny as he tried to get a license—and how his reputation, deserved or not, had finally come back to haunt him. The first one, written by Peterson, is dated September 7, 1960: "On September 1, 1960, I received a telephone call from Bob Moore, Gaming Control Board, Carson City, Nevada, who was seeking information on singer Frank Sinatra. . . . Moore informs me that Frank Sinatra and a group including Dean Martin, Hank Sanicola . . . and Paul D'Amato . . . have applied for a gambling license. . . . He stated that he understands that in February 1947 Sinatra flew to Havana, Cuba, with gangster Rocco Fischetti and other gangsters, and while there Sinatra met Charles 'Lucky' Luciano. I understood Moore to state that Sinatra admits that his picture was taken with Luciano, but denies that he knew him."

Another memo, sent by Peterson sometime later, included this: "Frank Sinatra is extremely close to Paul D'Amato, who runs the 500 Club in Atlantic City. Sinatra is trying to get a joint in Nevada which he wants to have operated by D'Amato. D'Amato is associated with all the big hoodlums such as Jerry Catena, Longie Zwillman and Willie Moretti in New Jersey. It is stated that Sinatra has been very close to D'Amato for a number of years. The 500 Club in Atlantic City has not been too successful, but D'Amato gets out of the hole each year when Sinatra appears as an entertainer for a couple of weeks gratuitously."

Finally, this from LaFrance: "Thank you for your letter of March 8th. . . . We are expecting Mr. D'Amato more or less momentarily, and the date that you gave, namely June 29th, will probably be the official opening date of the Cal-Neva Lodge. . . . We expect Mr. D'Amato to file an application for a license, as it is known he has retained counsel in this state for that purpose. . . . I think I wrote you some time ago that D'Amato was an applicant at this same casino for the seasonal year 1960. The day before the Board met to consider this application, he withdrew. While I cannot state what action the Board would have taken, it is my belief that he would have been denied had he allowed it to have been processed at that time. If anything should come to your attention indicating hoodlum associates, etc., on the part of D'Amato, I would appreciate hearing from you."

In the summer of 2001, I was in Las Vegas working on a story for a magazine and decided to stop by the University of Nevada, Las Vegas, Libraries. I had heard that the building was a great modernist piece of architecture and that it featured a fantastic special collections room. When I got there the man who ran the place turned out, of all people, to be David Schwartz, the son of Sonny Schwartz, the *Atlantic City Press* columnist who was one of Skinny's closest friends in the last fifteen years of his life. David saved me hours of work by fetching for me the most interesting document in the collection. As part of an oral history project that the library started several years earlier, Edward Olsen, who was the Nevada Gaming Control Board chairman from 1961 to 1966, had submitted to a lengthy interview in the early 1970s.

The section titled "Frank Sinatra and His Friends" was the most pertinent. Olsen begins by explaining that the board's relationship with Frank began in 1960, when he was first approved for a license to operate the Cal-Neva. Sinatra had been approved earlier for an interest in the Sands in Las Vegas, but he never took part in its operation. The Cal-Neva was different. Frank and his partners spent nearly $2 million renovating the place, and the source of that money has been the subject of much speculation over the years, whether it was from the Mob or the Teamsters Union or some other source. Skinny maintained that it was from a bank loan in Nevada. The renovation included the building of the Celebrity Room (a small but acoustically high-tech showroom where Frank and his friends performed) and a helipad on the roof. An I. Magnin clothing shop and a high-end beauty parlor were housed on the premises for the ladies.

"The summer of '61, as I recall, went fairly quietly," said Olsen, "although there were a number of rumors about undesirable people in the . . . north Lake Tahoe area. But it wasn't until the summer of '62 that the operation began to draw more and more attention, not only from the gaming board, but from the Washoe County Sheriff's Office and the FBI and other law enforcement agencies.

"There were a number of peculiar incidents that year . . . one of which involved a man who was killed in an auto accident, and his wife was an employee of the Cal-Neva Lodge. There were a number of circumstances that led to suspicions that . . . it wasn't an accident. . . . Then, later, there was a shooting right at the front steps of the Cal-Neva Lodge. One man shot another, but he then disappeared and wasn't found for . . . about a week. He was located in the Carson Tahoe Hospital. He was severely battered and bruised . . . and explained to the hospital employees that he fell from a horse. I later talked to the physician who treated him, and [he] commented wryly that it must have been an awfully high horse. . . . Then there were also federal investigations that year into the transport of women by airplane from the San Francisco area to engage in prostitution at the Cal-Neva Lodge. And apparently the operation was conducted quite openly from the main registration desk.

"But it wasn't until . . . the spring of '63 [that] we did sit down with Sinatra's attorney, a very charming gentleman by the name of Mickey Rudin. . . . And we outlined to him . . . a variety of incidents that had come to our attention the year before and suggested that perhaps some of these could be corrected by a little more careful selection of personnel up there, to which Rudin agreed. And we also had a discussion at that time of Frank's reported associations . . . with . . . Sam Giancana. Mr. Rudin . . . carried the gist of our discussion to Mr. Sinatra, and Mr. Sinatra had agreed that more care would be taken in the selection of his executive officers and that certainly Mr. Giancana had never been around the Cal-Neva.

"That year, they did go out and hire . . . an experienced hotel man, for the first time, to ostensibly be in charge. But as it subsequently developed, he didn't really have the authority usually associated with the hotel manager, and the real individual in charge was one Paul 'Skinny' D'Amato. Skinny was a character with whom we'd had previous association. He was forever making quiet overtures indicating he would like to get a gambling license and be approved for an ownership interest in Cal-Neva. He never, as I recall, openly applied. By the same token, his overtures were pretty much discouraged because he had a more questionable nightclub operation in Atlantic City and was the subject of considerable investigation by both the Internal Revenue Service and the FBI. But Skinny did show up for the third year, 1963, as what Sinatra subsequently described as his personal representative."

From Skinny's FBI file, April 24, 1962: "He stated that his application before the Nevada Gaming Board will be granted, as he has many character witnesses who will testify on his behalf. He said that because of his acquaintance with people who are alleged to be in the rackets, his character has been ruined. He stated that he cannot deny that he knows many of these persons, most of them who have become known to him through his contacts with them at the 500 Club. He stated he cannot now tell them to go away. . . . He is obligated to be friendly with them, as they are patrons and spend money at the club. This association has tarnished his character, and it is because of this that he is having trouble in obtaining a license from the Nevada Gaming Control Board. D'Amato added that he has not been arrested since 1941, has led a clean life, and has not been involved in anything since that time. He said all of this will be brought to the attention of the board, and he is confident his application for a license will be granted."

But the 1962 season at Cal-Neva did not go well. In fact, that summer and fall the whole fantasy of the Rat Pack mixing it up with the president and the Mob and having a little clubhouse in the Sierra Nevadas began to fall apart. The real trouble surfaced in February 1962, when Robert Kennedy's initial investigation into organized crime came to a head and a report was compiled by the Justice Department: "Sinatra has had a long and wide association with hoodlums and racketeers which seems to be continuing. The nature of Sinatra's work may, on occasion, bring him into contact with underworld figures, but this cannot account for his friendship and/or financial involvement with people such as Joe and Rocco Fischetti, cousins of Al Capone; Paul Emilio D'Amato, John Formosa, and Sam Giancana, all of whom are on our list of racketeers."

Around the same time that this report was filed, the FBI discovered that the president of the United States was carrying on an affair with Judith Campbell, a woman who had been, for all intents and purposes, Sam Giancana's girlfriend, not to mention one of Sinatra's occasional lovers. On March 22, J. Edgar Hoover had a private lunch with JFK, but what was said at that meeting will forever remain a mystery. One can only imagine that Hoover must have confronted his ostensible boss with the fact that nearly everyone in his secret parallel life was under constant surveillance. It was also around this time that Robert Kennedy impressed upon his brother the need to disassociate himself from Frank Sinatra and to stop seeing Judith Campbell Exner. In January, JFK had announced plans to visit Palm Springs in March, and the entire presidential entourage was to stay at Sinatra's newly built presidential guest wing. Frank, who had already been working with an architect to expand his place, was ecstatic, and he had the entire spread remodeled and redecorated expressly for Kennedy's visit; he even built a helipad. Peter Lawford, always caught between Frank and the Kennedys, was given the unfortunate assignment of having to tell Sinatra that JFK would now be staying at the home of Bing Crosby—a Republican!—and Sinatra, as anyone who watches biography specials on cable TV now knows, flew into a beastly rage.

"I was with Frank at that time," said crooner Sonny King. "He was building that $1.5 million addition. Those guys had an argument with each other because Lawford was the one who had to break the news. Frank was so enraged, he threw Lawford down a flight of stairs."

The Cal-Neva Lodge had been completely overhauled and remodeled in the spring of 1962, all of it overseen by Skinny. In fact, Skinny told an FBI agent that the expansion cost $2.2 million and that it included a new dining room that seated five hundred, new shops, the new showroom that seated seven hundred, and redecorated rooms. Frank and company originally tried to procure a $3 million loan through the Teamsters Union by way of Giancana to pay for the expansion, but Jimmy Hoffa turned them down because of all the heat on the Chicago crime boss, so they wound up borrowing $1.5 million from the Bank of Nevada. The lodge opened that season on June 29 with Frank headlining in the Celebrity Room for a week, for which he flew in dozens of his Hollywood friends. But on the second night of the big opening weekend, Frank got into a fight in the kitchen with a sheriff's deputy recently married to a waitress at the lodge who had previously been involved with Frank. The cop hit Frank so hard that he couldn't perform for a couple of days. Frank had the cop suspended, and then two weeks later the man died in the mysterious car accident near Cal-Neva that Edward Olsen alluded to in his oral history.

Not long after the opening, there were rumors that Giancana had been turning up at the Cal-Neva Lodge to visit his girlfriend, Phyllis McGuire, who with her two sisters was one of the many acts that performed regularly at the Celebrity Room over the three years that Frank owned the resort. Giancana was on the List of Excluded Persons, more popularly known as the Black Book, which was started in Nevada in 1960 and has over the years contained the names of thirty-eight people, most of whom are reputed mobsters. The list is distributed to the owner-managers of all the casinos in Nevada, and it states very clearly that if any of the people on the list show up on their properties, they are to throw them out or risk losing their gaming license. In 1962, there were eleven people on the list. Sam Giancana was number eight.

On a drive from Palm Springs to Las Vegas that summer, Hank Sanicola, Frank's manager and partner in Park Lake Enterprises, a corporation that included a film company as well as Cal-Neva, told Frank that he was worried about Giancana's visits to Cal-Neva to see McGuire, as it would threaten not only their gaming license, but Sanicola's own $300,000 investment in the property. Sanicola was already worried that the expensive renovation and subsequent losses at Cal-Neva were erasing the profits of Park Lake films. The two men had a bitter fight, and there on the spot Frank bought him out of all their partnerships by offering him the rights to five of his music publishing companies. Sanicola ordered the driver to stop the car. He got out and took his suitcases out of the trunk, and off Frank went, leaving his friend and ex-partner standing on the deserted highway. They never spoke to each other again.

(Just as he did when Manny Sacks died, Frank asked Skinny to take his place as trusted sidekick. When Skinny said no he went up another notch in Frank's estimation. "My father wouldn't do it because he didn't want to become a flunky," said Skinny's son, Angelo. "And that is what you become, sooner or later. My father would go to New York and be with Frank and then come back to Atlantic City. The next day, Frank would call and say, 'Come back,' and my father would say, 'Whaddya mean? I just left you!'" In the end, Frank would pay restaurateur Jilly Rizzo to be his constant companion.)

Shortly after the Hank Sanicola fiasco, things got even worse for Sinatra. On June 29, Peter and Pat Lawford brought Marilyn Monroe to the Cal-Neva Lodge when Sinatra was opening the resort for the season—despite the fact that Peter and Frank were not speaking. Apparently, the Lawfords thought it would be good for Monroe's fragile state of mind to get away from Hollywood for a little vacation. Her rejection by the Kennedys had finally pushed her to the edge, and she had been behaving more erratically than usual. Years later, Skinny told writer Anthony Summers, "I knew—*we* knew—about Monroe and the Kennedys, and about Robert especially, but I'm not going to be quoted on it. Imagine it, a friend of Frank Sinatra being quoted as saying what we knew about Marilyn."

Frank and Marilyn had met several years earlier, in 1954, at Romanoff's, a restaurant in Hollywood, just as Marilyn's ten-month marriage to Joe DiMaggio came unraveled. The night before their divorce became final in a Santa Monica courtroom, Joe and Marilyn reportedly holed up in Sinatra's L.A. apartment in some misguided effort to console each other; when the marriage was dissolved, Frank was the one who held Joe's hand, as he was out of his mind from jealousy and heartsickness. Years later, while Marilyn was still married to Arthur Miller, Frank invited her and the cast of *The Misfits* up to the Cal-Neva. "Frank had a party for them," said Langford, the bell captain. "Clark Gable, Marilyn, and a few other actors came up to Cal-Neva, and that's when Sinatra started chasing Marilyn." In fact, it was Skinny D'Amato who admitted to Anthony Summers years later that Frank and Marilyn did indeed carry on an affair behind DiMaggio's back.

In 1962, a reporter asked Sinatra how well he knew Monroe. "Who?" he said, joking. And then: "Miss Monroe reminds me of a saintly young girl I went to high school with, who later became a nun." When Marilyn was told of this exchange, she shot back, "Tell him to look in *Who's Who.*" Frank's affair with Marilyn began in the spring and summer of 1961, just after her divorce from Arthur Miller, which was finalized on January 20, the same day as JFK's inauguration. Frank even bought her a white poodle, which she promptly named "Maf"—short for Mafia. But Marilyn was too big a mess even for Sinatra. Not long after their affair he got engaged to Juliet Prowse, an attachment that lasted only a few months.

DiMaggio never got over Marilyn, and he eventually hired detectives to follow her around. It seems he knew she had been spending time at Cal-Neva and that he suspected she was having an affair with Sinatra. "Skinny loved Joe DiMaggio *and* Frank," said Sonny King, "and he was caught in between them. Those two guys didn't speak to each other. There was an incident that happened in Hollywood. Joe said to Frank, to his face, 'I don't ever want to see or hear from you again.' And they had been the closest buddies. It was all over Marilyn. And Marilyn loved Skinny because he was a pal of Joe DiMaggio's, and everybody knows she loved Joe till the day she died." Harry Hall, a friend of DiMaggio's, told Anthony Summers, "[Joe] was very upset. She went up [to the Cal-Neva]. They gave her pills. They had sex parties, and Joe thought—because at that time he was a friend of Sinatra's—it should never have happened. I don't think Joe ever talked to Frank again. He felt he should have had more respect for Joe. He should've left her alone."

Skinny must have been beside himself. Here he was, caught between the two most celebrated Italian Americans in the country . . . and he had introduced them to each other! And now they were making his life—not to mention their own—exceedingly complicated. Everyone knew that Marilyn was in serious trouble, and Frank wanted to keep an eye on her, so he had her flown in his private jet to the Cal-Neva on July 27, 1962, when Dean Martin was appearing in the Celebrity Showroom. There has been all manner of bizarre, even gruesome, gossip and speculation about what went on in those last days, most of which sounds exaggerated, but a few facts rise up out of the muck.

During the last days of her life—spent in the Cal-Neva snake pit— Marilyn drank and drugged herself into a stupor every night and nearly died right there in Chalet 52, one of a grouping of cabins on the grounds behind the main building that Sinatra reserved for his friends and special guests. More than once, people rushed to her room to revive her from the lethal combination of champagne, vodka, and downers. A kitchen worker named Ted Stephens told Sinatra biographer J. Randy Taraborrelli, "All I know is this: We got a call from Peter Lawford. 'We need coffee in Chalet 52!' he screamed into the phone, then he hung up. He sounded frantic. No less than two minutes passed, and it was Mr. Sinatra on the phone, screaming, 'Where's the goddamn coffee?' I learned later they were in 52, walking Marilyn around, trying to get her to wake up." Mickey Rudin added: "Frank is a very, very compassionate person. He brought Marilyn to Cal-Neva to give her a little fun, a little relief from her problems. If she was upset during that time, well, she could have a crisis over what she was having for lunch. . . ."

On that second visit to Cal-Neva, wrote Nick Tosches, Marilyn "spoke to Skinny D'Amato of things of which, as he told, people ought not to speak. . . . Dean knew what was wrong with [Marilyn], beyond the pills, beyond the booze, beyond the whole endless lost-little-girl thing. She just could not handle the dirty knowledge into which she had wandered, the black forest of Sam Giancana and Johnny Rosselli and her darling scumbag Kennedys, that world that lay past the dreamland she had shared with those who paid to see her. She wanted back into the fairy tale, but there was really no way back." In a way, the same thing could be said for Skinny. Those summers at Cal-Neva must have made him wish he could slip quietly back to being "Mr. Atlantic City."

The strangest part of the 1962 season at Cal-Neva is that Joe DiMaggio turned up that weekend and hovered around the edges of the property—a pathetic ghost of his former self. It is unclear why he came or how he knew Marilyn was there—perhaps she called him—but he checked into the Silver Crest Motel less than a mile down the road in Kings Beach. "He drove up in a car from Harrah's [on the south shore]," said Ray Langford. "He could have had a room there for nothin', but he wanted to be nearby. He didn't want to stay at the Cal-Neva. He said, 'No, I gotta find another place to stay.' He didn't want to be with the guys. Usually, he would stay in the caretaker's cottage with Skinny. I guess somebody must have lied to him or something. So I got him a room where Jimmy Mancini and I lived, at the Silver Crest. I took him fishing with me and everything, but I didn't want to get involved too much."

Sinatra was annoyed when he found out DiMaggio had shown up.

Frank told Joe Langford, Ray's brother, who also worked at Cal-Neva, "If the guy don't want her, why doesn't he leave her the fuck alone? He's just making things worse here." On the morning of July 29, Ray Langford was called down to the group of chalets on the California side. "Marilyn was just sitting there with a kerchief around her head and straw hat and dark glasses. Sinatra ordered martinis, and I think Peter Lawford was there. She looked very sad. It was in the morning, and I guess they may have been up all night. It looked like they were getting ready to leave."

Indeed they were. Sinatra's private jet, *Christina*, named after his youngest child, was a $6 million wood-paneled, wall-to-wall-carpeted flying swinger's pad with a piano bar. His pilot was called to Lake Tahoe on short notice to pick up Monroe, her hairdresser from San Francisco, and Pat and Peter Lawford. Monroe arrived back in Los Angeles after midnight, stupefied and barefoot. A limousine took her home. The next day, on July 30, 1962, she made her final call to Bobby Kennedy. The Justice Department phone log shows that the call lasted eight minutes. Six days later, she was found dead in her bedroom in Brentwood.

On August 5, Ray Langford was at the front desk at the Cal-Neva Lodge when Mickey Rudin was trying to reach Skinny. "The operator called me," said Langford. "It was in the morning, like ten or eleven o'clock. That's when Skinny used to come up out of his cottage at the end of the parking lot to check his mail. The operator said, 'Have you seen Skinny?' I said, 'Not yet.' She said, 'Well, I got an important phone call for him.'"

Bettyjane, Paulajane, and Cathy had traveled to Cal-Neva by train in early July that awful summer to stay with Skinny till the end of the 1962 season. Paulajane was only twelve years old, but her memory of that day is indelible. "I was in my parents' bedroom in our cottage, and my mother was in another room when the call came in," she said. "There wasn't a lot of time to spend with my father, so whenever he was around I would hang out. Like when I heard him get up in the morning and go into the bathroom, I'd run into his bedroom because I knew sooner or later he was going to come out and I'd get to talk to him. I always watched him shave. And he was in the bathroom when this phone call came, and I leaned over and picked up the phone. My parents had this huge bed that I loved to play on. The room was very dark. It had knotty pine paneling. The window shades were pulled, because my father had just gotten up. And this guy said, 'Put your father on the phone.' I handed the phone to my father. I was going, 'What? What?' because he was going, 'Ohhh, God . . . Ohhh, God . . .' He called my mother in, and they asked me to leave. And then I remember coming back in and them telling me what happened. And then he called Joe DiMaggio."

That phone call was the last time they spoke for nearly seventeen years. "DiMaggio had this crazy relationship with Marilyn Monroe," said Joe Del Raso, "and she was a fragile human being to begin with, and he blamed her death on the combination of Sinatra and the Kennedys and viewed Skinny as a conduit between all of them. Joe figured Skinny should have recognized she was in trouble and taken care of her. Nobody could have taken care of her by that point. Was she pushed over the edge by her own demons, or did somebody take care of her because she knew too much about the Kennedys? Who knows? Skinny told us, way back, right after Jack Kennedy died, that her biggest problem was Bobby, it wasn't Jack. It was Bobby who she really fooled around with. Jack, back in those days, had an eye for Angie Dickinson."

Marilyn's biographer, Anthony Summers, was the last person to interview Skinny D'Amato before he died. In his book *Goddess*, he writes: "Paul D'Amato confirmed to me in 1984 that Marilyn had been [at the Cal-Neva] just before she died. Chain-smoking Marlboros, while sitting in his pajamas in what would prove to be his deathbed, D'Amato spoke of the visit and the flight that took Marilyn away for the last time. Then, pursing his thin lips, D'Amato murmured, 'Of course, I didn't say that.' He added, 'There was more to what happened than anyone has told. It would've been the big fall for Bobby Kennedy, wouldn't it?'"

When Sinatra turned up at Marilyn's funeral in Westwood Memorial Park that August, he discovered that DiMaggio had given clear instructions to the guards not to admit him, Skinny, or the Kennedys. DiMaggio blamed them all for Marilyn's death.

✦

On August 17, two weeks after Marilyn died, Dean Martin and Skinny flew together from Los Angeles to Philadelphia and then drove to Atlantic City in preparation for a performance at the 500 Club. From his room at the Claridge, Dean gave an interview to a reporter, who was obviously trying to get Dean to talk about the resort's decline since the last time he had been there five years earlier.

REPORTER: *What brought you back to Atlantic City?*
DEAN: I'm here because Skinny is a friend.
REPORTER: *Have you noticed any changes?*
DEAN: All I've seen are the cops that escort me, and the club. I eat backstage between shows, do another show, and they escort me back here.
REPORTER: *Have you noticed any changes in the 500 Club?*
DEAN: It looks pretty good to me now. Five years ago, it was as big as a pool table.
REPORTER: *Are you and Frank and Sammy part of the Clan?*
DEAN: What about the Clan? There's no clan, just a group of right guys—friends.
REPORTER: *Anything to say about the death of Marilyn Monroe?*
DEAN: No. She was a wonderful girl. This is the longest interview I've had in two years.

A week later, Frank Sinatra joined Dean in Atlantic City for three nights of shows, with Sammy showing up for the last night. Police captain Mario Floriani delivered the singers in his car to the entrance to the club every night, where there were at least one thousand screaming fans waiting outside, bringing traffic to a standstill. Frank, as usual, rented out the entire first floor of the Claridge Hotel while he was in town for that week. His FBI file shows that President Kennedy called Frank, perhaps for the last time, on August 23. That phone call led J. Edgar Hoover to fire off a memo to Robert Kennedy, letting him know that the two men had been in touch again for the first time in several months. Frank, who had been humiliated and betrayed when the Kennedys brushed him off—*after* he helped get JFK elected—now seemed to be saying "fuck you" to everyone by throwing a huge, mobbed-up party at the Claridge. The Newark FBI office reported to Hoover that several known hoodlums were in the Atlantic City area "for two-fold purposes, that is to attend the wedding of Angelo Bruno's daughter on August 26, 1962, and a performance of Frank Sinatra–Dean Martin–Sammy Davis, Jr., at the 500 Club. Frank Sinatra arrived in Atlantic City . . . for the above scheduled appearance with Dean Martin and took over the first sleeping floor of the Claridge Hotel . . . which consists of approximately 40 rooms. Sinatra's representatives allowed no one on the hotel floor, including the hotel management, except by invitation. . . . Sinatra and Martin were appearing at the 500 Club as a personal favor to Paul D'Amato . . . for which they would receive no money but would have all of their expenses taken care of by D'Amato. . . . Sinatra's personal airplane landed at the Atlantic City Airport . . . and he departed from the Airport in an unmarked Atlantic City Police car." The report stated that Giancana was "observed . . . in a private dining room on Sinatra's floor of the Claridge Hotel."

At eight-fifteen A.M., after five shows, Frank and his entourage hit the town with Skinny and Sammy. They stopped at Grace's Little Belmont across the street from Club Harlem on Kentucky Avenue to visit Sammy Davis Jr.'s mother, Baby Sanchez, who was now a barmaid at the famed jazz club, and then on to Timbuktu at Kentucky and Arctic Avenues, Frank handing out folded $100 bills to every bartender, porter, doorman, cook, waitress, and washroom attendant who crossed his path.

✦

By 1963, Robert Kennedy's assault on organized crime had reached a crescendo—with the Senate committees, the Department of Justice, and the IRS all coordinating their efforts. That year, the paid testimony of Mob turncoat Joseph Valachi before the Senate's Permanent Subcommittee on Investigations brought the Italian phrase *La Cosa Nostra* into the vernacular; Valachi ratted on his brethren by identifying the twelve overlords of the dozen or so Mafia families in the major metropolitan centers of the United States as if they were board members of a corporation. Valachi singled out Sam Giancana, whom he had never even met, as the major figure and head of the Chicago underworld.

Giancana was subpoenaed to testify before a grand jury in Chicago, but he declined, pleading the Fifth Amendment. The U.S. Attorney's Office in Chicago took the unusual step of offering Giancana immunity from prosecution, thereby putting him in a situation where he *couldn't* plead the Fifth. Again Giancana declined to testify under those conditions, and the federal government began contempt proceedings against him.

Meanwhile, the FBI had been keeping Giancana under twenty-four-hour surveillance and had given up any pretense of secrecy. They taunted each other openly in public as the FBI followed him literally everywhere he went except into his own home. Then Giancana pulled off a risky legal maneuver: he sued the FBI, hiring famed civil rights attorney George Leighton, who in turn hired a film crew to record the agents' every move as they recorded Giancana's every move. In court, he maintained that the agents harassed his golf game, disturbed his home life, and invaded his privacy—and he won. The federal judge ordered the FBI agents to stay a reasonable distance away—for example, they couldn't play golf in the foursome directly behind him; they had to have at least one other foursome in between. Not surprisingly, the FBI, in protest, withdrew their surveillance and turned the matter over to the Cook County Sheriff's Office in July 1963. Within a matter of hours, the sheriff's office lost track of Giancana and, as one official put it, "he disappeared from the face of the earth."

All of this—the unusual offer of immunity, the suit filed by Giancana—made headlines in newspapers around the country and brought an extraordinary amount of unwanted attention. Giancana hadn't, of course, "disappeared." He had made his way to the Cal-Neva Lodge and was hiding out in Chalet 50 with his girlfriend, Phyllis McGuire, who would soon be appearing on the stage of the Celebrity Room with her sisters during the last week of July. After the opening-night performance, the McGuires, their road manager, Victor LaCroix Collins, and Giancana retired to Chalet 50 for a little private hoo-ha, where a violent fistfight erupted between Giancana and Collins that eventually brought Sinatra, his valet, George Jacobs, and headwaiter Eddie King into the cabin; King wrenched Collins off Giancana and then held him down so that Giancana could beat the stuffing out of him.

Giancana left Cal-Neva the next day, but a few days later, word leaked out that he had been there in violation of his Black Book listing, which forbade him to enter a Nevada casino for the rest of his natural life. By the time Edward Olsen, chairman of the Nevada Gaming Control Board, had launched an investigation into the incident, Sinatra was performing at the Sands in Las Vegas. On August 2, a headline appeared in the Chicago *Sun-Times:* MOE'S VISIT PERILS SINATRA LICENSE. By August 8, investigators were sent to Cal-Neva, but no one was talking. Skinny declined to be interviewed on the advice of his attorney. Meanwhile, Olsen interviewed Sinatra that same afternoon in his office in Las Vegas; Sinatra conceded only that he had seen Giancana coming out of Phyllis's cabin, that they had exchanged greetings, and that he'd had nothing to do with Giancana's visit. He vehemently denied any knowledge of a fight. But, as usual, his ridiculous pride set off alarm bells. When Olsen suggested that it was not such a good idea to associate with the likes of Giancana, Frank would promise not to associate with him only *in Nevada.* "This is a way of life," he told Olsen, "and a man has to lead his own life."

When Olsen asked if he knew that the hotel staff were taking care of Giancana while he was there, Sinatra suggested that he should interview the staff and gave Olsen a list of names, including Skinny's. Olsen promptly issued subpoenas to everyone on the list. "I still have that subpoena," said Jimmy Mancini, the bell captain who had delivered a pot of coffee to Giancana during his stay. "He had a fedora on and a set of golf clubs, and he pulled out the thickest wad of bills I've ever seen and handed me a twenty." Said Ray Langford: "Giancana never came into the casino. He was just there. He had a beat-up old Chevy, and he bought a lot of fancy clothes from the I. Magnin shop for Phyllis." When they started "passing out subpoenas," said Langford, "I got a call from Eddie King, the maître d'. He was in a diner somewhere on the road, and he said, 'Ray, get that little Ford, go down to my cottage, and load up everything I got, and I'll see you in Palm Springs. Leave the car at the gas station with the keys on the floor.' He wanted to get the hell out of there."

Meanwhile, the investigation had become, as Olsen said later, "a wild and woolly news story all over. We were just absolutely besieged by the press of all kinds." So much press, in fact, that even JFK began to feel sorry for Sinatra. The president made a stop in Las Vegas to speak at the Convention Center that August. Grant Sawyer, the governor of Nevada, later recalled that on the way from McCarran Airport, Kennedy asked the governor, "What are you doing to my friend Frank Sinatra?" The media feeding frenzy had upset Sinatra, who assumed that it was the result of the issuance of all those subpoenas. On Labor Day weekend, when Sinatra and Dean Martin were performing at the Cal-Neva to close the season, Frank had his accountant, Newell Hancock, call Olsen. In a memo Olsen wrote on September 4, 1963, to document the tumultuous holiday weekend, he stated, "Hancock opened the conversation with: 'Ed, what in the hell are you doing to us with all this publicity?' I explained to Hancock that the publicity did not originate with the Board. . . . Hancock went on to say that 'Frank is irritated' and would like to meet with me. . . .'"

Hancock suggested that Olsen come up to Cal-Neva, have dinner with Frank so that the two men could have an informal talk, and then catch the show afterward. Olsen declined. About half an hour later, his phone rang. It was Sinatra. "To describe him as 'irritated,'" wrote Olsen, "was a masterful understatement. He was infuriated."

"You're acting like a fucking cop," barked Sinatra. "I just want to talk to you off the record." When Olsen continued to resist the offer, Sinatra said, "Listen, Ed, I haven't had to take this kind of shit from anybody in the country, and I'm not going to take it from you people. . . . It's you and your goddamn subpoenas which have caused all this trouble." The two men argued for a while, Sinatra's rage escalating with every word. "I'm never coming to see you again," he said, to which Olsen replied that if he wanted to see him, he'd send a subpoena. "You just try and find me," Sinatra said. "And if you do, you can look for a big, fat surprise . . . a big, fat, fucking surprise. Now listen to me, Ed. . . . Don't fuck with me. Just don't fuck with me."

Within minutes after Sinatra and Olsen hung up, two gaming board agents showed up at Cal-Neva at six P.M. for their previously scheduled count of the gambling table drop boxes, a routine gaming board program that had been conducted on Labor Day weekend in Lake Tahoe for the past three summers. It was merely coincidence that they arrived just as Sinatra's blistering phone call to Olsen ended. When the agents requested admission to the count, Skinny fled to confer with Sinatra, who said, "Throw the dirty sons of bitches out of the house!"

When Skinny returned to the casino, the agents had already left, none the wiser. The casino manager, Irving Pearlman, had told the agents that the count had already begun, and they agreed to come back for the six A.M. count on Labor Day. The agents had absolutely no idea that Sinatra and Olsen were in the midst of a meltdown.

As planned, the two agents came back Monday morning and observed the count. Everything went fine—"totally routine," said Olsen. "The count had been concluded, and they were verifying and about wrapped up, and one of the boys was standing . . . with his arm crooked. D'Amato comes along, and he could feel [Skinny] touching his arm, and Skinny says, 'Here's one for each of you.' Then D'Amato just takes off and the agent turns around and here's two $100 bills stuffed into the crevice of his arm.

"Well," continued Olsen, "this was just—you know, horrifying! They didn't know what to do about that! So the one agent tossed it out on the table so the other agent could see it. And the two guys were really hilarious characters. They shuffled it back and forth trying to get rid of it, you know. And finally, D'Amato comes back in and he says, 'Aw, you can take that.' And D'Amato explained it was just because he'd put them to all the trouble on Saturday night before by not letting them into the count. But that wasn't the case at all. . . . They'd determined that it had already started, and they'd left. But ultimately they managed to get the two $100 bills back into Mr. D'Amato's hands."

As soon as the agents got out of the Cal-Neva Lodge, they called Olsen at home around eight A.M. and woke him up. "We need to see you immediately," they said. He told them to come right over, and they arrived shortly thereafter, at which point they detailed for Olsen Skinny's attempt to force money on them. "Well," said Olsen, "that was the straw that broke the camel's back, as far as I was concerned. I couldn't get straight answers to anything, and they were just nothing but headaches, the whole business up there. I felt that continuation would be detrimental to the entire gambling industry in Nevada. So as quickly as I was able to get the lawyer to work and legal papers drawn up, we prepared a complaint, seeking the revocation of Mr. Sinatra's license at both Lake Tahoe and at the Sands in Las Vegas."

Skinny tried to grease the wheels with money, as he had done hundreds of times before. He spent so much of his life in Atlantic City using cash as a salve that it must have been impossible for him to realize just how foolish a move this was. On that Monday in September 1963 when Skinny put two $100 bills in the crook of the gaming board agent's arm, the good times collided head-on with the bad. Skinny had lived and breathed illegal gambling since he was a child, and now he was expected to run a kind of legalized-illegal casino for his friend Frank Sinatra, and none of his old tricks were going to get him out of this particular jam. Handing money to the wrong person had serious consequences in Nevada's new, hyper-regulated era and, in this instance, brought the entire enterprise of Frank Sinatra's Cal-Neva Lodge— "Heaven in the High Sierras"—to a screeching halt.

A few days after Labor Day, Edward Olsen went to visit Governor Sawyer in his office, bringing along with him all the documents and memos and evidence of the last month of investigations as backup. When he told Sawyer that he was about to file a complaint for the revocation of Sinatra's license, "the man just dropped his teeth!" said Olsen. "This was the last thing he needed at the moment!"

"Why?" said Sawyer. Olsen showed him the memo that he had written about the long, strange Labor Day weekend and the transcript from the menacing, obscenity-laced phone call with Sinatra and the story about Skinny's attempt to force money on the agents. Sawyer looked it all over very carefully and finally said, "When?"

"Just as soon as all the legal details can be worked out," said Olsen.

"Well," said Sawyer, "you'd better be right."

Sawyer could smell a political shit-storm coming, and sure enough, he was later accused of engineering the whole thing as a publicity stunt to ingratiate himself with the Kennedys—Bobby in particular.

On September 11, Olsen filed a formal complaint that Park Lake

Enterprises, Inc., had violated gambling laws in Nevada. The complaint alleged that Giancana "sojourned to Chalet No. 50" with the knowledge and consent of Cal-Neva's owners, managers, and employees. Count number two stated that Sinatra said that he would continue to associate openly with Giancana. Count three: Sinatra engaged in a telephone conversation that was designed to "intimidate" Olsen, "maligned and vilified" the gaming board, and used "repulsive language that was venomous in the extreme." Count four: Skinny tried to force money on the two agents, which was "tantamount to an attempt to bribe them."

When the complaint was filed, "all hell broke loose," said Olsen. The one thing that infuriated Frank and Skinny was the allegation of bribery. "They didn't look upon it as bribery at all," said Olsen. "They looked upon it as a kindly gesture. Yet in all the time that I was in office, we never once had an incident of someone trying . . . to give you money of any kind."

On September 12, stories appeared in newspapers all over the country—including the *Atlantic City Press*. SINATRA IS ACCUSED OF HOSTING MOBSTER; D'AMATO UNDER FIRE blared a headline on the front page underneath head shots of Skinny, Frank, and Sam, in that order. Hundreds of letters from all over the country poured into the Nevada Gaming Control Board offices. "The unfortunate thing that I found out," said Olsen, "was that so many people had apparently an ingrained resentment of Sinatra because he had been successful, or he came from a poor background and made money, or something like that. And so many of these [letters] had racial overtones. People were just *bitter* about the man."

Sinatra hired a well-known Las Vegas lawyer named Harry Claiborne to defend him. The Sinatra camp was prepared to argue that not only had Frank not invited Giancana there, but, in fact, he'd never even been there in July 1963—despite the piles of evidence, including half a dozen eyewitnesses, to the contrary. But on October 7, Frank decided to throw in the towel; he released a statement through Claiborne to the press that he was divesting himself of all gambling interests in Nevada and devoting himself exclusively to the entertainment business. When it all fell apart, Giancana was furious with Frank for unleashing his ill temper on Olsen. "Sam lost a bundle because he was a secret, part

Sinatra and friends
at the 500 Club.

Sinatra presents
Skinny with the
"Sinatrama Award"
in 1959, for bringing
"the world's finest
entertainer of all
time...to the play-
ground of the world."

Smokin':
Sinatra
onstage
at the
Five.

Sinatra, onstage at the 500 Club,
backed by the Peter Miller Orchestra
(Joey Bishop's in the wings, yelling).

Skinny and his early-sixties business partner, Herbie Friedman. Paulajane stands on the famous Martin & Lewis bench.

One...two...three strikes, you're out! Paulajane sings "Take Me Out to the Ball Game" on the stage of the 500 Club, in 1955.

Cathy and Paulajane onstage with Patti Paige, singing "How Much Is That Doggie in the Window?" in the mid-fifties.

The Three Stooges and the two girls: Paulajane and Cathy get special access, as usual.

Mickey Rooney leaves his footprints on Missouri Avenue, in the summer of 1954, while Skinny and Paulajane look on.

Paulajane gets a piggyback from Joe DiMaggio near the 500 Club in the summer of 1961.

Paulajane and Cathy, with their mother and brand-new little brother Angelo, in the apartment above the club, in 1958.

Peggy Bramson, Milton Berle, Bettyjane, and Sam Bramson at Skinny and Bettyjane's tenth wedding anniversary party in 1959.

Bettyjane and Skinny at their tenth wedding anniversary party at the 500 Club, in 1959.

Frank, Sammy, and Dean onstage at the 500 Club, in summer of 1964.
(COURTESY OF RICK APT)

Frank Sinatra and his pal Skinny, whom he always called Paul.

Prominent New Jersey attorney Angelo Malandra, on the left in dark glasses, waits while Skinny talks to the future president of the United States, at a rally held in a tent in Camden, New Jersey, in 1960.

Skinny, Eddie Fisher, and Frank S. "Hap" Farley at the 1964 Democratic Convention in Atlantic City.

Donald O'Connor, Irving "Swifty" Lazar (in glasses), Skinny, Keely Smith, George Raft, and Louis Prima at the Cal-Neva Lodge, in Lake Tahoe, in the early sixties.

Nancy Sinatra Sr., Paulajane, Cathy, and Nancy Sinatra Jr. at the Cal-Neva Lodge, in the summer of 1961.

Skinny opens a new restaurant in 1969, naming if after his only son, Angelo.

On June 10, 1973, the 500 Club and Angelo's restaurant burned to the ground. One of the few things that went untouched by flame was a portrait of Frank Sinatra that hung in the main showroom. "It's a miracle," Skinny said.

Not long after the fire, Angelo travels to New York to hang out backstage with his father's pal. "So you met my kid," Skinny said to Sinatra after he saw this photograph.

Cathy, Jerry Lewis, Paulajane, and Skinny in his bedroom, in 1979. Skinny spent the last several years of his life in his pajamas, rarely venturing out of the house.

Skinny and Sammy Davis Jr. enjoy an afternoon cocktail in the backyard of 12 South Suffolk Avenue. The footprints from Missouri Avenue were moved there after the fire.

Frank Sinatra plants one on his pal Skinny, who was honored in 1981 as Man of the Year by the Hebrew Academy of Atlantic County.

The Last Good Time: Frank Sinatra, Skinny, Paulajane, and Dean Martin celebrate Skinny's seventy-fifth and final birthday at the Golden Nugget, in Atlantic City, on December 1, 1983. He died six months later.

Frank Sinatra, kneeling between Paulajane and Cathy at Skinny's funeral, June 10, 1984, at St. Michael's Church on Mississippi Avenue.

Sinatra, along with Paulajane's ex-husband, Bobby Palamero (far left), and other pallbearers, carries Skinny's casket out of St. Michael's, as Paulajane follows behind.

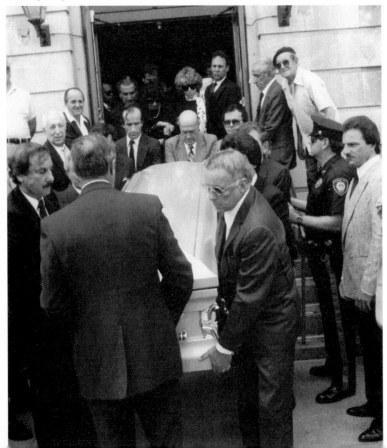

owner of Cal-Neva, and the whole thing went belly-up," said Tommy DiBella, a friend of Giancana, Skinny, and Frank. "So for a while there, Sam didn't know what to do with Frank. And I know that Frank was pissed at Sam, because, as he put it, 'that fucker shouldn't have been there in the first place. Look at the trouble he caused. This is *his* fault, not mine.' It wasn't the same buddy-buddy relationship between Frank and Sam, not after Cal-Neva, that's for sure."

At the very end of the Olsen transcript that David Schwartz dug up for me, there is one other little story about Skinny, kind of dangling out there, disconnected from the plot of that weird summer of 1963. "I might as well throw this in the record," said Olsen. "This guy D'Amato—who was a character—all these guys are *likable*! That's the trouble with them. You can't help but like all of them, just personally, to sit down and chat with them. . . . D'Amato, who wanted a license so bad at one point, had an intermediary in the Reno area invite Dick Ham, who was executive assistant to the governor [Grant Sawyer], to dinner at Cal-Neva Lodge. When he got there . . . who shows up at the table but D'Amato! It was a three-way dinner instead of a two-way dinner. And at that point, D'Amato made what, to my knowledge, was the only really open offer. . . . He offered $25,000 if Sawyer would take care of the license for him." Olsen laughed. "I guess this is the way he operates."

After I read the Olsen transcript, I called Sonny King, who lives in Las Vegas, and asked him about this last bit. "Skinny was a real spender and one of the nicest gentlemen I've ever met," said King. "I mean, of that era. Money was never any object. He was an amazing man, Skinny D'Amato. He loved nothing more than to sit down to a game of gin. You could tell him forty celebrities were outside, but if he was playing gin, he wouldn't come out. And everybody understood that. He was a plain, simple, lovable guy. I hate this cliché, but he was from the old school, where respect was a very important thing in his life. They tell me he had a terrific temper, but I don't think I ever saw him mad. But his anger was over the fact that they never gave him a license. I was deeply hurt when I read in the papers that he was denied. I also think Skinny really felt that it was Frank's fault that they lost Cal-Neva."

When Sinatra and Skinny pulled up stakes in Lake Tahoe and sold Cal-Neva, said Ray Langford, "the whole town died. The whole north shore. Everything was for sale, and nobody made it anymore. Then the clientele changed. There we were, just the summer before, and we had the Kennedys and all the movie stars, who don't care what it cost. I went up there a year later and you could get a room for nothing."

A month after Sinatra sold the Cal-Neva, his son, Frank Sinatra Jr., was kidnapped from the house Frank kept for his family just down the road from the resort in Crystal Bay. A month after that, John Fitzgerald Kennedy was assassinated.

Chapter Nine

When Skinny came back to Atlantic City from Lake Tahoe at the end of the 1963 season, he was, according to Rita Marzullo, "woebegone." Rita, who had known Skinny for well over a decade, had never seen him so depressed. "He wouldn't take any calls, he didn't want to see or talk to *nobody*," she said. Making matters worse, Skinny and Frank blamed each other for the Cal-Neva debacle. Skinny felt that Frank's temper—and his ill-considered phone call to Edward Olsen in particular—was what brought them down; Frank felt that it was Skinny's responsibility to keep Sam Giancana off the property in the first place and that his attempt to force money on the Nevada Gaming Control Board agents was, indeed, the last straw, as Olsen said years later.

By the following summer, however, they had forgiven each other, and in August 1964, Frank made his final appearance at the 500 Club. *Atlantic City Press* columnist Sonny Schwartz would note that, without Sinatra, the city had finally bottomed out. Between 1960 and 1970, nearly eleven thousand year-round residents left the resort, bringing the population to just under forty-eight thousand. In 1940, half of the population of Atlantic County lived in Atlantic City; now it was just one-quarter. The city had lost nearly one-third of its white population during the 1960s, and the resort became—as it remains in certain neighborhoods today—a place that feels very poor and very old. *Newsweek* declared that with one-fourth of its permanent residents over sixty, Atlantic City had the second oldest population in the country, after St. Petersburg, Florida.

A 1965 investigation into poverty in Atlantic City revealed some very telling statistics: 91 percent of the housing had been built before 1939; the resort ranked first in the state in tuberculosis and pneumonia deaths and, compared with other cities its size, first in syphilis as well. Unemployment rose to 15 percent during the off-season, while one-third of the population was on welfare. The investigators came to a grim conclusion: "Atlantic City is the poorest city in New Jersey." A couple of years later, the FBI's "Uniform Crime Report" added insult to injury: Of the 528 cities in America with a population of twenty-five thousand to fifty thousand, Atlantic City had the highest total number of crimes in all seven standard categories.

But the social fabric wasn't the only thing that was breaking down in Atlantic City. State Senator Hap Farley's political machine—which had moved mountains to build the Atlantic City Expressway, the Garden State Parkway, Stockton State College, the Atlantic City Racetrack, and Frank S. Farley State Marina—was beginning to work against the resort. Farley, while still the most powerful politician in south Jersey, who had served the longest of any legislator in state history, was losing traction in the larger political arena of the state; his old-fashioned ways and unfailing tendency to thwart investigations into corruption (largely his own) began to antagonize other, more progressive and powerful politicians in northern Jersey. Even though Jersey City was even *more* corrupt (thanks to its notorious mayor, Frank Hague) than Atlantic City, and Newark and Camden were decaying just as badly, Atlantic City's deterioration and fall from grace were of much greater interest to the national press because the resort had always attracted attention disproportionate to its size and stature. It didn't help that Farley—in protracted denial about how bad things had actually gotten—kept right on promoting the city as if it could still lay claim to being "the World's Greatest Resort"—or whatever preposterous slogan he was foisting on unsuspecting conventioneers ("the World's Playground!" "the Queen of Resorts!"). It was as if Farley, and the city itself, needed to be brought down to size and forced to come to grips with reality once and for all.

Ironically, it was Hap Farley's denial about Atlantic City's deplorable condition that led to both his greatest triumph and the final nail in the coffin for the resort. Farley managed to convince the Democratic National Committee to choose Atlantic City as the host of the 1964 Democratic National Convention, during which Lyndon B. Johnson, who had become president when Kennedy was shot, would choose his vice presidential running mate. On August 24, the political and media hordes descended on the Boardwalk hotels. Jackie Kennedy, making her first appearance at a political function since the assassination of her husband, turned up in Atlantic City and held a reception in the ballroom of the Deauville Hotel. Bobby Kennedy gave a brief, moving speech, in which he quoted Shakespeare and Robert Frost, and received a sixteen-minute standing ovation. He was ultimately passed over as a running mate for LBJ in favor of Hubert Humphrey.

After Johnson chose Humphrey to be his running mate, the press turned their attention to the resort itself. When Hap Farley had first learned that the convention would be held in Atlantic City, he had called a press conference and told an elated crowd that the world's attention would be focused on the resort for a week and that it would be "the pinnacle of prestige" for the city. His hopes were dashed when nearly every television and print media outlet did a story about the deterioration of "tawdry," "dirty" Atlantic City. The *Cincinnati Enquirer* described their visit as "paying for poverty at peak prices. Our room looked like something out of a Charles Addams cartoon book." Mocking Sinatra's Rat Pack (which was also on its last legs), the *Washington Star* wrote: "As a convention town, this is strictly Endsville."

On the last day of the convention, as LBJ was accepting the nomination, a woman hurled herself from a window of a hotel on Pacific Avenue right near Convention Hall, landing on the pavement in front of a crowd of delegates. A few weeks later, in the same esteemed hall where the leader of the free world had stood under a banner that read "Let Us Continue," Miss America 1965 was crowned. Even as every aspect of American society was shifting, this one thing remained stubbornly unchanged. As Frank Deford wrote in his definitive Miss America book, *There She Is*, "Donna Axum [the 1965 winner] declared that Doris Day was her favorite actress and that rock 'n' roll was surely just a passing fad. She would not even discuss such a woman as Elizabeth Taylor."

✦

Without Frank Sinatra, Skinny had a difficult time booking anyone of note into the 500 Club, as there was now a whole wing of the show business world that followed Frank around the country. If Atlantic City was good enough for Sinatra, then it was good enough for, say, Vic Damone. When Frank could no longer bear coming to the decrepit resort, everyone else stayed away, too. To survive, Skinny decided to build a big new restaurant; in 1968, he knocked down portions of the club that had been built for another, long-gone, era and erected an addition. He named it Angelo's after his then eleven-year-old son.

"It was like a big barn," said Joe Del Raso, who worked for Skinny in the summers. "It was the place to be seen for lunch in Atlantic City— like a really private lunch club with good Italian food. A lot of politicians and bigwigs came there every day. And Skinny was always up at the front table holding court." By now, Skinny had a lot of behind-the-scenes political power. "I remember him telling off a politician one night at a dinner," said Del Raso, laughing. "'You wouldn't be where you are unless it was for me. You couldn't get elected *dogcatcher!*'"

The restaurant was a success, and it kept the 500 Club alive, though just barely. But Skinny had bigger problems to deal with. His tax troubles—uncovered during Bobby Kennedy's tenure at the Justice Department—finally came back to haunt him. On August 15, 1966, U.S. Attorney David Satz Jr. filed an indictment in federal court in Newark, charging Skinny with evading corporate taxes on more than $1.2 million from 1960 to 1963. The story, which noted that the man who had been chosen Citizen of the Year in Atlantic City just ten years earlier was now facing three years in prison, got picked up in newspapers all over the country. Skinny was humiliated, and the ordeal dragged on for five years, with Skinny going in and out of federal court in Newark several times as the fines and penalties piled up. At one hearing in 1968, Skinny's lawyer contended that because his client lacked formal schooling, he relied on his accountants to file returns—not exactly a powerful defense. Besides, Skinny told the *Atlantic City Press*, "I was spending most of my time running Frankie's place [in Lake Tahoe], and I left the 500 Club operation to the auditors." In private, he blamed Herbie Freedman, his partner in the 500 since taking on Cal-Neva, who he felt should have filed the tax returns in his absence.

At the end of the *Press* story about his tax troubles, Skinny spoke of the increasingly loud whispers about his Mob connections: "In this business, you meet an awful lot of people. So you meet someone, and later—maybe years later—the Feds come along and say, 'He's a mobster.' What are you supposed to do? Say, 'I can't know you, I can't talk to you, because now they say you're a hood'?"

Eventually, in August 1971, the IRS padlocked the club for two days and placed it in receivership for Skinny's failure to pay what was now determined to be $120,000 in back taxes. Skinny blamed his troubles on an article published in *Philadelphia* magazine in 1970 linking him—and several other public figures—with organized crime. "I was negotiating with the government for a settlement," he told a reporter from *The Philadelphia Inquirer*. "I had an application for a loan and it was approved by the IRS. The party from whom the loan had been made telephoned me after the story appeared and canceled the loan."

A U.S. district court ordered the IRS to give Skinny a breather so that he could raise the money, and he regained control of the club after a promise to pay off the taxes within the following two summers. The first payment of $50,000 was due on November 30, 1971. So on a Sunday night, November 14, five hundred people attended a "surprise" benefit dinner at the 500 Club to help raise the first payment. The usual groups of politicians, businessmen, entertainers, and ever faithful locals paid $100 a plate for roast pig and champagne. Frank Sinatra's mother, Dolly, flew in from Palm Springs. "Frank was really sorry he couldn't be here tonight," she told the crowd from the stage. Skinny got up to speak, but just for a second. "I'm so happy, I'm just overwhelmed," he said in tears, before he went back to his cigarettes.

A couple of weeks later, Atlantic City's festering racial problems were revealed in a rare bit of Skinny bashing in *The Philadelphia Inquirer*. A columnist named Art Peters wrote a piece headlined ROYALTY LOOKS AFTER ITS OWN, BUT THE POOR? "It seems somehow ironic that this money was raised to help pay a nightclub owner's back taxes when so many people are jobless and hungry on Atlantic City's North-side," he wrote. "Many of the same politicians who remain so indifferent to the plight of the shore resort's poor blacks, feasted on roast pig and champagne at Skinny's bash.... Royalty has always looked after its own.... If she were alive today, Marie Antoinette would be enthralled by the new royalty. 'Let them eat roast pig at $100 a plate,' she would proclaim."

✦

The summer before her junior year at Atlantic City High School, Paulajane was spotted by the Ventnor beach lifeguards, who were responsible in those days for asking pretty girls to compete in the Miss Ventnor contest. She had been strolling along the water's edge with her friend Sugar McBeth, and the lifeguards asked the two girls to enter the pageant. Paulajane was wearing a back brace because she had broken four vertebrae in an auto accident on Father's Day, the first night that Bettyjane had let her daughter go "offshore" with friends, unchaperoned. On the beach that day, Sugar said, "I'll enter if you do it," and Paulajane agreed. But when she went home and announced this decision to her parents, Skinny objected. Bettyjane—who was, no doubt, thrilled to have her daughter take an interest in her old "sport"—told a reporter that she had a difficult time convincing Skinny. But when Paulajane was crowned Miss Ventnor, "no one was happier than my husband," said Bettyjane.

Paulajane loved to sing, even as a little girl. There are pictures of her at the age of five or six or seven, standing on the same stage and with the very mike that Frank Sinatra or Dean Martin used till dawn the night before, singing "Volare" or "Witchcraft." Paulajane was, in the words of her father, "a big ham."

Right from the get-go, Skinny discouraged his daughter from taking singing and dancing lessons, because, his thinking went, why waste your time? In fact, once, when he was out of town for Paulajane's birthday, he sent her a telegram that read, "Happy Birthday Paula, If you're going to sing today just make sure that this will be your last performance as a singer. As I've told you before you have two choices, to be a nun or a schoolteacher—you dig—have fun, miss you all, take care of Momie and Cathy and Angelo see you next week love and kisses = Daddy. . . ." Skinny knew all too well the dangers of the world he inhabited—and the way that beautiful women were usually treated by the very men who were his pals. (These rules extended to his son; once, Cooks Books, the family chauffeur, dressed Angelo as Santa Claus and put him on a local variety show without Skinny's knowledge, and, says Angelo, "he was not happy.") But there were a couple of songs that he wanted Paulajane to learn—"Volare" and "Mamma," the latter being his favorite. He cried every time he heard it. Paulajane eventually recorded a 45 of "Mamma," and it was on the jukebox in the lounge at the 500 Club. The only time Paulajane was allowed to perform in front of an audience was on Easter at a big party that Skinny threw at the club every year following Atlantic City's famous Easter Parade.

The responsibilities required of Miss Ventnor were minimal. She had to show up at grand openings, after which her picture would appear in the paper, but she didn't actually have to *stand* for anything, nor did she ever speak publicly. But by the following summer, Paulajane was required as Miss Ventnor to enter the more serious and organized Miss Atlantic County Pageant. She put together a patriotic song-and-dance number of George M. Cohan songs, including "The Yankee Doodle Boy," and came out onstage in an old army coat, which she peeled off to reveal a much sexier, leggier outfit. "It's about time somebody became patriotic," Paulajane told a reporter, revealing her alienation from her rebellious peers, most of whom were not feeling particularly warm and fuzzy about America's war in Vietnam.

When Paulajane won the contest in August 1968, Skinny wept. "It was his sense that it didn't matter that I was Skinny's daughter," said Paulajane. "He was so, so proud because of the fact that his reputation didn't harm me." The day after she was crowned Miss Atlantic County, Frank Sinatra called and said, "How you doin', baby? How's it feel to be a queen?"

Suddenly, she was a local celebrity. GIRL WHO KNEW THE STARS MAKES LIMELIGHT HERSELF, read a headline a few weeks after Paulajane won the title. The profile included this bit about her aspirations: "Hearing of her ambition, [Skinny] tried to convince Paulajane that show business was not all glamour . . . and she remembered pleading with him to be allowed to try her luck. 'Just six months,' she said. 'If I make it in six months . . .' But his blessing never came. It didn't need to come because Paulajane changed her mind. 'I liked the feeling at first, then I began to find out what it was like, how it was backstage, seeing the whole picture—that it was a tough grind,' she explained."

A month after Paulajane became Miss Atlantic County, the Miss America contestants from around the country made their annual pilgrimage to Atlantic City for a week of preening, primping, forced camaraderie, and, ultimately, silly yet deadly serious competition. And while the pageant may have seemed like the only thing in the resort that still had a little sheen left on it, cracks were beginning to form.

In the late 1960s, "radical" feminists began staging dramatic and provocative demonstrations, which they called "zap actions," to draw attention to their struggle. The first and most famous of these occurred on the Boardwalk in Atlantic City. About one hundred women turned up in front of Convention Hall to picket the Miss America Pageant. They carried signs with slogans like "Let's Judge Ourselves as People." They crowned a live sheep and dumped girdles, cosmetics, high heels, and bras into a "freedom trash can." The press ate it up, and the demonstration wound up on the nightly broadcast of all three networks. Not a single feminist ever stripped off her bra and tossed it onto a bonfire, but the papers ran a memorable photograph of brassieres going into a trash can.

On September 7, 1968, Judi Ford, a trampolinist (!) and bottle blonde, was crowned Miss America. The pageant officials' worst fear was that the American public would find out that she smoked cigarettes. As Frank Deford noted in *Here She Is*, the feminists produced the only "original news to emanate from Atlantic City during Pageant week since the bland TV era began" in the 1950s. *The New York Times* piece on the protesters was ten times as long as the story of Judi Ford's victory. "To the Women's Liberation Movement," wrote Deford, "the skirmish at Convention Hall is roughly analogous to the Boston Tea Party."

It makes a certain amount of sense that the women's lib movement would choose Atlantic City as a staging ground for its first demonstration, and not just because it's the home of the ultimate beauty pageant. Atlantic City was the spiritual birthplace of the Rat Pack, a group of men who called women "broads" and treated many of them like whores. For his part, Skinny was an old-school Italian who believed that women should stay at home and have babies. In his world, a woman needed no further education beyond high school, because, of course, a man would take care of her—no matter how unfaithful he was. But he was a contradiction, said Paulajane, "because he admired women like Gloria Steinem and Helen Gurley Brown, women who were bright and clever and made something of themselves. He was proud of the fact that I was working and wanted to go to college. I think he thought the feminists were going about it the wrong way. I would never have behaved the way some of those women did because it would have embarrassed him. But he didn't think it was all wrong. He was never black or white on anything. He never traded in negative stereotypes—only positive ones. Like, he thought all Jews were smart. He would say, 'I never met a dumb Jew.'"

By the summer of 1969, Paulajane was climbing the pageant ladder, preparing for Miss New Jersey in Cherry Hill. By then, she was being referred to in newspaper headlines by her first name only: PAULAJANE'S BIG MOMENT RIGHT AROUND THE CORNER, read one. PAULAJANE, GOOD AS EVER, went another. "Paulajane was back in town this weekend. She was belting out songs as strong as ever at the 500 Club where she served as co–master of ceremonies for the Miss Columbus Day festivities. Delivering a hard sock version of 'Frankie and Johnny' with just enough softness in the soft parts, she once again won the hearts of more than 1,000 localites at her daddy's club." One paper ran a big photograph of the eighteen-year-old "star" and her mother; both of them stood on the steps of the mansion on Suffolk Avenue, looking like twin-coifed blond beauties in almost matching suits as Paulajane packed to leave for a week of swanning in Cherry Hill. But on the first day of competition, the *Atlantic City Press* hit the newsstands announcing that Skinny had been indicted on voter fraud. He was eventually cleared of the charges, but the fact that the paper used only *his* name in a headline displayed in an unusually large point size suggested that there were at least a few people who wanted to take Skinny down a peg. It was the first time that Paulajane began to understand that being "Skinny's kid" wasn't necessarily always a good thing. She was favored to place at least as a runner-up, but she didn't even make the top ten.

When she went away to college, Paulajane was relieved to be in a place where no one knew her, to see what she had going for her besides a pageant title and Skinny D'Amato as a father. She packed off to a junior college called Vernon Court in Newport, Rhode Island, in 1969 and studied journalism. The day she graduated in 1971, Skinny gave her a card in which he wrote: "You are me. Love, Skin." She came home to work for Atlantic City's public relations department, writing press releases about the town that provided the backdrop to her odd fairy tale. But things had gotten even worse while she was away, and there was no more telling sign of the crushing failure of the resort than that of the once glorious hotels in the Boardwalk, most of them now filled with senior citizens living out their own twilight years in tandem within these hulking, bedraggled beasts overlooking the ocean. In 1970, Atlantic City staged a celebration of the one hundredth anniversary of the Boardwalk. *The New York Times* coverage said it all: "It is a barely believable experience to walk a few steps from pinball machines and foot-long hot dogs and step into the vast Turkish-carpeted silences of the Marlborough-Blenheim." But at least that hotel was *open*. The Ambassador, which had been closed since 1966, was sold at federal bankruptcy court in 1970 for only $2 million. It had been built in 1929— *for $8 million.*

In 1971, movie director Bob Rafelson came to town to shoot his dark, strange film *King of Marvin Gardens*, starring Jack Nicholson and Ellen Burstyn. Much of it was shot in the Marlborough-Blenheim Hotel, a setting that perfectly matched the pathetic, end-of-the-road lives of the characters. As the Atlantic City historian Charles Funnell wrote, the film "was pervaded by the mood of a late afternoon in winter, as it traced the collapse of a euphoric young man's world of illusion amid the peeling paint and rusty fixtures of a Boardwalk hotel." Skinny's beloved Traymore, which he had watched rise above the Boardwalk as a child and where he'd spent so many summers with his family in their private cabana by the pool, was sold by his friend Robert

Tisch, who couldn't make a go of it after twenty years in the business. Despite its landmark status, the humongous structure was imploded with dynamite in a single, awful blast in May 1972.

Slowly but surely, the city began to destroy all of its history, and Skinny—who had a kind of special landmark status all his own—was not immune to the unstoppable forces of destruction in the resort. In fact, the downfall of the D'Amato family seemed to match the city's, disaster for disaster.

The headaches started during the summer of 1963 at the Cal-Neva Lodge. They were so intense that Bettyjane would stay in bed all day, with the blinds pulled, as she had become hypersensitive to even the dimmest light. A nurse massaged her temples, put cold compresses on her forehead, and told her that it was probably from the high altitude. The headaches would come and go over the next few years, but Bettyjane, not wanting to face the truth, wrote them off as particularly bad migraines. Then, one night in December 1966, she was visiting her parents, who were both in the hospital—her father was diabetic, and her mother was always sick with one thing or another. She caught a cab home to Suffolk Avenue, and just as the driver pulled up in front of the house, she had a convulsion and slumped over, unconscious.

Paulajane was talking on the phone in her bedroom when suddenly there was a man in the street in front of her house yelling like a lunatic. By the time she made it downstairs and outside, her mother was coming to. "What happened?" she asked. Paulajane helped her inside and then called Bettyjane's friend Chris Owen, a nurse who lived eight blocks away. When Chris got there she called Dr. Donald Davidson, who showed up in a tuxedo because he had been on his way to the Century Ball. Someone called Skinny, who was at the club. Before long, they were all standing around Bettyjane, trying to figure out what was happening to her.

"I left the hospital," said Bettyjane. "I got in the cab, and I remember passing the Knife & Fork and the high school, but I don't remember anything after that until now. I just had this strange sensation that went from my legs and up into my head, and—" Just then, the look on her face changed and she said, "Oh, here it comes again. . . ." Then she slipped into a grand mal seizure right in front of everyone. Her head flew back and her body became rigid. Dr. Davidson kept her from swallowing her tongue, and then just that quickly, it was over.

The next day, Bettyjane was put through a battery of tests at Atlantic City Medical Center and misdiagnosed with a brain tumor; the neurological team wanted to operate immediately, but Skinny was having none of it. He took his wife to the University of Pennsylvania Medical Center, where a doctor determined that Bettyjane had an aneurysm that was pressing on the part of the brain that controls memory and personality. Paulajane remembers that there was too great a risk that she would become a vegetable if the operation didn't go perfectly, so the doctor put her on a variety of different medications to stave off the seizures. "It was basically a combination of uppers and downers," said Paulajane. "She never had another full-blown seizure again, but her personality would change. You could see the panic on her face—her color would change, her expression would change."

After several months of outbursts—"unbelievable anger," as Chris Owen put it—Bettyjane took Skinny and Paulajane to see the doctor so he could explain what was happening. "He told us that she will lash out at the one that she was the most connected to," said Paulajane. "If Skinny was at home, it would be him. If he was not home, it was me. If both of us weren't home, it was Cathy. If no one was home, she would call her best friend and torture her over the phone." The doctor advised Paulajane and Skinny to get out of the house during Bettyjane's episodes.

"It would happen just like that," said Paulajane. "She could be sitting having a very normal conversation and then just turn on you and lash out. She would exert so much energy that it would exhaust her afterward and she would have to go to sleep. She'd throw things, destroy things, run up and down the stairs. She was not in control of her behavior. She became like a maniac, a madwoman." As Joe Del Raso said, "The aneurysm gave her the personality of a schizophrenic."

One time, said Paulajane, "she ran down the street after me in her nightgown as I drove away in my car. Or I would call my grandparents and say, 'Come get me. Mommy's having another one of her *feelings*,' as she called them. The next day she would call me sobbing and say, 'What did I do?' It was terrible. She'd wake up and see the destruction, and no one would be home. It was just sad. I can picture her so vividly. I would sit on the edge of her bed, and she had the most magnificent brown eyes. And her lip would start to quiver and she didn't know how to apologize. How do you ask somebody, 'What did I do to you?'"

One can't help but think that some of the rage that was spewing forth from this controlled, proper, beautiful woman had been deeply repressed and that her illness—and all the drugs—made it impossible for her to control her feelings. Skinny was known to be unfaithful over the years, but by this point, he had a full-fledged girlfriend. And she was only nineteen. Mer Lyn was a singer who worked at the club. She was half Philippine and half Irish—and gorgeous. Skinny had a weakness for Asian girls, and for a while the 500 regularly showcased a group who called themselves the Tokyo Happy Coats because he was hitting on them all. Mer Lyn was talented, and Skinny tried to push her career for a time, but then he eventually broke off with her. Bettyjane cried and cried about Skinny's affair with the girl, and at one point when he was out of town, she confronted Mer Lyn and told her to "get lost."

When I asked Paulajane if her mother's illness had anything to do with his infidelities, she said no: "With her being sick, he was more careful. He didn't want to hurt her. He was very afraid of her illness. My father truly loved and respected my mother, and he was fearful of not having her in his life." On February 14, 1967, Skinny took Bettyjane to Miami to spend a few days with Frank Sinatra and his lovely—and very young—new wife, Mia Farrow. It must have been an uneasy experience seeing Frank with a beautiful young woman the same age as her own husband's girlfriend. Frank was performing at a nightclub and Skinny and Bettyjane attended the show and then flew to New York for a two-week cruise to the Caribbean. Bettyjane was always dragging Skinny on cruises, insisting that he get away from the club once in a while, but this one was *his* idea; he thought the cruise would be good for Bettyjane. But it turned out to be a bit of a disaster; she suffered a seizure on the ship, during which she fell and cut her head severely enough to require seven stitches. Making matters worse, he and Bettyjane were stopped on their way back through New York by customs agents. In Skinny's FBI file, it was reported that Skinny was "questioned regarding his knowledge and associations with . . . members of La Cosa Nostra." It could not have been a pleasant experience for Bettyjane to finally come face-to-face with the part of her husband's life she was usually shielded from.

But there were other tensions in the marriage. Even though Bettyjane had been born to parents of limited means, she comported herself as a well-bred WASP. "The women in Atlantic City had a lot of respect for Bettyjane," said Joe Del Raso. "In today's parlance she would be considered the perfect trophy wife, although it was his lifestyle that magnified her glamour and movie star quality. I think, looking back on it, some of her glamour may have been superficial. She didn't have the same character as Skinny. He was a man unto himself and beloved for it. I never heard anyone speak a bad word about him, but some of the envious women around town would sometimes refer to Bettyjane as a snob. She ran with a group in Atlantic City, some of whom were hangers-on—the social crowd, mostly people who were not Italians. In one respect, I think she may have been a little snobby about Skinny's Italian friends. She wasn't too excited about them, while on the other hand, the social types were attracted to Skinny because he was the celebrity of the town. He was 'Mr. Atlantic City.' Every Friday night, he would host the social elites at Arnold Orsatti's restaurant. They rarely met at the 500 Club. For years, Skinny picked up the tab for this gathering. I remember my parents went a few times and my father preferred paying his own way rather than glomming off of Skinny—I think he felt that some of the supposed 'elite' crowd were nothing more than freeloaders."

Skinny's infidelities and the couple's ethnic and quasi class differences, not to mention their vast age difference, were complicated, to be sure, but were ultimately part of a contract that the two knowingly entered into when they got married. Bettyjane was getting access to the fabulous life, while Skinny added a further layer of legitimacy to his reputation through his marriage to such a refined, beautiful, and non-

Italian woman. But there was something more troubling between the two of them that neither had seen coming.

✦

Right from the beginning Angie, as everyone called him, was bad news. He was born on December 14, 1957. Skinny stayed up all night celebrating with his friends, buying everyone drinks. It must have seemed at least vaguely meaningful that his first and only son was a fellow Sagittarian. Skinny, who was born on December 1, and Frank Sinatra, born on December 12, often celebrated their birthdays together. In the dead of winter, Sinatra would sometimes surprise Skinny; his helicopter would land on the Boardwalk, and a limousine would take him to the 500 Club. "When Sinatra came in December," said Rita Marzullo, "you not only paid your rent for three months, but you had Christmas money left over, because money came in from all over. People would fly in from Chicago or New York for one night to be there with Sinatra. Skinny and Frank would drink and laugh and joke together—always with a hundred girls around. But Sinatra always came in with a girl."

Bettyjane hemorrhaged so much during childbirth that she required a transfusion, from which she contracted hepatitis. In the 1950s, hepatitis patients were quarantined, so Bettyjane—with a newborn and two little girls, five and seven, at home—spent three months in the hospital. But unlike most families in Atlantic City, the D'Amatos had Lillian, their live-in maid, and Miss Goetz to take care of the children while their mother recovered. As if they weren't pampered and special enough, Joe DiMaggio came to live with them in the apartment while Bettyjane was in the hospital. During the day, Joe would play with the girls; at night, he'd head downstairs to party with their daddy.

When Bettyjane finally made it out of the hospital, Skinny threw a christening party to end all christening parties at the club for hundreds of people, many of whom came from all over the country. It was here, on this day, that a subtle psychic split in the family began to form; Angelo was baptized Catholic, while Paulajane and Cathy had been raised as Protestants. Angelo, Skinny seemed to be saying, will be reared *my* way. Angie was a very unhappy—or, as they said then, "colicky"—baby. "He had this nurse," said Rita, "and she would walk him up and down the street in his beautiful English pram with a net over it, and she wouldn't let nobody touch him. If you leaned over the pram, she'd say, 'Are your hands washed? Don't breathe on him. Don't touch him.' She always wore a uniform, and in the winter she wore a cape. And every day she'd sit on a bench across the street, facing the club, with the baby."

When Skinny and Bettyjane were at the 1958 World Series in New York with DiMaggio—and Miss Goetz had the day off—Lillian was left to take care of Angelo. For whatever reason, she beat him so badly that day, he had to be iced down to slow the swelling. When Skinny and Bettyjane returned from New York, they fired Lillian but declined to press charges. "I was there that day of the beating," said Genevieve Norato. "He wasn't even out of the crib yet, and he was an adorable blond-haired boy, and he had an angel face with big brown eyes like his mother's. Lillian always wanted to be a Mrs. D'Amato type. Bettyjane was an elegant woman. Everyone adored her. She was a class act. Slim, beautiful, blond hair—she just floated. As soon as Bettyjane would leave the apartment, Lillian would put on one of her robes and walk around the apartment smoking cigarettes, and I think it just got to her—that she wasn't who she wanted to be. Lillian was a really nice woman, and she was very attractive: pretty brown eyes, dark skinned, perfectly tweezed eyebrows, and she straightened her hair. But she just, like, wigged out one day when Angelo was being ornery. When Bettyjane came home, she was so upset. That baby was head-to-toe black and blue. She beat him simple. Paulajane and I had been swimming at the pool at the Traymore, and when we got back we went in to see him, and, oh, that boy, that baby. He was still smiling. Sitting in his crib, smiling, covered with bruises."

From an early age, Angelo suffered from bizarre behavioral problems that only seemed to be exacerbated by the tense—and intense—relationship he had with his father. Angelo began to work at the 500 Club as soon as he could reach the bar without standing on his tiptoes. At the club, he lived the pampered, undisciplined life of a celebrity's child; Skinny's friends gave him $20 bills as if they were candy bars.

Partly because of this, at home on Suffolk Avenue, he became increasingly difficult and disruptive. At night, after everyone had gone to bed and while his father was at the club, he would go downstairs to watch TV all night, lighting matches and tossing them behind the couch or into the drapes, or setting pans on fire in the kitchen. In the morning, his father did not hesitate to discipline him with brute force. Skinny often bragged to his friends about how Angie cowered in the corner of his bedroom to shield himself from the blows, never trying to flee, crawling away only after he had been dismissed. Skinny—who dislocated his thumb during one of these "spankings"—made up for the violence the only way he knew how: by letting Angie back into the dark, glittering world of the nightclub.

Bettyjane, on the other hand, was adamant about seeking therapy for her son, despite the fact that Skinny forbade it. "Only crazy people go to psychiatrists," he would say, dismissing her pleas for professional help. Eventually, with her household allowance, she took Angelo to a psychiatrist behind Skinny's back. During the evaluation, the doctor asked Angelo to draw a picture of his home. He drew an exaggerated house with tiny windows and doors. The doctor told Bettyjane that this signified that Angie didn't feel loved at home—and that he was shutting people out.

Fearful that Angelo was going to injure himself and the rest of the family, the psychiatrist suggested that Bettyjane put a lock on the outside of his door to keep him in his room at night. Always a clever kid, Angelo got a knife, hid it in his room, and whittled away at the wood, eventually getting free. On other occasions, he would throw everything in his room that he could lift out the window. In desperation, Bettyjane bought restraints and, at night, anchored her son to the bed. By fifth grade, Angelo started stealing. One night, he took one of his mother's diamond rings, hid it under the mat outside on the back steps, picked it up the next morning on his way to school, and gave it to a girl. When Bettyjane discovered the ring was missing, she marched down to city hall and had her son "arrested" later that day at his Little League game. He was only ten years old.

A couple of years later, Bettyjane thought she had misplaced several hundred dollars earmarked for Paulajane's car insurance (the family paid for everything in cash). By this time, Bettyjane was suffering memory blackouts from her aneurysm, so she was blaming herself for the missing money—she was literally losing her mind. Angie came home from school one day to find his mother tearing her closets apart. "*I'll* help you!" he volunteered. Together they looked through hatboxes, coat pockets, and dresser drawers, to no avail. A week later, the owner of Phil's Pizzeria—a block from the junior high Angelo attended—called Bettyjane. "I don't know if I should be calling you," he said, "but your son came in here with $700 and said, 'Here's money for me or any of my friends. Just deduct from it when we come in.'"

When Angelo was only eleven years old, one of Skinny's friends hired a prostitute to deflower the young boy, a favor that would be repeated many times before he was out of puberty. He was learning from his father's world all too well. Bettyjane was jealous of Angelo because Skinny spent so much time with him, singled him out and raised him almost separately from the girls. After a while, admitted a family friend, "Bettyjane just didn't want to be bothered with Angelo."

Finally, the decision was made to send Angelo to Archmere Academy, an exclusive private boys' school in Claymont, Delaware, where Joe Del Raso was going to school and where Joe's father, Vince, was on the board. On a warm September day in 1972, Bettyjane—driven by family chauffeur Cooks Books—took Angelo to Archmere to drop him off for his first semester. There were about three hundred boys enrolled, and out of those, only about ten actually boarded there. Bettyjane spent the day with her son, getting him settled in his room, and then spent the evening with the Del Rasos in Valley Forge before she and Cooks drove back to Atlantic City. It was the last time Angelo would see his mother alive.

Not surprisingly, Angelo has a very different take on his childhood. "Cathy told me that it was true," he said of the trip to the shrink. "That they said I made a house and the windows were small. I don't believe any of that stuff. I did *not* feel unloved. I don't look at it like that. I had a good time growing up." When I mentioned that someone told me that Bettyjane was jealous over how close he and Skinny were, he said, "Well, I didn't know my mother too well. I regret it. I always wanted to be with my father, and I would just go to the club. My mother was always very close to Paula because maybe she was living her life through her. But I always felt that my father loved Cathy the most. Forget it. He loved Cathy. I think it was just bad for Cathy because she was the middle one and my mother was pushing for Paula with the contests and all that.

"But I always wanted to be at the club. I didn't care what time it was. My mother was sick, and I didn't know it because I was too young. I would stay at the club until six in the morning and hang out with all my father's friends. They would fix me up, too, thinking they would get in good with my father. I would never tell my father if I was with a waitress or something. Here I am thirteen years old, what am I supposed to do? One time, I was showing Frank Sinatra's mother around the club and she hands me $100. She said, 'Is that your friend?' and she handed him $20. I would hang out and cook and watch the shows. Sometimes I worked the spotlight. One night I was there making sandwiches and I sliced my thumb and they took me to the hospital. And there's my mother on another gurney because she had one of her attacks. I said to the doctor, 'You gotta take care of her before you take care of me.'"

September 11, 1972, was a beautiful, sunny day. Skinny was up and getting ready to leave for the club by around eleven A.M. Bettyjane was still in bed, and before he left, he brought her a glass of milk. Cathy, who was now attending classes at Atlantic County Community College, was off at school. Paulajane spent the day in the backyard, sunning herself. When Cathy got home around two P.M., Paulajane said, "Wake Mommy up. She has a hair appointment at three." She and Skinny were to attend a charity benefit later that evening.

Bettyjane often slept very late. She kept her room cold and dark, with the air conditioner blasting all night. When Cathy came back into Paulajane's bedroom and said, "I can't wake her," Paulajane stood straight up as if she had been given an electric shock. She ran into her parents' room, turned on the chandeliers, and knew instantly that her mother was dead. The aneurysm had finally burst, and there were bodily fluids leaking out of her eyes and ears and nose. Paulajane called

Chris Owen, and then she and Cathy jumped in Paulajane's Corvette and raced over to get her. When Chris got to her bedside, she leapt on top of Bettyjane and pounded on her chest, screaming, "Jesus Christ, Bettyjane, breathe!"

Eventually Paulajane called her father at the club as well as Dr. McCracken, who lived two doors down. The doctor came over to pronounce her mother dead. Skinny left the club and brought with him Reverend Conklin, who had been having lunch at Angelo's. As Skinny arrived at the top of the stairs, Dr. McCracken was just coming out of his bedroom and said, "I'm sorry, Skinny." He became lifeless and silent as he hugged his daughters. Then he went into his bedroom and closed the door and stayed in there alone with his wife's dead body for what seemed to Paulajane like an eternity. Friends started showing up at the house, which within a few hours was filled with dozens of people.

Angelo had been at Archmere for only a week. He was outside playing football when a priest told him that the headmaster wanted to see him immediately. "I go to this office with a big desk and a big chair. He said, 'I have something to tell you. It's very bad news. Your grandmother died.' So I say to myself, Well, she is only nine thousand years old, and he said, 'Did you hear me?' and I said, 'Yeah, you told me that my grandmother died,' and he said, 'No, your *mother* died.' I was in shock. They drove me home right away, and my father heard I was pulling up to the house and he came outside and brought me in. I'm not trying to sound like a creep here, I'm basically trying to be honest, but I was really more just sad for my father. And I will say this—and this is not a shot at my mother at all—but if she hadn't died, I think my father's life would have been so much different. Because my father would never have stayed at the house for those last ten years of his life."

Paulajane has long felt that her mother's death was the major defining moment of her life—not just because she lost her mother, but because, in a way, she had to *become* her mother. Her relationship to her siblings and her father changed almost that very instant. The next day, she picked out the coffin, the flowers, and the clothes her mother would be buried in. "My father couldn't do any of that," said Paulajane. "He was the adult, but he just couldn't do it. I had help, but generally people at that age don't plan funerals. Unfortunately for me, in my life,

I've gotten very good at planning funerals. That's one thing I know how to do well."

Skinny was adamant that it be a Catholic ceremony and he wanted Father Pasquale Dibuono (whom everyone called Father Pat) at St. Michael's to preside over the ceremony. "You can't do this to Mommy," Paulajane would plead with him; Bettyjane had said over and over to her daughters, "Don't let your father bury me Catholic." Apparently, she had agreed to renew her marriage vows in a Catholic church in 1969 only to appease Skinny. Paulajane had always rolled her eyes at her mother's protestations, but now she understood. She and Skinny argued over the burial, and then finally Paulajane proposed a compromise: Why can't it be both? Skinny acquiesced. They had the service at the funeral parlor with both Father Pat *and* Reverend Conklin presiding. Toots Shor came from New York with his wife, and Frank Sinatra cabled regrets from England. The *Atlantic City Press* reported that it was the largest viewing in Atlantic City in many years. "That was the first time that my father and I compromised," said Paulajane. It was the beginning of her efforts to take control of the D'Amato legend.

Angelo finished out the year at Archmere, but because of his terrible grades, he failed and had to repeat ninth grade the next year. He eventually convinced his father not to send him back, and for his third year of high school, he enrolled in Holy Spirit, a Catholic school just outside Atlantic City known for producing rowers and lifeguards and surfers. But Skinny had returned to his premarried life of living above the club, and he had a new girlfriend named Terry. In fact, after Bettyjane's death but before the club burned down, Skinny spent not a single night sleeping at home. He stayed at the 500 Club nearly twenty-four hours a day, coming home only to have dinner with his kids. More often than not, though, if they wanted to see him, they had to go to the club. "There was no supervision over Cathy and I," said Angelo.

Paulajane became responsible for her brother—and she was afraid of him. In the mornings, she made sure he got on the bus to go to school, but she couldn't stop him from getting off a few blocks away, which he did nearly every day. There were times when Paulajane would try to discipline Angie, but invariably he would react with violence, sometimes pinning her to the ground. Angelo never took to Holy Spirit, never fit in among the jocks and preppies, and before his sophomore year was over he was thrown out for lack of attendance.

Angelo eventually dropped out of school altogether and began working full-time at the restaurant named after him. He enjoyed being around his father's powerful friends, and most of the people who knew him well as a kid agreed that Angie wasn't all bad, that there was another side to him—he could be charming and funny, and like his father, he was tall and good-looking and had a dazzling smile. He also had his mother's beautiful, sad brown eyes. Angie discovered, to everyone's surprise, that he liked to cook, and he was beginning to thrive at his father's game of entertaining people. Everyone, including Angelo, assumed that he would take over the old man's business one day.

✦

It was a Sunday, just before noon on June 10, 1973, and Paulajane was trying to be happy, trying not to think too much about the loss of her mother several months earlier. She was distracted by the company of friends as she tanned herself on the rooftop of a building where her boyfriend, Bobby Palamaro, lived, just a block from the 500 Club. Bobby was an Atlantic City cop. He was sixteen years older than Paulajane and had five children from a previous marriage that had ended shortly before he met Paulajane. Skinny liked Bobby, but he disapproved of their relationship because Bobby already had a family, and he wasn't confident that he would be able to "provide" for his daughter. But after five years of fighting it, even Skinny could see that they were in love and there was nothing he could do. When he finally showed up at a birthday party Paulajane held for Bobby and gave his blessing, there wasn't a dry eye in the room.

Bobby lived on Arkansas Avenue in a very small one-bedroom apartment on the third floor of a brick walk-up, where in the summer, Paulajane and her friends spent time hanging out on the roof with the other tenants in the building. But on that hot summer morning, billowing black smoke dirtied the sky, a little too close for comfort. "It's the club!" yelled someone from the street.

Paulajane bolted down the stairs and across the street, through a little alleyway that came out behind the 500, where she found the porter, Paul Stoneburner, in a panic. "Where's my father?" she screamed.

"Out front!" he yelled. "In the street!"

She raced around the side of the building, through the parking lot. She found Skinny in the lot across Missouri Avenue, staring up at the club, holding back tears as flames shot through the roof and smoke belched skyward. It was Stoneburner who had discovered the fire in the stage area of the club's main showroom, and he'd run to get Skinny, who was sitting at a table in Angelo's Restaurant with Jimmy Ceres, a club employee. Angelo had been asleep in the apartment upstairs. "I had just moved all my stuff from Suffolk Avenue into the front room, above the club," he said. "I worked that night from ten P.M. until six in the morning, and I'd gone to bed at eight A.M. Next thing I know, Jimmy Ceres is at the door. Fire! Fire! The firemen had to break down the door to get me out. I lost everything, all my stuff."

Eventually Cathy arrived, and then the press. "That's where my kids were born—where they grew up," said Skinny, pointing to the second-floor windows as tears began streaming down his sunken cheeks. He lowered his head, wiped his face, and looked up. "I'll rebuild. I don't know how, but I'll try. I'm going to keep going. I was born on this street." A moment later, he was entertaining reporters with stories about Dean Martin and Frank Sinatra.

Turned out the fire was electrical and started behind the stage of the showroom, climbed up the stage curtains, spread very quickly to the ceiling, and raged for four hours, destroying the entire complex, including the Next Door tavern and most of Angelo's Restaurant. More than two hundred firefighters from all over Absecon Island battled the blaze while hundreds of spectators watched from behind barricades that had been set up to redirect traffic on Atlantic Avenue. Hundreds more stood on the Boardwalk a block and a half away and watched as a piece of history turned to ash and rubble. In a front-page story the next day, *The New York Times* described the club as "one of the most famous entertainment spots on the East Coast" and noted that the damage was estimated at $2 million. The piece went on to describe other, more painful, losses, including "Mr. D'Amato's collection of photographs and signatures of the famed entertainers who played there over the years since he acquired the club in 1942."

Like Grauman's Chinese Theatre in Hollywood, the 500 Club had a cement pavement outside that was an attraction unto itself, featuring hand- and footprints and signatures of nearly an entire generation of celebrities. Over the years, as the cement was poured and stars made an appearance to "sign" their names and push their hands or feet in the cold, wet cement, the club's house band would set up and play outside while hundreds of people gathered to witness this odd, distinctly American spectacle. The *Times* listed them: "Frank Sinatra, Paul Whiteman, Sophie Tucker, Milton Berle, Patti Page, Sammy Davis Jr., Perry Como, Walter Winchell, Joe DiMaggio, Donald O'Connor, Eartha Kitt, Jack E. Leonard, Joe E. Lewis, Jersey Joe Walcott, Nat King Cole, the McGuire Sisters, Roberta Sherwood, Jimmy Durante, Zsa Zsa Gabor, Eddie Fisher, Alan King, Louis Prima, Keely Smith, Liberace, Jackie Gleason, Mickey Rooney, Danny Thomas, Joey Bishop, Johnny Rae, and Joey Adams."

The cement imprints survived the fire and were eventually moved to a warehouse in Philadelphia owned by Vince Del Raso, Dolores's husband and Joe's father, until they could be installed in Skinny's backyard in Ventnor. But just after the fire had been brought under control that day, Skinny toured the smoking ruins and discovered that the only thing in the club itself that had been untouched by flames was a huge framed photographic portrait of Sinatra, still hanging in what was left of the front room of the club. "This has to be a good omen," Skinny said to a reporter. "It's God's way of assuring me that the future is secure. It's a miracle." But, of course, it wasn't a miracle. It was just dumb luck.

✦

What the *Times* didn't report, and what most people didn't realize, was that Skinny's dream of turning the 500 Club back into a casino—this time legally—also went up in smoke that day. Throughout the late 1960s and early 1970s, the FBI kept Skinny under surveillance pretty much around the clock. They seemed particularly interested in his finances and any expansions or modifications he was making to his property on Missouri Avenue, which is to say that they were watching to see if he was turning to his old tricks and bringing back gambling to keep his enterprise afloat. From his FBI file, 1968: "The renovations at the club are going to cost $200,000 which D'Amato claims he does not have. He has decided to discontinue having shows during the winter months and confine them to . . . summer. He said . . . he had not made any plans to have Frank Sinatra appear. He said there is talk every year about Sinatra coming to the club, which is unfortunate for him as a number of persons hold off on their vacations in Atlantic City thinking that they will plan them for the time Frank comes and he does not show. He said Sinatra is only doing one show a night as he is apparently slowing down."

In March 1968, two agents sat down with Skinny at the 500 Club at Skinny's request. "D'Amato stated that there was a rumor in Atlantic City to the effect he was fronting for XXXXXX [most likely Angelo Bruno] and was taking over gambling and shylocking in Atlantic City. He stated he wanted to set the record straight. . . ." The report went on to detail how Skinny had been offered a book in a cigar store as well as a horse book and that Skinny declined the offers: "D'Amato further advised that he does not have any money out as a shylock and in fact borrowed $3,000 himself from a shylock last week. . . . D'Amato denied membership in La Cosa Nostra (LCN) and said that for years he was accused of activities which in fact were the activities of XXXXXX also known as XXXXXX [again, probably Bruno]. He said that he could have avoided considerable trouble with the IRS had he been in a position to refute these allegations but that anything he might have said would have injured XXXXXX and as a result he remained silent. . . . D'Amato stated further that he knew of no outside influence in Atlantic City nor was there any connection with organized crime in Atlantic City. He stated he would not countenance anyone coming into Atlantic City in an effort to take over the town and if such an effort were made he would notify the FBI."

Then there was this report in his file from December 1969: "D'Amato said he has not seen or heard from Sam Giancana since 1963, and as far as he knows, Giancana has not been East. There would be no reason to expect that Giancana would contact him should he come to either New York or New Jersey. He said the last time Giancana got out of jail, he left immediately for Mexico were he spent some time. He described Giancana as being a very quiet person. . . . He said it was his impression that the 'money' boys in Las Vegas were getting old and tired of trying to run the gambling casinos with the Government and everyone else on their back, along with the unfavorable publicity they were getting. He said that they would have sold out much cheaper than they did, but apparently Howard Hughes' organization offered them top dollar for the clubs."

In 1999, I began meeting surreptitiously with a black woman in her mid-sixties who worked undercover at the 500 Club when she was in her mid-twenties. She got the job through her husband's brother around 1967. Every week, the FBI wired money to a Western Union office on Tennessee Avenue, which she picked up and used to create the illusion that she was a pricey lady of the evening. "And it was a lot of money," she said, "because in order for me to have the look, the ambiance, I had to wear furs and expensive dresses and jewelry and perfume." Officially there were no women FBI agents at the time, but they used women frequently. "They told us, 'If you get caught in a compromising situation, you're on your own.' They didn't give us much protection."

Once a week she would meet up with two agents, who took notes on her reports of the shenanigans at the 500. The FBI were mostly interested in catching "crooked cops," she said, but she was also there to "watch Skinny, the gambling, people who came and went, organized-crime figures." Occasionally, she would get invited to the back room by a Mob guy or a half-baked entertainer who wanted to act like a big shot. "When you walked in the front door," she said, "you would turn left and there was a hall, just after the coat check. If you went down the hall and veered to your right, there were these . . . *offices*. That's where the gambling took place, because . . . they were not offices. There were some very high stakes card games. Money would be all over the tables. People would make $100,000 bets. It was unbelievable. And there was a roulette wheel in one room. Skinny had some very sophisticated gambling equipment brought in primarily because he thought that, at some point, gambling was going to be legalized in Atlantic City and he wanted to be the first casino to open. He had plans to turn the large showroom into a casino, but . . ."

When I met this woman, she was a faceless bureaucrat in Atlantic City, with a big office at city hall and an inflated title stenciled on her door. The few times I visited her, she seemed to have absolutely nothing to do. She showed me pictures of her kids, both in their thirties, and said I couldn't use her name because she had never told them about Mama's shady past. It occurred to me that if anyone would know whether Skinny was in the Mafia, it would be this formidable woman. I said to her: Skinny is constantly described as a "pimp" or an "underworld figure" or a "gangster." "No," she said impatiently, "he wasn't any of those things. I never saw anything on Skinny that indicated he was in the Mob. He was just a man trying to make a living. His brother Willie used to try to shake down the girls [read: prostitutes] at the bar, but Skinny had nothing to do with any of that."

I asked her, What was your gut feeling about Skinny—as a person, not somebody the FBI was watching? She looked at me for a long time and then said, "I don't know." Long pause. "I didn't like him." Why? "He was oily." I must have looked dumbfounded, because she nearly shouted, "I don't know any better way to describe it!" When I told her that she was the first and only person to say a single bad word about him and reminded her that *oily* was a not-so-subtle slur, she said dismissively, "Oh, please. Him being Italian has nothing to do with it! I looked at him in a different way than most people did. Everyone looked up to him and idolized him because he had money—or at least he appeared to. He probably could have cursed them out and spit in their face and they still would have said he was a wonderful guy because he was up there and they thought they were down here. But if you were in my position and you looked at him, what you saw was a person who was *oily*. You don't associate with the kinds of people he associated with on a day-to-day basis and think you're going to look like snow. You're going to be oily. And you *have* to be oily to do it. The nightclub business is a dirty business. I think Skinny was *somebody*—he became a somebody—but I don't think he became all that he wanted to be, in spite of the fact that he hooked up with so many people from so many walks of life."

We talked for a while about the city and the almost clownish aspect of its corruption, and she laughed and said, "I have never seen a police department so crooked. It was *unbelievable*. Today, it's cleaned up. You have a few dirty cops, like anywhere, but you can't do the things you used to be able to get away with in those days. It was a different world and a different time. A person like Skinny D'Amato couldn't exist today. He had so much influence. He was friends with entertainers *and* the Mob guys *and* the politicians. A president wouldn't associate with a guy like Skinny D'Amato today. And if he did, it would be all over the news in two seconds. Everybody would know his name. He would be so famous. Skinny was able to operate in the way he did because he lived before the media went crazy."

✦

One can clearly see from Skinny's FBI file that they were also keeping a close tab on the ever noisier rumblings in the ever crazier media about the notion of legalizing gambling in Atlantic City in general. But, as usual, all roads eventually led to Skinny. Talk of legalization began in earnest at a stag party at the Shelburne Hotel on the Boardwalk in December 1968. It was a surprise black tie birthday dinner for Skinny that also doubled as a miniconference of influential Atlantic City and Philadelphia businessmen and politicians to discuss legalization. The ruse the group came up with to get Skinny to the party without him knowing was that they were having a formal dinner for Mack Latz, then owner of the legendary (and still open) Knife & Fork Inn. "I don't know why I gotta put a goddamn tuxedo on for *that* guy," Skinny complained. "He doesn't even wear *socks*!"

"Gambling in Atlantic City was born that night," said Vince Del Raso, who attended the dinner. "I came down from Philly and took Skinny to the dinner, and he was all excited. He said, 'Geez, Vince, everybody's here.' The group included Skinny's best friends: Tony

Maglio, who owned a sausage company in Philadelphia now run by his son; Joe Dykes; chief of Atlantic City police Mario Floriani; Judge Angelo Malandra; and *Press* columnist Sonny Schwartz. Also seated at the horseshoe-shaped table that night were John Kenny, the legendary political boss from Hudson County, New Jersey; Hap Farley; Atlantic City commissioners Arthur Ponzio and Karlos LaSane; the mayor of Ventnor, Mike Segal; and about fifteen others.

"We went around the table," said Vince, "and everybody had to say something. We discussed how depressed Atlantic City had become and how gambling was the only thing that could save it. We all decided to unite behind legalization. We heard later that somebody from Las Vegas approached Mike Segal and told him to forget about the whole thing." It was at this party that Skinny was informally anointed Mr. Atlantic City; the title was conferred as well as displayed on a huge banner, and it stuck.

On January 31, 1971, a piece by Herb Wolfe appeared simultaneously in the *Trenton Times* (D'AMATO ENJOYS ROLE AS RESORT'S NO. 1 CITIZEN) and the *Atlantic City Press* (CASINOS SPELL PLUSH TIMES FOR "SKINNY"). The piece, which was the first to publicize the movement toward legalization, began with a strange introduction that foreshadowed the difficulties ahead for Skinny: "His fans say he's the best of the good guys. His detractors charge he's the worst of the bad guys . . . ," but he's "the man to be reckoned with if and when casino gambling is introduced in New Jersey's No. 1 resort."

When Wolfe asked Skinny if he planned to open a casino, he said, "What do I need that for? I'm getting old. All I want to do is sell this place." But then he conceded that, yes, in fact, he would like to convert the club's main showroom into a casino. "The best way for the city to handle legalized gambling," Skinny said, "would be to tear down the old hotels and build plush new casinos in their place. Make it another Vegas." (That, of course, is exactly what happened ten years later.) Skinny also expressed doubts that the state legislature would vote to hold a referendum on legalizing gambling, and he placed the blame squarely on the shoulders of New Jersey governor William T. Cahill. "I don't know why he's against it," said Skinny. "He doesn't have anything to do with it. You know, he's even written letters against it." Then, in a rare self-aggrandizing burst of ego, Skinny asked Wolfe, "In this whole country, who do people think of when they think of Atlantic City?"

"Hap Farley," said Wolfe.

"No!" said Skinny, slapping his palm on the table, voice rising. "He's not even best known in New Jersey. It's me, Skinny D'Amato."

But then Skinny's dreams burned to the ground. Exactly three months after the 500 Club fire, Skinny's friends once again threw a big party to help him rebuild the 500 Club. The $100-a-plate dinner in the Pennsylvania Room at the Haddon Hall was attended by 1,100. Comedian Corbett Monica performed, as did the ever loyal Cooks Books, who was a singing cabdriver when Skinny hired him as his chauffeur. Then Enzo Stuarti brought Skinny to tears by singing his favorite song, "Mamma." From the stage Stuarti proclaimed: "Skinny is immortal."

But by now, Skinny had come to expect that he would be held up as a model citizen one minute and reduced to common hoodlum the next. A month after the party, a piece appeared in *New York* magazine about the New Jersey gubernatorial campaign of Charlie Sandman, a Republican from south Jersey who was running against Brendan Byrne, a Democrat from the north. The damning piece included this rhetorical question: "Will Charles Sandman return campaign contributions he received from convicted felons and reputed underworld figures such as . . . 'Stumpy' Orman and 'Skinny' D'Amato?" The piece was illustrated with a picture of Skinny looking incredibly suave and handsome in his tux at the testimonial dinner at the Haddon Hall—shaking hands with Charlie Sandman.

Brendan Byrne won that election, a turn of events that favored Skinny and Atlantic City more than anyone realized. Shortly after being elected, Byrne publicly committed himself to placing the question of "casino-type gambling" on a referendum to save Atlantic City from sliding any further into hell. With that promise, Skinny's outlook on the resort's future—and his own—gelled into something like cynical optimism, if there is such a thing. D'AMATO TALKS OF REBUILDING CLUB, BUT THINGS WON'T EVER BE THE SAME, read the headline in the *Atlantic City Press* a few weeks after Byrne took office. In the front-page story,

Skinny said he planned to rebuild "on the order of a Holiday Inn operation with sleeping rooms, as well as banquet, dining and entertainment rooms. Of course, if gambling comes in, then that will be a whole new set of circumstances that would revamp all plans and considerations." He went on to say that the 500 Club was the best possible location in Atlantic City because it was situated at the mouth of the Atlantic City Expressway, and it was the first thing people saw as they arrived.

By early 1974, all the dreamy talk about legalized gambling in New Jersey had congealed into something a little more solid, which in turn invited real estate speculation in the resort. Anthony DiTullio, an Atlantic City native who was then president of Hyatt International in Chicago, announced that he was in negotiations to buy—as an individual—the Claridge Hotel for a little over $3 million. He said that he planned to build twin office and condominium towers behind the Claridge, to be dubbed Park Place Plaza. The 1929 redbrick hotel tower set back from the Boardwalk would be turned into a luxury hotel with several nightclubs for a total cost of $15 million. This was very big news, and it inaugurated the speculative Atlantic City gold rush that continues to this day.

It is hard to grasp the significance of an out-in-the-open discussion of legalized gambling in New Jersey in the early 1970s, because today, some form of gambling is legal in forty-eight states. All day every day there are ads on television for casino gambling. Lotteries are now conducted by thirty-seven state governments. Horse race betting is permitted in forty-two states, and nineteen states allow dog race wagering. Out of national guilt, we "let" Native Americans build casinos and keep almost all the money for themselves. More than $550 billion is gambled each year in the United States—more money than is spent on recorded music and movies together. There are more visits to gambling facilities than to all professional sports events combined. But just a few decades ago, legalized gambling existed in casinos in exactly one place: Nevada. Beginning with New Hampshire in 1964, state after state caved in and institutionalized lotteries—which are essentially cigar store books—as a way to raise tax revenue (gambling enterprises now produce over $16 billion in special taxes and employ 650,000 people nationwide). The vote in New Jersey was considered crucial to the legalization movement, as it would finally throw the doors wide open.

In October 1974, when it was certain that New Jersey voters were going to get the chance to vote in a gambling referendum, another article appeared in the *Atlantic City Press:* D'AMATO SEES CASINO PARADISE. Skinny held forth in the piece about the fact that "Atlantic City was the original Las Vegas," as it was brimming with gambling dens through the 1920s and 1930s. He also claimed he was broke and that the 500 Club property was heavily mortgaged.

On election day, voters decided against legalization in their state, and by December, Skinny was forced to sell all of his holdings on Missouri Avenue. Skinny talked neighbor Vince Del Raso into buying the parking lots across the street from the 500 Club at a tax sale. "So my father owned them for a while," says Joe Del Raso, "and then he sold it to the group that put Caesars together." Fred Davis of Reading, Pennsylvania, foreclosed on the mortgage he held on the 500 Club (in what Davis characterized as a "friendly foreclosure"), extinguishing debt of $395,000. A few years later, the land was resold to Donald Trump for several million, and he built a parking garage. Today, as you arrive in Atlantic City via the Expressway, the first two things you see are a gigantic Trump Plaza sign with a waterfall under it and a rather bland, monolithic parking garage owned by Caesars.

Less than a year after Skinny finally gave up on his dream of rebuilding and sold the property, he had his first heart attack. On April 24, 1975, he was at a friend's house in Brigantine, the island north of Atlantic City, having dinner with a bunch of his friends. As dinner ended, he wasn't feeling well; at first, he thought it was indigestion, so he took some Brioschi—the Italian Alka-Seltzer. As he was ready to leave, he realized something was wrong—he was feeling strange—so his friends took him to the Atlantic City Medical Center, where it was discovered after several tests that his heart was in bad shape.

Skinny had moved back home to Suffolk Avenue after the 500 Club fire, but almost immediately after his heart attack, it seemed as if he moved his entire *life* into his bedroom—a coffee urn, a refrigerator, the card table, a telephone, and, of course, all his meetings with friends and associates. People were constantly pulling up in their big cars and traipsing up and down the orange-carpeted stairs to pay homage to—or play gin or two-handed pinochle with—the great Skinny D'Amato. Other than occasional trips to Philadelphia, New York, or Florida, or parties and charity events in and around Atlantic City, Skinny spent much of the last ten years of his life hardly ever getting out of his silk pajamas and paisley bathrobe.

His very strange schedule went like this: He got up at eleven A.M. and stayed in his room until three P.M., at which point he would nap for an hour. Then he came downstairs to eat dinner at seven P.M.; sometimes Paulajane would cook him dinner, sometimes he would go next door to the Del Rasos' for dinner, where Dolores's mother would cook him all the dishes he'd loved when he was a child. In any event, he would retire to his room once again after dinner to watch television. *Sanford & Son* was his favorite show. He went back to sleep around nine or ten P.M. until twelve-thirty A.M. Cooks Books would bring his boss all the New York and Philadelphia newspapers for the next day, which he would read until he went back to sleep at seven-thirty A.M. Nearly every night, Skinny would receive visitors—movie stars, gangsters, local officials—and could play his beloved card games. When he was alone he played baseball solitaire, a game with strange and complicated rules that he had learned in prison.

Indeed, the clearest memory his only grandchild—Paulajane's daughter, Devon—has of Skinny is watching him, propped up in bed, playing cards on a yellow plastic TV table that he would cover with a piece of foam and a towel, his one long fingernail clicking against the cards as he shuffled and dealt. Devon was only five when he died. She also remembers his most important piece of advice. "Devon," he would say to his brown-eyed girl, "whatever you do with your life . . . don't be a stool pigeon."

Skinny smoked a hundred cigarettes a day, though he switched from Kent to Carlton, the lowest-nicotine cigarette available. He poked holes in the paper wrapping with a little contraption someone had given him in an attempt to inhale even less smoke. One friend remembers that, toward the end, he starting putting honey in his coffee instead of sugar because, as he once said, "it's healthier." On one occasion, Angelo noticed that every time the phone rang, Skinny had to get up from his card game to answer it. So he tried to help his father out. "I got a really long extension cord, hooked it up to the phone, and put it right next to him. So he plays cards all night, and when he finished, he pulled me aside and said, 'Listen. Don't do that.' I said, 'Don't do what?' And he said, 'Don't put the phone next to me.' And I said, 'Why not?' And he said, 'That's how I get my exercise!' I said, 'Your exercise? You gotta be kidding me!' He said, 'It rings twenty-five times a day! I get up, I walk over.'"

On those nights when he would get dressed, go next door, and sit at the Del Rasos' dinner table, it was as if Skinny were trying to achieve, at least for a moment, a sense of normalcy. The Del Rasos were, and still are, an extended, loving Italian family who, in an ever changing world, cling to their old-fashioned hardworking values and their unshakable sense of right and wrong. The D'Amatos, thanks to Skinny's choice in life, were in nearly every way unconventional, over the top, larger than life.

The young Joe Del Raso, out of a job the summer the club burned down, sat up many nights with Skinny watching westerns and Frank Sinatra movies and reminiscing about the glory days of the forties and fifties. Another young acolyte of Skinny's, Ricky Apt, who was a friend of Angelo's, recalled a story about visiting Skinny not long after Sinatra testified in 1981 before the Nevada Gaming Commission. Apt told Skinny that he was about to get his hands on a pilfered videotape of Sinatra's testimony. "You gotta bring that over when you get it," said Skinny. Only problem was that Skinny didn't have a videocassette recorder, so Apt had to bring his VCR. "I had to hook it up to his TV in the bedroom," he said. "Remember the early VCRs? In those days, they weighed about nine hundred pounds. Skinny's bedroom was on the second floor, and I remember carrying the damn thing up the steps, feeling like I was getting a hernia. So I hooked it up, and it was two hours of testimony by Frank, and I watched it with Skinny."

Every time Frank testified to one thing or another, Skinny told Apt what really went down. "Frank lied about everything," said Skinny. "They asked him about the Fischetti brothers. Frank said, 'Well, I may have been a passenger on the same plane, but we didn't socialize.' They didn't *socialize*? They stayed on his fucking boat for two and a half weeks! He should have gotten the Oscar for this, not for *From Here to Eternity*!"

Skinny, said Joe Del Raso, "had a mind that went a mile a minute. For someone without a formal education, he was nobody's fool. I think he was just born with natural talents and charisma. If he had been born to a family of wealth and means, he probably would have been a senator, but he wasn't, so he used his charisma on the streets to propel himself to prominence. Here was a guy who didn't have insecurities. He was *always* the top dog. The look, the way he held a cigarette in his mouth. He was older than Frank Sinatra. The relationships get blurred between the wiseguys and Skinny and Frank, but the glue that held them together was that when Frank was down, Skinny took good care of him. Frank never forgot that."

As Angelo pointed out, incredulously, "In Nancy Sinatra's book, [*Frank Sinatra: An*] *American Legend*, she's got that my father *asked* Frank to perform. My father would never do that. I've got my father on a tape from an interview in the sixties saying, 'I never asked Frank to perform.' Frank was a funny guy. He'd call up and say, 'Skinny, how ya doin'? Need anything?' And then he'd call a few days later and say, 'How about these ten days in August.' That's how it would happen. He'd never say, 'Listen, Frank, why don't you come perform in my club for me.' My father would never put him in that position."

Another mistake in *American Legend* that annoyed the D'Amatos is that Nancy Sinatra wrote that Sam Giancana owned the 500 Club. Of all the different versions of Skinny's ties to the Mob, that was a new one. To this day no one knows what, if any, Skinny's relationship was to the underworld. Some of the old-timers don't think he was "a member of the Mob," because he always ran his own show, had the ability to do big favors, and moved freely about the country, whether playing cards in Florida in the winter or running his club in Atlantic City in the summer.

Before Bettyjane died, she once asked Vince Del Raso's wife, Dolores, "Is Skinny in the Mob?" and Dolores said, "You're asking *me*?" Whenever anyone had the nerve to ask Skinny himself, he always said: "There is no Mob in Atlantic City." "All those years," said Joe Del Raso, "and you're not going to find anything. The other answer Skinny always used to give was that he was on the periphery of everything, including these guys who he grew up with as well as the rich and powerful. I worked the day shift at the club and never perceived the presence of organized crime in the late sixties and early seventies. I would assume they were around at different times—not unlike the businessmen and politicians who would come in for lunch and dinner. There is no doubt that Skinny was an influential man who did many favors and traveled in a wide circle. He moved about and did as he pleased without interference from any organized group. Skinny went to the debutante ball in New York City at the Waldorf-Astoria when my sister came out, and all these society people were coming up to him. He'd say, 'Oh, yeah, I remember that guy, he used to come into the place in Palm Beach.' We were walking into the '21' Club for lunch and Herb Siegel, the chairman of the board of Chris-Craft, smacks him on the back to say hello."

Father George Riley, a man who's been friendly with the Del Rasos for many years and who gives the invocation at so many Jersey-Philly events that he has been called the "George Jessel of the Catholic gentry," met Skinny through the Del Rasos shortly after Skinny took to his room. They became fast friends. "I knew Skinny the last eight years of his life," said Riley. "He and I went down to Florida to visit the Del Rasos a couple of times in the winter together, and it was like walking through the airport with Jesus Christ. One of the happiest days of Skinny's life was a day we spent together in New York in 1976. His wife had died, he'd lost the club. For some reason he was in New York, and I flew up from Washington to meet him. We went to the '21' Club and it was like his last hurrah. Everything clicked. It was wild. Every place we went. Then we were over at some place on Central Park South. Toots Shor was still alive. I never saw him happier. Everyone yelled, 'Skinny!' You walk down the street with him and he was a legend. He was a really charismatic guy. He was a very gentle guy. That's what I liked about him. He was smooth and kind. And sentimental. That was one of his nicest days. . . . And then the tragedy happened after that with his son."

On the very last page of Paul Emilio "Skinny" D'Amato's FBI file, there's a report dated May 12, 1976, that reads: "Spot checks have been conducted on a weekly basis of the subject's residence, 12 South Suffolk Avenue, Ventnor, New Jersey, during the period October 2, 1975, through April 16, 1976. No activity reported. The subject continues to convalesce from a series of heart attacks suffered last year and has been inactive during the period of this report. In view of the above, this case is being closed."

What those bored FBI agents—men who had been tracking Skinny D'Amato's every move since the winter of 1961—could not have picked up from their dwindling "spot checks" of the mansion on Suffolk was something much uglier than anything their ailing subject had ever been capable of. What they could not see from inside their black sedans was the jealousy and rage and confusion building up inside Angelo. Indeed, they were after the wrong guy. Exactly two months after the FBI closed their fifteen-year investigation into his father, Angelo D'Amato came home from work one steamy July morning to Suffolk Avenue, went into the basement, where his friend Ronald Bodanza was sleeping, bludgeoned him with a baseball bat, stabbed him fifteen times with a kitchen knife, and then partially dismembered his corpse with a knife.

Chapter Ten

Angelo D'Amato has always said that the 500 Club fire was the worst thing that ever happened to him, because if the club hadn't burned down, he wouldn't have taken a job at Tony's Baltimore Grille. And if he hadn't taken a job at Tony's Baltimore Grille, he would never have met Ronald Bodanza. Ronnie, as everyone called him, was the son of Anne Battista, the first cousin of Lee Norato, the woman who owned the Penn Plaza Hotel. Anne left her abusive alcoholic husband in 1958, and for several months thereafter, she and her five children lived in a Philadelphia project, where they spent some time on welfare and where, more often than not, Anne begged door-to-door for anything kindly folks could spare: firewood, coal, money, food, clothes. Her children, from oldest to youngest, were Joseph, Ronnie, Joyce, Anthony, and Joanne, who died from cancer when she was just four. Anthony died of liver failure in 1993, and, of course, Ronnie met his end in a basement on Suffolk Avenue.

In 1959, Anne brought her children to live at the Penn Plaza Hotel, next door to the 500 Club. Her cousin Lee gave her a job cleaning rooms. Ronnie was just nine, but he worked shining shoes in front of the 500 Club. He was, said his sister Joyce, always out in front of the club with his shoeshine box. Anne, who first went to the 500 Club in the early 1940s, always knew of Skinny D'Amato from seeing him at the club during those postwar summers. In the late 1950s, when she was working at the Penn Plaza, she'd see him occasionally, but they were never formally introduced. "We'd sit out on the porch of the hotel, and we'd watch all these people going into the 500 Club. Skinny's brother Willie would be standing out front, and my Ronnie would chat with him because he was always out there, shining shoes. Skinny came out a couple times and Ronnie would come home and he used to feel so big because he shined Skinny's shoes. I'd say, 'Charge him a buck! He *owns* that club!'"

Anne eventually moved her family back to Philadelphia, and Ronnie, barely out of adolescence, "became a huckster," said Anne, "selling fruits and vegetables up and down the streets of South Philly." He also pulled a wagon around with him and picked through people's trash, looking for things he could sell. When he was just fourteen, he bought a pony named Jitterbug, hitched a cart to her, and charged kids fifteen cents for rides around the block. "Mom, you're not gonna have to worry about nothing," Ronnie would say as he gave her all the money he made, "because I'm going to make a lot of money and I'm going to buy you a house someday."

Ronnie dropped out of high school when he was sixteen and started working full-time at a restaurant called Dewey's. Anne eventually remarried and moved to Mississippi, where she worked as the manager of a McDonald's. Ronnie went with her but left after less than a year because he couldn't stand the humidity. He moved in with Anne's parents on Georgia Avenue in Atlantic City and took a job as a cook at Tony's Baltimore Grille, where he worked for eight years.

Tony's is an institution in Atlantic City that opened at the height of the resort's—and Skinny's—Prohibition heyday. Its roots actually go back to 1911, to a hat-cleaning business and sandwich shop on Front Street in Philadelphia. In 1927, Giuseppe Tarsitano, who had emigrated from Italy at the turn of the century, and his son John moved the Front Street business to the Inlet in Atlantic City, at Connecticut and Atlantic Avenues. In 1966, Giuseppe's son Tony moved the establishment again, to Iowa and Atlantic Avenues, where it remains, utterly unchanged, to this day. The appeal of the Baltimore Grille is that you can experience, for an hour or two, a lost world, one in which a bowl of ravioli, two meatballs, a basket full of hot bread and butter, and an ice-cold glass of beer costs less than $10 and you can smoke to your heart's content. The Baltimore Grille has been in the Tarsitano family since it began in Philadelphia and is now run by Tony's son, Mike Tarsitano, who is in partnership with the Rich family. But when Mike's father moved the business in 1966, they had planned to go into partnership with Skinny, who was looking to supplement his dwindling fortunes at the 500 Club. But then Skinny's tax problems took center stage in his life, making him less attractive as a business investment. "Atlantic City was always a neutral town," said Mike Tarsitano. "Anyone from any organization could come here, go to the 500 Club, and be sure when they walked out the door they weren't going to get shot in the head. There were a few people other than Hap Farley and Stumpy Orman who ran things here, but they ran it as a haven—this was Switzerland for the Mob."

When Ronnie Bodanza came to Atlantic City in the late 1960s, he wound up at Tony's. "He was my best employee," said Tarsitano. In the summers, he sometimes took a second job selling pizza on the Boardwalk. When he was just twenty years old, Ronnie made a down payment of $5,800 on a house for his mother in Atlantic City.

After the 500 Club burned down in 1973, Skinny went to Mike's father, Tony, and asked if he would give his son a job. Tony was happy to help Skinny, and Angelo ended up working side by side with Ronnie Bodanza in the pizza kitchen. They quickly became friends, and before long, said Anne, "that little pain in the ass was forever ringing our doorbell on Ventnor Avenue. Angelo was a gambler, just like his father. A gambling *fool*. Ronnie would say to me, 'Mom, as soon as that guy gets paid he blows his money on gambling. He'd do anything for money.' Ronnie was so generous, and Angelo would take advantage of his good nature." Ronnie often worked until four A.M., but Angelo didn't care what time he showed up on their doorstep to ring the bell, usually looking to borrow a car—or some money. "He's sleeping," Anne would say.

"But I just want to talk to him," Angelo would plead.

Anne would relent and let him in. After he got whatever it was that he came for, Ronnie would say to Anne, "Mom, he's such a pest. He's nuts. That kid's not happy unless he has a pocket full of money, and if he does have a pocket full of money, he blows it in a second. And then he's looking for more money."

Ronnie also had a taste for the high life. He was forever renting limousines and taking half a dozen friends to the Latin Casino, a nightclub in Cherry Hill, just outside Philadelphia. (In fact, the Latin Casino sort of filled the void left by the 500 Club fire.) Ronnie also spent a small fortune on clothes; he was usually dressed in that flashy super-'70s open-collared look with a gold chain around his neck. And he loved spending money on other people—which, of course, sounds an awful lot like Skinny, whom Ronnie idolized, according to Joyce Bodanza. "He was very impressed and intrigued with that whole scene," she said. "He got involved where he shouldn't have been involved." Said Anne: "Oh, my Ronnie thought it was heaven on earth to be mixed up with Skinny. We were so poor, and Ronnie really wanted to get ahead in life. And to him, hanging out with Skinny made him feel so big. 'I made it,' he thought. 'I'm with the best.'"

Ronnie began palling around with Angelo more frequently, largely because it afforded him access to Skinny, and Angelo often brought him home to the house on Suffolk Avenue. Skinny immediately took a shine to Ronnie, and before long, he was holding him up as an ideal. Skinny would call Angelo a "bum" and say, "I wish you could be more like Ronnie." Or he would jokingly introduce Ronnie to his card game pals: "Have you met my older son?" He did this right in front of Angelo.

On the three occasions that I visited Angelo in prison, there was a quid pro quo aspect to the proceedings. He would tell me stories, and then he would insist that I tell him things I had learned about his father from my research and interviews. More than once he asked if I had found any proof that his father was in the Mob. Angelo is affable and funny. He does not strike you as a murderer—or even a tough guy. But he can be manipulative and clever and gossipy—and he tells a lot of lies. I kept trying to figure out whether he's a sociopath or just a man who made some terrible mistakes when he was young. When he talked about the victims of his crimes, he did not express anything that looked or sounded like remorse. The only display of real emotion came whenever he talked about his father. In fact, he choked up several times. When I asked if he looked up to his father when he was young, he said, "Yeah, there was no better guy than Skinny. He hit me, but I never hit him back. I never cursed in front of him. I never smoked in front of him.

There is nothing I could say that is bad about him. Even if I had a bad thought, I wouldn't say it. The closest I ever came was this one time when he yelled at me, and when he was walking up the steps and his back was turned, I gave him the finger."

In the year or two before Angelo killed Ronnie, he hung around the card games any chance he got. "I would make the guys a sandwich," he said, "or whatever they wanted, and they would take care of me, give me money. I guess it was easy money. I don't think my father did anything wrong by any of that stuff. People say you have to blame the parents, but I have no one to blame but myself. The way I see it, I'm in here now because I killed Ronald Bodanza. I shouldn't have done it. It was wrong. And this is how I deal with that. Listen, with my background, I should be jumping out a window. You would kill yourself. But I can't."

After Skinny's first heart attack, Angelo insinuated himself even further into his father's world. "After my father got sick," said Angelo, "he would never go to the shows, not in a million years. But I would go anywhere I possibly could." In September 1975, Sinatra was playing New York with Ella Fitzgerald and Count Basie, and Angelo called Jilly Rizzo and asked if he could go to the show. When he invited his friend Ricky Apt to join him, Ricky's mother said, "I bet you $10 you won't meet Frank Sinatra."

"So I get to the theater in New York, they let us in and put us up in the spotlight section," Angelo told me. "I said, 'This is not good.' So we go and knock on the backstage door, and the biggest black guy I have ever seen in my life to this day answers, and he said, 'What do you want, boy?' And I said, 'Is Jilly Rizzo here? Tell him Skinny D'Amato's son is here.' Now I'm shaking like a schoolgirl. My knees are wobbling; I'm nervous as hell. When he comes back his whole tune has changed and Jilly comes out and we went backstage and took pictures with Frank and it was really nice." A few weeks later, Skinny was sitting in his bed looking at the photograph of Frank and Angie; he called Frank and said, "So you met my kid." Said Angelo, "My father was pleased and happy with that story because I did it without him. I did it on my own."

On another occasion, Angelo saw Joey Bishop on the street in Atlantic City at three in the morning. "I went up to him and said, 'Why don't you come over and see my father?' And he said, 'I made a joke about your father and he hasn't spoken to me in seven years.' So I called him from a phone booth and said, 'Dad, listen, Joey Bishop is here and he wants to come over and see you.' And he said, 'I don't want to see him.' He was playing cards, and I said, 'All right, Dad, we'll be right over.' Then I said to Joey, 'Come on.' And Joey said, 'He said okay?' And I said, 'Sure he said okay. Let's go.' So we went to the house and Joey stayed until like seven in the morning, hugging and kissing and crying."

✦

In the spring of 1976, Skinny invited Ronnie to live in his basement, which he had fixed up into a studio apartment. It was a nice arrangement. There was a bed, a bathroom, and a living-sleeping area with a fireplace and a beautiful hand-carved freestanding wooden bar that was a gift to Skinny from Sam Giancana. Shortly thereafter, Ronnie was invited into the sacred world of the card game. "Skinny would let him sit at the game and cut the cards for him," said Anne. "He was twenty-five, but Angelo was just a punk kid. Ronnie got close to Skinny, maybe even closer than Angelo was to him."

Meanwhile, said Joyce, "Skinny sees his own kid being a pain in the ass and a worthless bum." One friend of the family put it this way: "Angelo thought he was Dean Martin. He was always walking around with a cocktail and a cigarette." If Angelo couldn't be taken seriously by his father and his gambling friends, he tried to play the big shot elsewhere. "We'd have card games each week, all the guys from the Baltimore Grille," said a former co-worker of Angelo's. "We'd be dressed in whatever disgusting clothes we had on, but Angelo would show up in a suit. He was an impeccable dresser." And there were plenty of girls who liked him, according to several who knew him, because he was boyishly handsome—and Skinny's kid. "When he was out with a girl," said one of his co-workers, "he was a perfect gentleman . . . and, you see, that's how his father was. But behind the scenes, he was terrible. Angelo would pitch a hissy fit. One time, he threw a deck of cards at me because he lost $200."

✦

On the afternoon of July 12, 1976, Skinny went to Philadelphia for a funeral. Before he left, he told his kids that he planned to stay overnight. Paulajane slept over at Bobby Palamaro's house that evening. Cathy was home early and in bed around midnight. Angelo worked at Tony's, and after his shift, he sat at the bar for a few hours and drank himself into a stupor. Because Skinny rarely traveled anywhere overnight, some people think that Angelo planned that day to kill Ronnie, knowing his father wouldn't be home. Someone who worked with Angelo at Tony's told Anne Battista after her son had been murdered that Angelo had been asking people, "If you were going to kill someone, how would you do it?"

One thing is clear: Just before dawn on July 13, Angelo arrived home from Tony's and went down to the basement and murdered Ronald Bodanza. He tried to dismember his body with a kitchen knife, but quickly vomited and then panicked. He went outside and backed Paulajane's white Cutlass Supreme up to the door that opened onto the basement stairs, then dragged Bodanza's body up and outside and tried to load it into the trunk of the car. Ronnie was only five feet nine, but he weighed 185 pounds, and the body was just too heavy. So Angelo took Bodanza back to the basement. Then he called Sonny Schwartz, the *Atlantic City Press* columnist and Skinny's longtime friend. Sonny died in 1998, but I spoke with his daughter, Pauline.

"Skinny was many years older than my father, so he was like an older brother or even a father figure to him," she said. "I guess that's why Angelo called him that morning. My father was a tough guy, but I'm sure he was really shocked by what he saw that morning."

Angelo told Sonny that he found a bloodied, dying Bodanza in the basement. Schwartz told him to call the police and then went straight to the house. Before Sonny arrived, however, Angelo went upstairs to get Cathy, who was the only one home at the time of the murder. "Cathy, wake up," he said to her. "You've got to come down to the basement. I found Ronnie dead in his room." Cathy, everyone agrees, has never fully recovered from the horror of that day. "She screamed and freaked out," said Angelo. "I'm not proud of that."

When the police arrived at eight-fifteen A.M., they found Bodanza's body on the floor, bound with electrical cord, one leg nearly severed, and a plastic trash bag tied around his neck. Blood was splattered everywhere—the walls, the ceiling, the bed. Angelo told the police that he had walked downstairs to find Ronnie tied up, bleeding, and still alive and that he had tried to keep him alive. The police were immediately suspicious, as Angelo had nary a speck of blood on him.

When the phone rang—unreasonably early—at Bobby Palamaro's apartment, he answered it and then woke Paulajane, who was asleep next to him, and handed her the receiver. "Something's happened," said Jimmie McCullough, a friend of the family. "Ronnie's been killed, and Angelo's involved. You need to get here." Paulajane hung up the phone and went berserk. In her gut, she knew the painful truth: Her brother had finally snapped.

Paulajane, always one step ahead of everyone, remembered that Skinny would be driving home from Philadelphia that morning, so she and Bobby jumped in his car and went straight to the Ventnor police station and asked them not to release any news to the press so that Skinny wouldn't hear it on the radio; she was afraid he'd have a heart attack on the road. Then she called his cardiologist and asked him to be at the house when Skinny arrived to receive the shocking news. When Paulajane got to the house, Cathy was a zombie, completely unhinged. Angie was strangely affectless, as if nothing of any consequence had happened.

By midmorning, the house on Suffolk Avenue was filled with a few dozen people: cops, detectives, friends of the family, Paulajane's good friend Georgene McCullough, and various others. When Skinny finally walked up the front steps, into the foyer, and through the French doors, he had a puzzled look on his face: Why were all these people here so early? Paulajane grabbed a chair from the living room and pulled it over, tried to get her father to sit down to hear the news. But she didn't get it to him in time. "Ronnie's been killed," said one of the cops, "and Angelo's been taken in for questioning." Skinny went weak in the knees and grabbed on to the back of the chair, nearly slumping to the floor.

He sat at the kitchen table for the rest of the afternoon, head in hands, devastated. Before long, as the story began to break on the news, he was fielding phone calls from people all over the country, including Frank Sinatra. When they first heard the story, many of Skinny's friends assumed it was a Mob hit or a card game gone bad. Throughout most of the day, the body—and half a dozen cops and detectives—remained downstairs in the basement, with blood tracked all over the floor. Always the consummate host, even on the worst day of his life, Skinny sent Georgene to the basement to get some liquor. The cops handed her up a few bottles. Cocktails were served.

✦

Paulajane had always been the "strong one" in the family, the one who could do everything, handle anything. Cathy, on the other hand, was a follower who had always let Paulajane speak for her and take care of all the details. On this day, things were no different. While Cathy eerily paced the floor in her bedroom—and at one point stood facing a wall and gently banged her head against it—Skinny sent Paulajane to the Atlantic City Court House to be the family representative. She brought with her the deed to the house in lieu of $5,000 bail. From there she went to Ventnor City Hall, where Angelo was being held in the basement holding cell. By the time she got there, reporters and television crews were waiting. She handed over the deed and filled out the paperwork, and Angelo was brought out of the cell. They tried to sneak out the side door, to no avail. Reporters descended on them, and a big picture of Paulajane and Angelo dodging reporters ran on the front page of the *Atlantic City Press* the next day.

For eight months, Angelo denied that he'd had anything to do with Ronald Bodanza's murder, and in the beginning, the family chose to believe his story. They knew he could be violent and that he had a vile temper—but murder? Skinny hired a battery of lawyers to prepare his son's defense, including his nephew Paul, the son of Willie and Grace D'Amato. Paul put Cathy and Paulajane through mock trials to test their mettle under questioning. Paulajane was able to remain composed. Cathy broke down every time.

Several months went by before a grand jury was convened, and during that time Angelo maintained his innocence and went on with his life, which included the usual rounds of parties and card games and trips to the Latin Casino. Joyce Bodanza, who was around twenty-three at the time, kept hearing from people that Angelo was seen all over town—wearing her brother's jewelry. The police had delivered Ronnie's belongings to the family months earlier, but some things had been missing. She became obsessed with vengeance and would often drive by the D'Amato house late at night. One afternoon, with her cousin in tow, she screwed up her courage and knocked on the D'Amatos' front door. A woman answered who Joyce assumed was the maid. "Hi," she said. "Is Skinny home?"

"Yeah, he's up in his bedroom," said the maid. "Go on upstairs."

Joyce's knees were shaking as she climbed the stairs. When she got to the bedroom door, she pushed it open. Skinny was propped up in bed in his robe, as usual.

"Who are you?" he said.

"I'm Ronnie's sister," she said.

"Oh, my God . . . Oh, my God," said Skinny as he got out of bed and approached her.

"I'm here to get my brother's things," said Joyce.

"Oh, we don't have anything of your brother's," said Skinny.

"Well, that's not true," said Joyce, "because your son has been seen around town wearing my brother's gold rings."

She didn't realize that Angelo was in the house until Skinny yelled down the stairs, "Angie, come up here!" When he arrived in his father's bedroom, he took one look at Joyce and turned white.

"Do you have things that belong to Ronnie?" Skinny asked.

"No," said Angelo.

Skinny started naming specific items that Joyce had described to him. "You don't have a gold ring with diamonds in it?"

"Well, yeah," said Angelo. "Ronnie used to let me wear that."

"I want you to go downstairs," said Skinny, "and I want you to pack up everything that belonged to Ronnie and get it ready to go." When Angelo left the room, Skinny turned to Joyce and said, "My heart is broken from what happened to Ronnie. I loved him like my own son. Please tell your mother how sorry I am."

Anne Battista eventually had her own run-ins with both Angelo and Skinny. About three months after the murder, she was working as a cashier in a convenience store in Ventnor when who should walk in to buy a pack of cigarettes but Angelo. She froze. And then she shocked herself with a scream that was anguished and primal: *"You murderer!"* Angelo ran out the door. She would have to wait seven long years before she could confront Skinny.

✦

Several weeks after the murder, an Atlantic County grand jury returned a six-count indictment charging Angelo with murdering Ronald Bodanza as well as possessing a baseball bat and knife as dangerous weapons, unlawfully disposing of a dead body, and obstructing justice. He was held in the county jail in lieu of $75,000 bail. Eight months after the murder, Angelo pleaded guilty to manslaughter, claiming he had killed Ronnie because his friend had made sexual advances toward him. Angelo told superior court judge Manuel Greenberg, the same judge who would preside over his next two trials, that he'd had fifteen to eighteen drinks that night and then went down to the basement to talk to Ronnie, who was in the bathroom. Angelo said he sat in a chair to wait. When Ronnie came out of the bathroom, he was wearing only a pair of underwear, and he leaned over and tried to kiss Angelo. To fend him off, Angelo said, he picked up a baseball bat and hit him over the head with it.

A family friend who knew Angelo from the time he was a baby told a reporter in 1983 that Angelo had told him that he'd plotted to kill Ronnie because gossip linked them as lovers—someone had pictures of the two of them at a gay club on New York Avenue. But most people who know Angelo think this is nonsense. He killed Ronnie out of jealousy, they say, because Skinny kept pointing to his friend as a success. "He moved into the basement," Angelo told a reporter after confessing to the murder, "and he was staying, and he was staying, and he was staying, you know? My father built a room for him down there. Was I jealous? At that point I did not believe I was. I can't stand fags. I'm not trying to bad-mouth the guy, but the first thing was . . . was the sexuality thing. People said they had a picture of me and him on New York Avenue. Now, I been on New York Avenue, but, like, I was with a *girl*, you know?"

To this day, Angelo insists that Ronnie was obsessed with him. "I *know* he was gay," he said. Angelo told me that he killed Ronnie because "it had all built up." It started, he said, at a New Year's Eve party, months before the murder. At midnight, Ronnie kissed him, and "I swear to God, I felt tongue. I was loaded, but I backed away real quick. We got in fistfights and everything, he was always on top of me. I couldn't turn around. He was always there. Then the pass in the basement happened. It was all that built-up frustration. There was a lot of anger there. I was working with him, I was on my days off with him, it was too much of him. Then I would try to hook him up with girls. He fell asleep in a car with one."

When I asked Angelo if he was jealous of the fact that Ronnie had weaseled his way into his relationship with his father, he replied, "There could be something there to that. . . . Maybe I didn't like what he was doing, but I know where my father stood. There was too much of him. The main reason is, you look for an excuse and you found it and you use that excuse. Quite possibly there was jealousy. But it never went that far. It just got tiring. God, this guy is *here* again. It was one of those kind of things."

✦

In a controversial plea bargain in March 1977, Angelo pleaded guilty to manslaughter in exchange for an indeterminate reformatory sentence at the Garden State Youth Correctional Facility in Yardville, New Jersey. Atlantic County prosecutor Richard Williams called a press conference to explain that the manslaughter bargain had been agreed upon because, he claimed, there was insufficient evidence to convict D'Amato of first-degree murder. This tested the limits of credulity for many of those familiar with the details of the crime. "Ronnie was bludgeoned to death, and then Angelo tried to cut up the body," said Albert DiOrio, Bodanza's cousin. "Obviously this was first-degree murder, and so there were a lot of rumors flying around and the DA is defending himself and saying, 'The evidence wasn't there.' Well, of *course* the evidence was there." The most persistent rumor, which gets repeated to this day, was that Frank Sinatra paid someone off—the judge? the prosecutor?—to the tune of $35,000. Angelo himself even admits that *something* shady transpired, some kind of pressure was brought to bear on someone, and that he believes his father was directly involved, but he will not elaborate any further than telling a cryptic story about Skinny borrowing someone's car and "running an errand" late at night, in the middle of a marathon card game that, he thinks, led to some kind of a deal. Skinny never left a card game in the middle of the action, and he never drove himself anywhere. That night, he did both.

In a weird way, one can't help but see shades of patricide in Angelo's crime. Ronnie was a poor kid from a big, working-class family who figured out how to make a living when he was just fourteen years old. He took care of his family, lent a lot of people money, and was clever, generous, and well liked in the extreme. He was so much like Skinny that even *Skinny* couldn't resist him. By inviting Ronnie into his home, where he slowly but surely took Angelo's place—at the card game, no less—Skinny was practically daring Angelo to come unhinged.

Angelo was paroled after only thirty-three months. During those three years, Skinny visited his son only a couple of times because, like everything else to do with the heartbreak of Angelo, he just couldn't handle it; once again, the responsibility fell to Paulajane. She and Bobby made the hour drive to Yardville nearly every weekend, even while Paulajane was pregnant with Devon.

Angelo was released on December 14, 1979, his twenty-second birthday, just two days after Frank Sinatra's birthday—which, too bad for Angelo, meant that Skinny wasn't even in town when his son came home from prison. Skinny was at Caesars Palace in Las Vegas for a party: Frank Sinatra's fortieth anniversary in show business. Bobby Palamaro picked Angie up at Yardville and drove him to the big empty house on Suffolk Avenue; there he was welcomed home by his sisters, who tried to make him feel as comfortable as possible, though they were obviously afraid of him.

About a month after Angelo got home, one of Skinny's friends gave him a job working as the timekeeper for the Morse Diesel Corporation, one of the general contractors working at the Playboy Hotel & Casino construction site. The job gave him access to the payroll. By then, Resorts and Caesars had opened, and Angelo could not resist the call of Atlantic City's decadent nightlife and the strangely seductive promise of gambling in the vast, new, carpeted, clock-free, air-conditioned, smoke-filled, noisy, cacophonous, open-all-night theme parks that are modern-day casinos. Before long, Angelo started stealing from his own family in order to rent limousines and to buy expensive dinners for women whom he would take out on the town. He stole his dead mother's jewelry and his father's money to finance his profligate lifestyle. Skinny, a man whose life had been built on an unspoken but deep and abiding trust and love among great men, learned to sleep with his ever-present wad of bills in the breast pocket of his pajamas because he loved—but did not trust—his own son.

t is impossible to overstate the significance of the opening of Resorts International Hotel & Casino on May 26, 1978—the beginning of Memorial Day weekend. It was the first legal casino in the history of the United States that was not in Nevada, the only casino in the Northeast, where a quarter of the population lives just a drive away from Atlantic City; and it was the first and only casino in the resort for the initial fourteen months of the new era of legalized gambling.

Resorts International was run by James M. Crosby, board chairman, and I. G. "Jack" Davis, president—two ambitious iconoclasts who had molded a nothing little paint company based in Tampa, Florida, into one of the most surprising business turnarounds in U.S. history. In the mid-1960s, after they bought a casino on Paradise Island in the Bahamas, they sold Mary Carter Paint for $9 million, and Resorts International was born. With a vision to open casinos around the world, the two men began traveling to places like Tunisia, Greece, Yugoslavia, the Philippines, and Haiti, looking for opportunities. Not long after the referendum to legalize gambling in New Jersey failed to get enough votes in 1974, Crosby and Davis heard that New Jersey assemblyman Steven Perskie was sponsoring a bill for a new referendum in New Jersey, but this time it would limit casino gambling to Atlantic City.

In quick succession, Crosby and Davis commissioned a survey of the area, including aerial photographs of the old Boardwalk hotels, took a tour of the city, picked up an option to buy a fifty-five-acre Boardwalk-front tract of land, put several local power brokers on their payroll, and then, in the summer of 1976, came to New Jersey and contributed hundreds of thousands of dollars to the Committee to Rebuild Atlantic City, the chief pro-casino lobby. The committee hired Sanford Weiner, a media wizard and pollster from San Francisco, to launch a full-scale campaign. Weiner had orchestrated 174 political campaigns in eighteen years, and all but 13 had been successful. After arriving in Atlantic City and learning the lay of the land, Weiner quickly discovered that 98 percent of the black population of New Jersey were in favor of legalized gambling, though black voters were unlikely to get to the polls in great enough numbers to make a difference. Weiner called on Willie Brown, now the flamboyant mayor of San Francisco, to come to New Jersey in the summer of 1976 to get out the black vote. On election day, they spent thousands of dollars to pay for baby-sitters, bus fare, and taxis to get black folks to the polls.

The strongest and most vocal opposition to legalization came from the Council of Churches and law enforcement. "I learned a lot about politics in this thing," said Jack Davis. "It was fun, actually. We had an ex-sheriff from Bergen County who was in charge of influencing the law enforcement people. For the Catholic Church, we made a deal that we wouldn't have bingo, so they were neutralized. There were various other people in charge of the Italian vote, the Jewish vote, and we all went around the state giving speeches. I was mainly involved in influencing the banks and the businessmen by talking to them about how good it was for business. We campaigned all summer, and were the largest financial contributors to the effort. And then the referendum passed."

With gambling officially legalized in Atlantic City, Davis and Crosby had tremendous influence over how the laws—what became known as the New Jersey Casino Control Act—were written and what the rules of the games in casinos would be. For example, they insisted that a state representative be present at all times in the counting rooms, and they invented the "no peek" rule in blackjack. (This rule is now standard in Las Vegas; that little electronic machine "peeks" at the dealer's card instead of the dealer himself.) When at last the legislature finished arguing in Trenton, any concerns that Crosby and Davis might have had about excessively burdensome government regulation were assuaged. By the time the Casino Control Act became law in the summer of 1977, easy credit for gamblers was a given, drinks would be on the house (as long as you were gambling), casinos could operate eighteen hours a day on weekdays and twenty on weekends, and minimum bets would be set in a manner that benefited the casino operators. The New Jersey Division of Gaming Enforcement was formed to investigate casino applicants and would report to the regulatory agency called the Casino Control Commission, whose first commissioner was Joseph Lordi.

It should come as no surprise, then, that Resorts International filed the first application to operate a casino in Atlantic City. In December 1977, Crosby handed over a nonrefundable application fee of $100,000. Resorts was in a big hurry. Aside from the fact that several other states in the East were in various stages of considering legalizing gambling, Resorts had fast-encroaching competition right in their own backyard. Caesars World, Inc., which owned Caesars Palace in Las Vegas, was preparing to build on the site where Skinny's beloved Traymore Hotel had once been; Bally took out a long-term lease on the Marlborough-Blenheim; Playboy announced plans to build a glass tower right next to the city's famed Convention Hall; and Penthouse snatched up several hotels, including the old Mayflower Hotel and the Holiday Inn. To get out even farther in front of their competition, Resorts decided to "restore" the one-thousand-room Chalfonte–Haddon Hall instead of building a new structure. The seventy-year-old hotel had been the largest in the world at the time of its construction. The Casino Control Act required that a hotel-casino property be on the waterfront, either on the Boardwalk or in the marina, and have a minimum of four hundred hotel rooms. But that number was eventually knocked up to five hundred through lobbying from Resorts. This ensured that Resorts would have the town to themselves for many months, as the Chalfonte–Haddon Hall was the only existing hotel large enough to qualify. Everyone else had to tear down their hotels and build new towers, which Governor Brendan Byrne had encouraged. Indeed, new construction was one of the main reasons to legalize gambling in the first place. There would be no more "patch and paint" jobs, Byrne declared, so whatever was left of the old hotels—including historic landmarks like the Marlborough-Blenheim—was brought to the ground in massive heaps through spectacular implosions that were broadcast on the evening news.

✦

On May 26, 1978, Steve Lawrence and Eydie Gorme cut the ribbon to open Resorts, as thousands of people waited in a line that stretched for a mile down the Boardwalk. They waited for hours to get through the doors of the spruced-up old pile of bricks that sat in the middle of the worst part of the crumbling city. By Saturday night at three A.M. it was pouring rain, but there was still a line snaking down the Boardwalk.

After the long weekend, Jack Davis got a call from Steve Wynn, who owned the Golden Nugget in Las Vegas. "He was telling me that he had the biggest weekend he ever had at the Golden Nugget, and he said, 'How'd you guys do?' and I said, 'Well, Steve, we don't know yet because we haven't been able to count all the money. We just threw it into a room—bags and bags and bags of money—and we haven't had time to count it.' We were way over capacity. People were lined up behind each playing position, and some of those who had seats at a blackjack table wouldn't even leave to go to the bathroom. They'd just go on the floor. It was extreme."

Brendan Byrne had promised the people of New Jersey that Atlantic City would feature "European style" gambling, which meant what, exactly? That James Bond would show up in a tux with Pussy Galore on his arm? It was a ridiculous notion, but it was meant to soothe people's fears about gambling's dark side—the Mob, crime, and so on. Of the thousands of people who showed up to gamble at the opening, many were in jeans and T-shirts and sweats and shorts, and the state was quickly disabused of any pretense toward Monte Carlo. For the first few weeks, though, Resorts kept hundreds of suit jackets on racks in a room near the entrance, to be rented to men who showed up without one. "Can you imagine how ridiculous that was?" said Davis. "But we were trying to make it a classy place."

The most telling example of just how grand the delusions were about what kind of resort the "new" Atlantic City would be is that Davis persuaded Geoffrey Beene—whose clothes are, perhaps, the closest to haute couture in America—to open the only freestanding Geoffrey Beene boutique in the world in the Resorts complex. They spent a small fortune designing and building the space, which was gray and sleek and modern, and stocked it with $5,000 dresses. "It was like a museum," said Paula Arena, who worked at the boutique when she was nineteen. "The lighting was incredible. The people started coming and they never stopped coming, but no one bought a thing." Beene eventually closed up, and within a span of two years the shop changed hands a couple of times, sliding further downmarket until the space was finally occupied by a junk merchant selling . . . T-shirts.

"That is typical of Atlantic City back in the seventies," said David Spatz, a reporter for the *Atlantic City Press* at the time. "These entrepreneurs would come to town with big eyes: 'We will make a killing.' They would sink a ton of money into opening something, and no one would show up. What was frustrating to a lot of merchants was that there would be hordes of people jammed on the boardwalk waiting to get into Resorts, and they would just stand there in front of the stores and not go in. They didn't want to give up their place in line. They were all interested in gambling and that was it."

And gamble they did. Before the first day was over, Resorts had won over $1 million—pure profit. Overnight, the company's Class A stock, which had been selling at $2 in 1976, rose to $210, and its Class B stock rose to $185, making millionaires out of "friends and family," as they say. Within nine months, Resorts had recouped its entire investment.

The casino floor was only thirty thousand square feet—puny by today's standards—and it was the costliest part of the renovation, which was really just a glorified paint job. "Alan King or Buddy Hackett or one of those guys performed at Resorts in the beginning," said Fran Freedman, who founded *Atlantic City* magazine just before Resorts opened. "And he said onstage, 'Two months ago this was a shit house. Now it's a shit house with carpet.' They didn't do *anything* to that place. They just threw carpets and mirrors all over. It was never really right, Resorts. But they were in a hurry. They believed in the numbers."

No doubt! In its first year of operation, Resorts turned a profit that was more than half that of all the Nevada casinos put together. Because of their huge success, Davis and Crosby decided to institute a very ambitious and lavish entertainment policy. They commissioned a fellow by the name of Tibor Rudas to design and run the 1,750-seat Superstar Theater. "He's the one who really convinced me that we should be spending all this money on entertainment to create an image," said Davis, "even though we had more business than we could handle. But he was right, and that gave Resorts a cachet that kept the place in the running even when the facility was falling behind the newer places."

Rudas, who became known around Atlantic City as "the mad Hungarian," was born in Budapest. At eight years old, he began singing boy soprano for the Budapest State Opera, but he lost his voice after a few years from overuse. After earning a degree in business administration from the University of Budapest, he toured the world performing with a theater group. Eventually he settled in Australia, where he started a dance studio and began producing what he called "French-style" dance revues that featured a lot of tumbling and acrobatics and sexy costumes. In 1963, he moved to the one place in America where his services were needed most: Las Vegas. He eventually produced a show on Paradise Island in the Bahamas, so he was an obvious choice when Jack Davis needed to bring a little pizzazz to Atlantic City.

"He was the impresario," said Fran Freedman, "and he was such a temperamental guy, but he was the beginning and he brought everybody to Resorts." "Tibor was such a character," said David Spatz. "This was in the days when they didn't care how much money they spent on entertainment, so he was spending a bundle. He was the first person to pay Sinatra $50,000 a show. And that kind of set the precedent."

Bob Chambers, who worked at Resorts for twenty years, was the stage manager at the Superstar Theater when it opened in 1978. "Frank Sinatra was the first major star to play Atlantic City again. He broke the ice. Atlantic City was viewed in the entertainment community as a dead place. This is where you went if there was no place else to work. The days of the 500 Club, when it was a hot town, were long gone. But even after Resorts opened and things started happening, there was still a resistance. Steve and Eydie opened Resorts, and it was not a good experience—it was chaos. You had to pay people a lot of money to get them to come here. Don Rickles, Alan King, Vic Damone, Joey Bishop, Sammy Davis Jr., Jerry Vale, it was a small group, and most of them were from the Northeast, especially among those who played Vegas, a genre of entertainment that Sinatra was obviously the head of. When he got reports back that Resorts was not terrible and that the audience reaction was great, he agreed to come. Because it's different in New Jersey for these guys. It's different from Vegas. East Coast people have a different mentality. If I say hipper, I sound like a snob, but it was true. It's less true today than it was then."

When the East Coast boys who played Las Vegas began showing up in town, Skinny's life and mood improved immeasurably. "When Resorts opened, that was the happiest I ever saw my father," said Cathy D'Amato. "Suddenly he had a life again, because the entertainers respected him so much, and because of that the owners of Resorts gave my father respect. It was almost as if he had the 500 Club back."

David Spatz concurred. "When Resorts signed Frank, that was when Skinny was really, really happy. Skinny was on home court whenever Frank was in town. Skinny would be at a ringside banquette and then backstage and then at one of the restaurants for dinner, and Frank and Skinny would sit at a table and trade war stories. Play remember when. Skinny was a happy camper then. You could see it on his face."

Many people thought it was an outrage that Skinny wasn't offered some kind of management position at Resorts, but given how onerous the licensing process was—and how deep the background checks were—it should not have come as a surprise. "I don't think, given his past," said Spatz, "that he would have been able to get licensed in Atlantic City, which is probably why no move was ever made to offer him even some sort of ceremonial position. But as long as Frank was in town, Skinny was happy."

"Frank Sinatra played over one hundred shows in our casino," said Jack Davis. "Dean Martin, Sammy Davis . . . we had them all, and I hung out with those entertainers because that was part of my job, and that's where I got to know Skinny and know *about* Skinny. They were all just so indebted to him, and every time those guys came to town, they would not only spend time with Skinny, but they would make such a fuss over him. They all had tremendous respect for him. At one point we had thought about putting a 500 Club in our casino as a lounge."

Resorts eventually built Sinatra a huge suite, decorated according to his tastes. It was like a sprawling, fabulous apartment that could have passed for a classic Manhattan prewar three-bedroom . . . except everything was orange. "Initially," said Chambers, "we just put him in a regular suite. His contract came up for renewal, and he said he'd like to have someplace where he could cook. So they redid this whole suite with a kitchen. It was pretty opulent and very big. Several rooms. Art deco. And yes, a lot of orange. It stayed that way until Merv Griffin bought the property and redid it. It had a plaque on the door: 'Sinatra Suite.'"

Once Jack Davis and Tibor Rudas figured out how important Skinny was to Sinatra, they rolled out the red carpet for the D'Amatos, their extended family, and any hangers-on. Besides their table for twenty, Skinny was provided with fifty tickets to sell to people who came to see him in his bedroom. Skinny being Skinny, he would lose money on this deal because he couldn't help himself and gave most of the tickets away. "It was always a major event when Frank had dinner after the show," said Bob Chambers. "It was never just Frank. It was always Frank and eighteen other people. The D'Amatos came to many shows. There would be a ringside table that sat twenty people, and it would stay empty until about five minutes before the show, and then Skinny and his guests and Barbara Sinatra would fill it up. And they would all come backstage afterwards and then to the bar, the Rendezvous Lounge, where they would listen to Sam Butera or the Turniers. Sylvia Syms was a singer that Frank liked, so we hired her a lot when he was in town. He'd go hang out, and they'd rope off a whole section for Frank and his party. Always with a couple of AC cops in tow, usually Bobby Palamaro, Paulajane's husband, who was Frank's bodyguard when he came to town."

Despite what many people think, Skinny, even back in the early days of the 500 Club, rarely if ever sat at a table to watch a show in his own club. He did not enjoy being a member of a captive audience. "So," said Paulajane, "for my father to go to Resorts and sit and watch Frank's performance was a very big deal because he hated it."

Fran Freedman put Paulajane on one of her early covers of *Atlantic City* magazine. The newsstand at Resorts was perhaps the most important venue for her publication. It was run by an irascible character named Eddie Devlin, who also owned several stores on the Boardwalk. Devlin hated the magazine and refused to stock it. When Fran called to object, he screamed in her ear and threatened her. Fran went through her formidable list of contacts in the city—and got nowhere. Finally, she called Paulajane and asked if she could please talk to Skinny. "Not half an hour later my phone rang, and it's Skinny," said Fran. "I tell him what happened. Three o'clock that afternoon the magazines were on the newsstand at Resorts. I never heard a peep out of Eddie Devlin again. In case you doubt that Skinny had any real power."

Not long after that, Fran called Skinny because she had a friend in town whom she wanted to impress and she needed Sinatra tickets, as did so many others when Frank was playing Resorts. "He said, 'How many do you want?' I said, 'I don't know, ten?' He said, 'What night? Whatever.' So I go over to his house—big, beautiful house—the doors open, and there's a couple of guys hanging out in the kitchen. They say, 'Up the stairs, to your right.' It's afternoon, and it was just exactly like the movies. He was sitting in this huge master bedroom, on the bed, talking on the phone, in his bathrobe. He welcomes me, very friendly, this and that, and what do you think he shows me? His *closet*. Skinny, as you know, had a wardrobe to die for—a whole room with clothes in it. He was very dapper. He handed me an envelope with ten tickets in it, and he said, 'I'm tired of it already. I don't even feel like going up there to see the show, but you know, Frank sends the car, I have to go.' I saw him many times up in that big restaurant at Resorts, the one that looked like a medieval castle, at a big long table with Frank and Barbara and Paulajane and Cathy and the whole group."

✦

A few weeks after the first opening weekend at Resorts in 1978, Steve Wynn couldn't get the phone conversation with Jack Davis out of his head: *We couldn't count all the money.* "After the referendum passed in 1976," said Davis, "I went to Las Vegas to see friends of mine who ran casinos there—Steve Wynn, Cliff Perlman, who ran Caesars, and Al Benedict, who ran MGM Grand Hotels. They came to Atlantic City and they said, 'This isn't going to be anything. This town is such a junk pile. It's gonna be a truck stop for slot machines, and we're not interested in coming here.'"

But when Resorts opened, they quickly changed their tune. As Steve Wynn told *Fortune* magazine: "Coming to Atlantic City took about as much perspicacity as biting into this cheesesteak [I'm eating]. I took one look at Resorts. It was June 16 [1978], a couple of weeks after it opened, and I'll never forget standing on the steps [to the casino]. I saw more people betting more money than I'd ever seen in my life. It made Caesars Palace [in Las Vegas] on New Year's Eve look like it was closed for lunch."

Davis took Wynn for a walk down the Boardwalk when he came to visit that June. They walked all the way to the other end of Atlantic City, to the Strand Motel, and asked to see the owner, Manny Solomon. "I asked him how much he wanted for the place," said Wynn. "I was standing there in my sandals, wearing my Willie Nelson T-shirt, with my tie-string beach pants, and he looked at me like I was crazy." Half an hour later, the two men had agreed that Wynn would pay Solomon $8.5 million in cash for the property. Wynn tore down the Strand and spent sixteen months and $160 million building the Golden Nugget, Atlantic City's sixth and most fabulously over-the-top casino-hotel. It opened the day before Skinny's birthday, November 30, 1981.

In the first six months the Nugget was open, Wynn reported $17.7 million in profit, more than all seven other Atlantic City casinos combined. The Nugget was so successful that Wynn hired Frank Sinatra away from Resorts, paying him $10 million over three years, plus generous stock options, to perform for high rollers at invitation-only shows. He began appearing in television commercials with Wynn, had use of Wynn's private jet, helicopters, and limousines, and was given free access to one of the six deeply luxurious twenty-second-floor suites for high rollers that Wynn had built and decorated at a cost of $4.5 million. Plus he got free rooms in the hotel for his entire entourage.

Sinatra's first appearance over a four-day engagement brought in $20 million in revenue. One high roller lost $3.7 million at the baccarat tables that weekend.

Wynn, as a favor to Frank, offered Skinny a job as a kind of ambassador—and a magnet for big players. He offered him a secretary, phone line, and computer, but it didn't work out, said Paulajane, because Skinny wasn't "feeling up to it." However, that's probably not the reason. Skinny actually had an application into the Casino Control Commission, dated as received on July 20, 1981, just four months before the Nugget opened. Among the many documents in the packet is the résumé of Father George Riley, vice president of university relations at Villanova, offered up as the one and only character witness. There's something distinctly old school and almost naive about having a priest vouch for character; it seems to say *guilty*, even if you're not. The very next page in the application packet is a copy of Skinny's rap sheet on FBI letterhead: "Material witness to a murder, 1934; violation of the White Slave Act, 1938; maintaining disreputable house, 1943; income tax evasion, 1963." In the cover letter, Skinny's lawyer and nephew, Paul R. D'Amato, wrote: "We are revealing any criminal matters which we have genuine knowledge of. No effort whatsoever has been made to attempt to hide any matter on this application."

If Skinny couldn't pass muster in Nevada in the early 1960s, he surely wasn't going to in New Jersey in the 1980s. Besides, said Fran Freedman, "Skinny was too much of an individual to work in this new corporate casino culture." It hardly mattered, though, as by this time Skinny had graduated to the status of living legend, and his life seemed to consist of nothing but card games, gala events, and testimonial dinners. At one such event, Jimmie McCullough, the publicist for the 500 Club, was honored with the Super Sportsman Award at the Atlantic City Country Club for having attended every game of fifty-three consecutive World Series. Joe DiMaggio and Monte Irvin were the guest speakers. Skinny and Joe, estranged for seventeen years, were reunited that evening, and Joe finally forgave Skinny for the disastrous Marilyn Monroe weekend at Cal-Neva. Not long after that, the Atlantic City Medical Center staged a Frank Sinatra concert at Convention Hall to raise money for improvements. With the D'Amatos front and center,

Sinatra called Skinny the "Ziegfeld of saloon keepers." Several months later, the hospital held a dedication ceremony when they unveiled the new Frank Sinatra wing to Frank and his wife, Barbara.

Skinny was honored as Man of the Year in April 1981 by the Italian Social Circle, which coincided with the renaming of a portion of Missouri Avenue to 500 Club Lane. Shortly thereafter, the Hebrew Academy of Atlantic County chose Skinny as Man of the Year, and they asked Tibor Rudas to produce the event. When Frank Sinatra left Resorts for the Golden Nugget, Rudas decided to return to his roots to distinguish Resorts entertainment from the rest of the city's venues. In a risky move, he began booking classical performers into the Superstar Theater, including Zubin Mehta and the New York Philharmonic and Itzhak Perlman. In October 1983, Rudas convinced Luciano Pavarotti to come to Atlantic City. It was the first time an opera singer had ever performed on a casino property. "We're replacing one Italian singer with another," Rudas told *The New York Times*. Pavarotti had reservations about performing in the casino showroom, so Rudas commissioned the construction of a fifty-thousand-square-foot, five-story-high, blue-and-white-striped tent on an empty two-acre lot next door to Resorts. Five thousand tickets sold out in three hours, so they made the tent bigger still, ultimately packing in 7,500. The concert was such a huge success that Rudas left Resorts to produce Pavarotti's concerts throughout the world and was the brains behind the extraordinarily successful Three Tenors concerts that have made untold millions for all involved.

But while Rudas and Frank and Skinny were still calling Resorts home, Rudas produced the evening in May honoring Skinny as Man of the Year. Skinny was the first non-Jew to be honored by the academy in its history. The event was held at the Grand Ballroom of the International Hotel. The place had once been a kosher hotel called Teplitsky's. Bob Eubanks, known mostly as a game show host, was the MC, and Jerry Lewis and Frank Sinatra attended. Skinny had no idea that it was to be such a big deal. Rudas secretly sent a camera crew to get video toasts from Danny Thomas, Dean Martin, and Sammy Davis Jr. When Skinny walked into the ballroom with Paulajane and Cathy by his side, a spotlight picked them up and the entire room stood and applauded for what seemed like an eternity. Skinny, who had assiduously avoided the spotlight his entire life, squirmed and blushed. "He was mortified," said Paulajane. As he approached his table and realized that he had to sit alone with just his daughters on an elevated platform right in front of the stage, he froze.

He eventually sat down as Paulajane picked a thread off his tuxedo jacket. Just then, Dean Martin appeared on a big screen, very tan and leaning against a fence outside on his ranch in California. He had a red bandanna tied around his neck, a crisp, white shirt, and a cocktail in his hand. He was doing his "drunk" act. "Hey, Skinny," he said, slurring his words. "Tibor just called to tell me you're already drunk. *Shame on you, Skinny.* Tonight is your big night, and I should forgive you for drinking that way . . . and that *heavy.* Remember when you were stupid enough to forgive me at the 500 for all those years for doing the same thing? Sorry I can't be with you tonight. Skinny, you're the greatest dago that ever lived . . . outside of Frank Sinister and me. Tonight I'll celebrate you on my own, and just for a change, *I'll* get stoned."

Sammy, in all his lachrymose pomposity, was up next. He was wearing a red sweater vest over a blue-striped button-down, gold chains around his neck, and those great big ridiculous glasses. "I remember the first time playing the 500," he said out of the corner of his mouth. "It was long before the Chez Paree and the Copa and Riviera. You booked us in—my dad, my uncle, and myself. And it was the beginning of something, because you allowed me to become a friend of you and your family. And I'm not being maudlin or oversentimental when I say the following: Without your friendship and without the support to stretch out as a performer at the 500 Club, I would have never ever attained what I have now. You taught me a great deal, you taught me about audiences—even though you're not a performer—and friendships, which you're *tremendously* good at. The 500 Club was something special. I remember seeing Dean and Jerry for the first time there. And I remember the fun we had when we snuck in on the man who's there with you, my man, Francis Albert. And those friendships happened directly because of you, Skinny."

When the video portion of the evening was over, Eubanks introduced Jerry Lewis. "At *Teplitsky's?*" he shouted when he took the stage. "It doesn't make sense! What did you do? Change your name tonight? They couldn't get a Jew to honor? I'm in New York making a film, I got no time to ride three hours on the turnpike. They wanted me to make a tape. And I think distance is certainly of no consequence. I don't care how great the distance when it comes to a friend." Pause. "So, I left Margate at about five-thirty. . . . I don't know where thirty-five years went. I was twenty years old when I went to the 500 Club, and I was befriended, protected, guided, helped by this man. The flowers out there . . . I really thought it was your funeral, to be honest. There's an Italian singer in the lobby doing a novena. I don't ordinarily work with singers, but I'd like to introduce this gentleman, needless to say, he's one of the mob— No, let me rephrase that. He's one of the *group*—the original group: Dean, Sammy, Skinny . . . myself, I guess it was the five of us. I'd like you to meet the Chairman of the Board, Mr. Frank Sinatra."

As the piano player twinkled out "New York, New York," Frank made his entrance to a roaring, standing audience. When he arrived onstage, Skinny stepped up to him, and the two men hugged and kissed. The microphone in Frank's hand picked up their private greeting. "Hello, Paul," Frank said in his ear. "How are you, buddy? How d'ya feel?"

"Not bad," said Skinny. Pause. "I love you."

"Sit down," said Frank. "I'll be about an hour and a half." He made a crack about Sammy being there via video, calling him a "jungle bunny" in the way that only Frank Sinatra could—and *almost* get away with it. "This is a nice room, too," he said. "I've got a dressing room at home bigger than this." He waited for the room to get quiet. "This man has been the most famous name in Atlantic City since I can remember, which is back in 1934–35. I also feel that a lot more should have been done over the years in regard to Skinny—or Paul, as I'd rather call him. Skinny was an old neighborhood joke. He hasn't gotten any fatter, but I like to call him Paul. Just imagine what the two of us looked like together when I was young. We looked like number 11. When Fat Jack E. Leonard was with us we were 101.

"I'd like to just say as clearly and as simply as I can," Frank continued, "that without Skinny and his club . . . a lot of us wouldn't have had a chance to be known nationally, because that's what happened to many of us after we worked there. It wasn't really local. The magazines and newspapers"—he spat on the floor—"started to write about us right after we played Skinny's place, because the 500 Club on Missouri was a place that became internationally famous. He helped everybody's career jump a little higher a little quicker. I know that because I played the Steel Pier and I got nowhere. All I got to know was the goddamn horse that used to jump in the water. But when I went to Skinny's, people knew me. They'd say, 'There's Skinny's friend.' That was it. They didn't know the name. Just Skinny's friend. Obviously, you know that Jerry and Dean made the biggest noise in the U.S. when they came into Skinny's. And then went on to great things. If Skinny's was open today, or for the past several years, we might have had a little more talent come before us. *Real* talent. I don't mean the guys with the funky suits and the funny shoes. I mean talented people like Sammy Davis, or his old man, or his uncle Will. There's a guy who made a million dollars a year with a gold tooth, snapping his fingers. The word *gonif* was invented for his uncle. There's not much more I can say. I love Paul D'Amato and his whole family. And I will continue to be his friend as long as we both breathe. And I hope sometime in the future, some bright manager or owner of a building in this town will build a room in honor of Skinny and call it the 500 Club."

Skinny was overwhelmed. By the time he finally got onstage and took the microphone, he could barely speak. "You know," he said, "I'm not much of a speaker." He paused for an uncomfortably long time as the room fell pin-drop silent. "I think this is the second time I've ever been onstage. There was the time that Dean and Jerry said, 'We won't perform unless you get onstage.'" He then thanked Rabbi Aaron Krauss, Father George Riley, and a short list of other men in the room, mostly his friends, like Tony Maglio and Sonny Schwartz. But he saved for last Jerry Lewis—whom he called "my kid"—and, finally, Frank: "My man . . . my brother . . . my everything . . . Mr. Sinatra." Tears rolled down his cheeks.

When Skinny got offstage, he sat down and turned his chair toward Frank—and his back toward Jerry. Frank lit Skinny's cigarettes, which seemed for some reason, in that moment, to be an expression of intimacy and love and tenderness. Paulajane was on the other side of Jerry, who lit her cigarettes; Cathy was on the other side of Frank, who lit *her* cigarettes. Everyone smoked and looked gorgeous and happy, as if they were all out on a big date together with not a care in the world. Everyone but Angelo, that is.

Just a few months earlier, he had pleaded guilty to theft by deception. While working at the Playboy construction site, he had invented phantom employees and then cashed their checks to the tune of $30,000. He was sentenced in April 1981 to a second "indeterminate reformatory" sentence and sent back to Yardville. But what no one yet knew—except for Angelo and a man by the name of Art Devine—was that Angelo had been involved in, if not entirely responsible for, something much worse than embezzlement. In the early part of 1981, Angelo had begun an affair with Keerans "Kerry" Carter, a troubled young woman who had left two children and an ex-husband behind in Baltimore and moved to Atlantic City shortly after the casinos began to open. A lot of Kerry Carters moved to Atlantic City in the late 1970s. Kerry was a very attractive and beguiling blonde with big blue eyes, and according to several who knew her, she became a high-end prostitute who often picked up rich guys at the Rendezvous Lounge at Resorts. She cleaned up her act for a couple of years while dating a local musician named Bobby Young, but she took a turn for the worse when she met Art Devine, a notorious drug addict. Devine, who was several years older than Angelo, had gone to Atlantic City High with Paulajane and Cathy. He owned an auto body shop on Dorset Avenue in Ventnor and was a former Green Beret. He was, from all reports, a scary guy—tough and muscular and prone to violent mood swings, "a monster," according to one person who knew him.

Kerry and Art moved into a town house condominium at 815 Marshall Court on the bay, in Ventnor, where apparently they did a lot of drugs—including crystal meth, a nasty, soul-destroying form of cheap speed that can be made in a bathtub with chemicals anybody can get hold of. One person who knew Kerry and Art claimed the two had a crystal meth lab in their home. In the later months of 1980, Angelo started hanging around Art and Kerry's apartment all the time—virtually moving in. Kerry had recently gotten breast implants, paid for with insurance money she'd received when her Camaro had been totaled in an accident. One day, Kerry asked Angelo if he'd like to see her new breasts. One thing led to another, and they wound up having sex. On February 17, 1981, Art found out about the affair, and things got even uglier at Marshall Court. In the early evening, the neighbors heard Kerry shrieking in terror, and someone called the police, who arrived to find Art in a rage, screaming at Kerry. She didn't want to press charges, and there was no obvious physical abuse, so the cops left.

The next day, Kerry vanished. Eventually the neighbors started wondering what happened to her, and again one of them called the police. When detectives turned up at Marshall Court to interview Art, Angelo was there. Both men were interviewed separately, and their stories matched perfectly and seemed rehearsed. It wasn't much of a story: Art said he didn't love Kerry anymore and he'd kicked her out. He had no idea where she went. There was no evidence that a crime had taken place, but the detectives turned up not a single person—cab-drivers, bus station employees, family—who had seen her or had any idea where she was. In April, Angelo was busted for the check-cashing scam. A month later, as Skinny was being toasted by Frank and Jerry at the International Hotel, Kerry's 1979 Camaro was found abandoned on Bainbridge Street in Philadelphia, not far from Jewelers Row. The mystery deepened. But after a few months, with not a single lead or clue, the detectives moved on to more pressing concerns.

Then, in November 1981, Ventnor police headquarters received a phone call from Daniel Bloom, captain of internal affairs at the Garden State Youth Correctional Facility in Yardville. An inmate named John Webber claimed to know "of a very serious crime committed some-where in the state of New Jersey." Webber said that a new prisoner, who had recently arrived from Ventnor, had told him in a bragging con-test about the "worst thing he'd ever done"; he claimed he had stran-gled a girl named "Karen," cut up her corpse, stuffed her body parts into trash bags, and disposed of them "in or near a body of water" in Atlantic City. Local investigators requested an interview with Webber, who said that at first he didn't believe Angelo—he thought he was just a braggart and a liar—but when Angelo began threatening Webber and his family by saying that he was connected to the Mob and was friends with Nicky Scarfo, Webber took him seriously and told the prison warden.

The detectives interviewed Angelo and put him under close observation. Still, there was no evidence of a crime. Then came a dramatic break. On May 28, 1982, a retired fireman was looking for driftwood in the salt marshes along the access road that connects Somers Point on the mainland to Longport at the southern end of Absecon Island. As he was poking his way through the tall grass and mud, he came upon a trash bag that was blown up like a balloon. When he ripped it open, noxious gases escaped and bones spilled out. It appeared to be a very small rib cage, but there was no skull or limbs. And it was not entirely clear whether the bones were human. "I don't see how they could ever identify who it was," said an investigator to the press. The bag and its contents were sent to the New Jersey medical examiner, Dr. Geetha Natarajan. When she examined the remains, she found something that she didn't immediately recognize—a round, clear plastic sack imprinted with a serial number.

Kerry Carter's breast implants had lived to tell her tale.

When the detectives confronted Angelo with the gruesome discovery—found in a place and manner consistent with John Webber's version of Angelo's supposed tall tale—he was forced, in the moment, to choose a story, to decide what tale *he* would tell. He has been telling that same story ever since, with less and less conviction. It goes like this: Art called him at two A.M. on the night of the fight about Kerry and Angelo's affair and asked him to come to his garage. When Angelo got there, he found Art with a mask on and Kerry's body parts spread out on a blanket on the floor. Art said that he would dispose of her body, but he needed Angelo to get rid of all her belongings in the apartment: her furs and her jewelry, the accoutrements of her life as a prostitute, and her gifts from the rich guys from Resorts. Angelo agreed to help because he was afraid of Art and because he knew that everyone would think he did it—because, indeed, he had killed someone before and tried to chop him up. He filled Kerry's car with her belongings and drove to Philadelphia, to a pawnshop, and sold her jewelry and furs.

Art Devine told a very different story. He wanted Kerry out of his house and out of his life, and the night the police came to Marshall Court it had reached a crescendo—he had actually threatened her. He slept on the couch downstairs in the living room that night after he and Angelo watched *The Godfather*, of all movies. At seven A.M. Angelo woke him up and told him that he had killed Kerry after an argument over a few hundred dollars. "There had to be something more [to it]," said Devine, "but you have to understand the kind of person Angelo D'Amato is. He's a braggart, a person who's used to getting what he wants." Devine said that he didn't turn Angelo in to the cops because he thought they would immediately pin it on him; they had, after all, just witnessed him in a rage threatening Kerry the night before. So they left her body under Art's bed while they disposed of her belongings together in Philadelphia. At ten P.M. that night, they took Kerry's corpse to Art's body shop, and Angelo cut her up with a hacksaw while Devine waited in his office. It took nearly three hours to complete the hideous task. Devine took the plastic bag containing her torso and threw it off Margate Bridge, while Angelo took the other bags filled with her arms and legs and put them in Dumpsters around the city. Devine said that Angelo stored her head in the rafters of his father's garage for a few days and got rid of it later. For whatever reason, he did not want to dispose of it on the same day.

Just before midnight, on August 11, 1982, Angelo, who had recently been paroled from Yardville, was arrested on a warrant at the mansion at 12 So. Suffolk, and bail was set at $250,000. It was duly noted in the paper the next morning that the "Suffolk Avenue address was the scene of a grisly slaying in the early morning hours of July 13, 1976." Skinny did not post bail, and he did not hire Angelo a fancy lawyer. He left his son in the hands of a public defender. The trial was set for June 1983. Over the following year, there were constant headlines in the Atlantic City and Philadelphia papers about the case. When the trial finally got under way, it was front-page news every day. The case was heard for three weeks. The jury deliberated for seventeen hours and could not reach a verdict. Judge Manuel Greenberg declared a mistrial.

The second trial began on September 6 and lasted two weeks. On the final two days, Angelo took the stand and testified for nearly seven hours in his own defense, with disastrous results. The first blunder happened on day one of his testimony, when he was provoked into talking about Ronald Bodanza's murder. Under the law, prior convictions can be used only to impeach a witness on the stand, and the details are usually inadmissible—unless, of course, the defendant can be coaxed into bringing them up himself. On the second day, under cross-examination by the prosecutor, Steven Rosenfeld, Angelo came unglued. At one point, he shouted, "I'm the victim!" The *Atlantic City Press* wrote that Angelo's "prolonged testimony was punctuated by emotional outbursts, dramatic accusations, sarcastic insinuations and almost constant objections from the defense."

When I first went to see Angelo in prison, I was not entirely convinced that he was guilty. Plenty of reasonable doubt had been raised during the trial. And Art Devine is about the least sympathetic witness you could find. But as one person involved in the prosecution said to Kerry Carter's family: "Sometimes you have to let a thief go to catch a murderer." Angelo maintains that he is innocent, but he has no illusions about getting out of prison anytime soon. He thinks the prosecution went after him because of the fact that he'd been insufficiently punished for Ronald Bodanza's murder, and on that count he might be right. But he is splitting hairs; both men were involved in the nasty business of disposing of Kerry's body, and both their lives have been ruined. Devine was a destitute heroin addict who lived on the streets of Atlantic City for many years.

When I went to see the prosecutor, Steven Rosenfeld, he assured me that he is absolutely certain Angelo killed Kerry and cut up her corpse. For one thing, he said, dismemberment is very unusual; that it occurred twice to people Angelo was involved with is significant, and unlikely to be coincidental. "Here he is, the son of Skinny D'Amato, a fabulously successful and esteemed person, and he's living this underground life with dope addicts. And this Kerry Carter, she was like Bonnie to Angelo's Clyde. They were ripoff artists. He killed her over $100! I also think that he was one of those people who was fixated on being a made man. I really think he idolized those local gangsters, and that's part of the initiation—that you're supposed to kill someone."

Angelo, it seems, wanted to be what his father actually wasn't.

As another friend of the family put it: "Angelo figured out what he did wrong the first time, with Ronnie, and he improved on his technique. He figured out how to get rid of a body."

Still, I wasn't convinced of Angelo's guilt. Then a friend of Angelo's told me this: "I know Angelo killed her because he called me the day after he did it and *told* me he did it. He was laughing about it, saying she was a piece of shit and she was on dope. Skinny's power got him off easy after the first one. The sheriff was Mario Floriani, and he and Skinny were really tight. Favors were called in. Today, a fourteen-year-old kid gets tried as an adult and gets life. That's what should have happened to Angelo."

On September 21, 1983—two days after Vanessa Williams was crowned the first black Miss America—the jury deliberated for three hours and twenty minutes and convicted Angelo of murder. On October 7, Judge Greenberg sentenced Angelo to the maximum: twenty-seven and a half years in state prison. "I'm a sincere con and you're not," Skinny would say to Angelo when he was a teenager. "You got bad con." Skinny made not a single appearance at either of his son's trials—effectively disowning him.

Two weeks later, Luciano Pavarotti performed in the big tent built by Resorts. Ronald Bodanza's mother, Anne Battista, was by then working as a waitress at Resorts. The night of the concert, she was assigned to "the chain gang," as she put it. "I was one of forty-two waitresses that worked in the tent that night because there were seventy-five hundred people there," said Battista. "Naturally, all my waitress friends knew that I had lost Ronnie by Skinny's son. That night, one waitress came up to me and said, 'Anne, guess who's sittin' down there at table thirty-three? Skinny D'Amato.' Ronnie had been dead for seven years, and I hadn't seen Skinny since long before that. I said, 'Oh, yeah? Watch my table.' I walked over to where he was sitting with a group. He had a gray suit on. I said, 'Mr. D'Amato?' and he got up, and he put his arms around me, and he said, 'Hello, honey! Hello, honey!' I said, 'You don't know me,' and he said, 'But I would like to know you.' I said, 'I'm Ronnie Bodanza's mother.' Well, the man starts shakin' like a leaf—shakin' like you would not believe—and holdin' me and shakin', and his friends finally sat him down, and he said, 'Oh, my God. Oh, my, my, my . . . Ronnie was *so* good . . . I loved Ronnie . . . Ronnie was *so* good . . .' I wanted to say to him, 'Ronnie was so good, but you didn't come to his funeral,' but I didn't say nothin'. Afterward, I was so sorry. The man was so shook up, and I said to my friend, the waitress, 'Well, I should never have done that to that boy's father.'"

✦

Two months later, on the night before Skinny's seventy-fifth and last birthday—December 1, 1983—Steve Wynn threw a big, lavish party to mark the third anniversary of the Golden Nugget's opening. Dean Martin and Frank performed in the casino's showroom for the high rollers, and then later that night, Frank, his wife, Barbara, Dean, Mort Viner, and Skinny wandered into the casino to play blackjack. Their dealer was a Korean woman named Kyong Kim. Frank bought $2,200 in chips, with which he and his wife began to gamble while the others looked on. What happened next is now the stuff of legend.

Sinatra asked Kim to deal them a hand from a single deck of cards, rather than dealing out of the shoe, which holds six decks. Kim tried to explain that it was illegal, and Sinatra shouted, "You don't want to play one deck, go back to China!" A Nugget shift manager and a Casino Control Commission inspector approved the request, and Kim dealt from one deck by hand. Sinatra lost about $20,000 in fifteen minutes, and then he and his group left. The next night, Dean and Frank threw a surprise birthday dinner for Skinny for about ten people at Charlie's, a restaurant at the Golden Nugget named after Charlie Meyerson, whom Skinny knew from his Cal-Neva days and who was now Steve Wynn's right-hand man. Tony Maglio was there and Sonny Schwartz and Paulajane and Cathy and a few other friends. Skinny sat between Frank and Dean, and they talked and laughed and teased one another. No one realized the significance of that evening, that it was the last time Frank and Dean would see Skinny.

The next day, Kim, the blackjack dealer, and four other Golden Nugget employees were suspended for two weeks without pay for violation of the state gaming laws. Sinatra and Dean both pleaded ignorance, claiming they were used to Nevada's more accommodating rules. The whole thing quickly escalated to absurd proportions until the Casino Control Commission's Joel Jacobson called Sinatra an "obnoxious bully." Celebrities like Sinatra, he said, have the "occasional unfortunate combination of an uncluttered mind and a bloated ego."

Sinatra was furious. He would be no one's "punching bag." In October 1984, he retaliated by not only canceling all his future engagements at the Nugget in Atlantic City, but also announcing he would never perform in New Jersey again. In a lifetime of overreactions, this one topped them all. Perhaps one of the reasons he was able to level such a threat was that his favorite thing about Atlantic City—about New Jersey—was now gone.

✳

On June 5, 1984, Skinny died of a heart attack in the Frank Sinatra Wing of the Atlantic City Medical Center. The time of his death—five forty-five A.M.—was about the time Skinny had gone to bed for the last sixty years of his life. He had been driven to the hospital around midnight, suffering from chest pains. "Paul E. 'Skinny' D'Amato, 75, the colorful former nightclub owner credited with 'single-handedly making Atlantic City swing' for three decades, died Tuesday morning," read the opening paragraph of his obituary in the *Atlantic City Press*. "While known primarily as the host of a nightclub where major stars like Frank Sinatra, Sammy Davis, Jr., and Nat King Cole performed, associates say D'Amato also established a reputation as an unusually kind and generous man." Skinny's obituary appeared in newspapers all over the world. On Friday night, June 8, a wake was held at St. Michael's Church, as no funeral home was big enough to handle the crowds. Paulajane and Cathy picked out a bronze coffin—"not too gaudy, not plain," said Paulajane. They agonized over what to dress him in. How do you pick out clothes for someone who was so particular about his look? They settled on a blue suit, white shirt, and white silk pocket square. They ordered the flowers—gardenias and white and yellow roses. "The throng was endless," said Paulajane. "Cathy and I stood there for hours accepting condolences." When everyone was finally gone, and before they closed the lid, Paulajane and Cathy put a deck of cards, a pack of cigarettes, a 500 Club matchbook, and some Tic-Tac mints into his casket.

The following day, they went back to St. Michael's to do it all over again for the mass and burial. "When we turned the corner from Arctic to Mississippi Avenue," said Paulajane, "the traffic was backed up and the motorcycle cops stationed around the church had to intercede. I could see the hearse holding Daddy's coffin up ahead and a sea of people standing along the sidewalks and on the stairs of the church. There were newspaper and television reporters, photographers and camera crews, all hoping to see the entertainers."

The church was filled with three hundred friends and family, and at one P.M., seven pallbearers carried Skinny's casket into the church as Cooks Books sang "Mamma." Father Riley gave the eulogy. "Skinny was forever a realist," he said. "He was a student of living—not of the schools. His summa cum laude was of the streets. His real degree came at the end of his life, not the beginning. He was not a person to dazzle but only to deliver, especially when the chips were down. . . . The laughter and love of friends were Skinny's reward on earth. The computerlike memory for stories, events, happenings, many of which never, or could never, be put in print, were a source of hope to all who came within his magic spell. He collected and attracted people around our nation with the care and concern of a rare book devotee. They all came to him, the bright and the dull, the direct and the devious, the saintly and the cynical, the lonely and the frustrated, the quick and the slow . . . and he embraced them all . . . from the gold and glitter of Hollywood and Broadway to the simple man in the street."

Before the service got under way, though, Frank Sinatra, who was performing in New York at Carnegie Hall later that night, arrived in a silver limousine with two bodyguards and parked behind the church, so that he could enter through a rear door to avoid the crowds. Nick Nardo, who was the maître'd at the 500 Club for 25 years, was sitting out back, smoking a cigarette and waiting for the service to begin, when Sinatra's limo pulled up. Nardo hated Sinatra. That afternoon, he saw him get out of the limo and start to walk toward the church. He stopped suddenly, started to weep, and then got back into the limo to pull himself together. When Frank emerged ten minutes later, he was wearing sunglasses. "That is when I liked Frank Sinatra," said Nardo.

Inside the church, Frank waited in the vestry until just before the services began, at which point he took his seat in the front row between Paulajane and Cathy. "He couldn't bear the thought of it," said Paulajane. "When we were sitting in the pew with him between us, he was concentrating so hard not to lose it, and his face was a mask of anguish. He couldn't even talk to us. He just sat there, looking down. I think Frank had a thousand friends in his life, but there was a connection that was more like a brotherhood with Skinny. They were more like equals. The times they spent together were the best times in both of their lives. When they were young and hot and everything they touched turned to gold and Atlantic City always represented good times to Frank. This was probably the saddest time he ever had in Atlantic City. Skinny's death represented his mortality. Skinny was the first one of all those guys to die. After my father, he saw every other friend die before he did. It's hard to be the last one."

"I know Frank was broken up by his death," said Tommy DiBella, a friend of Sam Giancana and Sinatra. "All these guys, connected to the underworld, were dropping like flies by the end of the seventies. None of the shit they did made a bit of difference in history, if you think about it, except Skinny, the nicest guy in the world, who made a big mark on Atlantic City with his nightclub. The rest were all full of big-talking schemes, murdering the innocent and not so innocent, setting people up so that their lives would be ruined, being big shots in a fucked-up business."

✦

In the last few years of Skinny's life, Rita Marzullo called him every week. "Sometimes," she said, "when he was lonely and he was crying and he didn't want the children to see him, he would call me. A couple of times I went to see him, but I couldn't do it no more. I cried too much. I'd leave and I'd be miserable for weeks. Nobody in this world knows how much I loved Skinny."

When he died, Rita jumped on a casino bus to Atlantic City. "I got off near Resorts," she said, "and I see Arnold Orsatti, who owned a restaurant, coming towards me: 'Hey, Momma Rita! What are you doing here? I heard you moved back to Philly.' So I said to him, 'I came to say goodbye to Skinny.' We were standing near this hot dog stand, and he said, 'You want a hot dog?' And I said, 'A hot dog? Why don't you offer me a filet mignon or a lobster tail? I could buy *myself* a hot dog.'"

She took a cab and got off on Mississippi Avenue at St. Michael's. "The place is jam-packed," she said, "but I'm fat at this point, so a lot of people don't recognize me. Skinny's brother Willie came up and said to me real nice, 'Rita, I knew you'd be here.' When I went to the coffin, my legs buckled and I almost passed out. Paulajane's ex-husband, the cop, Bobby, helped me up. Now, as you know, Skinny dressed out of this world. Every night, a custom-built tuxedo for work. And he had beautiful hair, but he always had to have a piece on his forehead. When I went to go sit down, right behind me was another girl who worked at the 500, that I hadn't seen for years, Dolores Turner. She said to me, 'Look what they didn't do. They don't have the curl on his forehead.' I said, 'Oh, my God, he probably won't rest in peace because his hair isn't right.' So I went up to Bobby and said, 'He's gotta have the hair on his forehead.' He said, 'It's too late, we can't do it now.' I said, 'I'll do it,' and he said, 'No, nobody can touch him.'"

Rita sat on the end of a pew on the left side of the church right next to Al Cohen, Skinny's nephew. "Everybody came to see Skinny from all over the world," she said. "All the big shots and politicians, when they passed by me they all came over to hug and kiss me, and I was crying in all their arms and everybody was watching. There were these men sitting behind me, and they looked to me like big men, businessmen or something. So when all these men were coming over to me, the men behind me were saying to each other, 'But who *is* she?' And one of them said, 'Maybe that was his girlfriend.' And I turned around and said, 'No, I wasn't his girlfriend. I was his *pet*.'"

Rita was flat broke by this time in her life, and she didn't have the money for a hotel room in the new Atlantic City. Besides, in the summer it's nearly impossible to get a room on a minute's notice. She also didn't have the nerve to ask people she knew if she could stay at their house so that she could attend the funeral the next day. "When I left the viewing, I looked all around the city. I went to a few of the casinos and I saw thousands of people, but not one person I knew. I wanted to kick myself in the ass that I didn't have enough money. I was even gonna stay up all night, but I couldn't. If Rocky Castellani's club was still there on Missouri and Atlantic, I could have gone there and would have found somebody to stay with, or I would have stayed at Rocky's all night. Atlantic City had changed so much. *Did it change!* The casinos ruined my Atlantic City. It's a sin to say it. My old Atlantic City . . . *what they did to our town.*"

The only thing that really surprised her at Skinny's viewing, she said, was that she didn't see a single Mob guy. "Not one. Not even Nicky Scarfo. Nobody."

As she told this story, she was crying. Then she took a deep breath and wiped away her tears. "That's one of my greatest regrets, that I didn't make it back the next day for his funeral. But then Sonny Schwartz sent me the picture of Sinatra carrying Skinny's coffin. I have it around somewhere. It always makes me cry." She paused for a moment and then said very quietly: "So many stories about Skinny . . . so many beautiful stories."

✳

People often talk about how the new Atlantic City is so different from the old, and they are both right and wrong. If Skinny were alive today, he'd probably dismiss all the complaining as nostalgic hair splitting. Legalized gambling saved the city that he loved so much from extinction and that was the point. Much of the old Atlantic City has been— or is in the process of being—knocked down, paved over, and rebuilt as a modern twenty-first century tourist attraction, but to Skinny D'Amato's near exact specifications. He wanted Atlantic City to be an environment where gambling was legal—not to make great big piles of money, but to make it possible for regular folk to *dream of winning* great big piles of money. Who cares if the old hotels had to come down.

Today, there are fourteen glittering, cacophonous casinos that stay open nearly all night and they attract millions of people. All that money changing hands would have made Skinny very happy because, in the end, that's really what he cared most about: the pursuit of gambling, the sport of betting, the *sound* of money. Shortly before he died he said, "I never cared one damn about money, except to spend it. I guess that's why I'm not rich now." As Skinny's cousin, Joe DiSanti, said, "If my father couldn't leave a hundred-dollar tip, we didn't go out to dinner, and Skinny was a hundred thousand times more like that than my father. Money, money, money, money. Skinny gave it all away. But that was the style because he was a kid with nothing who went to second grade and then worked his way up from the street. I would think to myself, Why would somebody let all that money go through their hands? If I hadn't seen it with my own eyes I wouldn't understand it myself. But the answer is, he was living a lifestyle. I mean, look at everybody he knew, from the actors and actresses to the judges and politicians. He had to be on the same level as them—he had to be *better* than them—and he just gave it all away."

The thing that *is* missing from the resort—what makes the new different from the old—is Skinny. *He* was the old Atlantic City. The lifestyle that Skinny seemed so effortlessly to embody is gone forever because the apparatus that was necessary to provide illegal gambling is no longer needed. In some ways, that was what made Skinny so cool—that he so successfully walked on the edges of the law and flirted with the underworld in order to create an environment where people could *spend their money* on something they weren't supposed to be doing.

Now it's all perfectly legal.

✶ Acknowledgments

I COULD NOT—perhaps *would* not—have written this book without the irrepressible force of nature that is Paulajane D'Amato. She is one of the bravest and toughest taskmasters I've ever met and I thank her from the bottom of my heart for opening herself up to me, sharing her life, home, Sambuca, archives, and photographs. I also thank her for her great instincts, friendship, and unflagging support over the last few years. FYI: Paulajane—after years of trial and tragedy (including the sudden death of her third husband, Jay Venetianer, on October 19, 1997)—is living happily in Delray Beach, Florida, with her beautiful daughter, Devon. I also thank Cathy D'Amato Schuppert, for sharing memories of her father and her childhood. Cathy, too, is living happily ever after in Marietta, Georgia, with her husband of thirteen years, Don Schuppert. I owe a debt of gratitude to Angelo D'Amato for those ten difficult hours we spent together under the hot lights at East Jersey State Prison.

Of all interviews, there are two people who stood out and made working on this book a far richer experience. Joe Del Raso went beyond the call of duty and spent many hours helping me get to know Skinny D'Amato. I thank him for putting his prestige on the line and for understanding the process of journalism better than any nonjournalist I know. I also thank him for introducing me to his wonderful family, especially his parents, Vince and Dolores. Second, and perhaps most important, I thank "Momma" Rita Marzullo for her tireless good nature, beautiful sense of humor, and extraordinary memory for vivid detail and conversations that took place many years ago. (I love you, Rita. I couldn't have written about Skinny without you. You're a piece of work!)

I'd also like to thank Ronald Bodanza's mother, Anne Battista, and his sister, Joyce Bodanza, for welcoming me into their home and bravely recounting the life and death of their beloved Ronnie. Anne Battista's fundamental decency is an inspiration. Additionally, I'd like to thank the siblings of Kerry Carter, Larry Graham, and Glenda Parker for sharing with me their memories of their sister. Also, a thank you to Linda Lu for same.

In no particular order, I also thank: Ricky Apt, Anthony Maglio, Sonny King, Steven Rosenfeld, Bryant Simon, John Almier, Honey Rizzo, Phyllis McGuire, Sid Mark, Jack Davis, John Schultz, Gary Hill, Bob Chambers, Howard Bacharach, Caroline Kimmel, Antoinette Malone, Michele Ruggieri, Fred Augello, Mike Tarsitano, Ed and Sissy Hurst, Bill McCullough, Manny Tischler, Johnny D'Angelo, Anita Widecrantz, Genevieve Norato, Tony O, Tina Sinatra, Reverend George Riley, Peter Miller, Kurt Koogle, Pinky Kravitz, Mary Koury, Chris Owen, Georgene and Sonny McCullough, Ray Harris, David Spatz, Jerry "Geator with the Heater" Blavat, Kevin Shelly, Robert Venturi, Denise Scott Brown, Ray Langford, Jimmy Mancini, David and Pauline Schwartz, Jim Barber, Sid Trusty, Les Kammerman, and Sue Pollack.

A special thank you to architectural historian and all-around smart guy George E. Thomas, whose knowledge of the lost Atlantic City is a thing to behold and whose book, *William L. Price: Arts and Crafts to Modern Design*, is . . . priceless!

Thank you to the writers who have come before me and to whom I owe a huge debt: Grace D'Amato (*Chance of a Lifetime*), Charles Funnell (*By the Beautiful Sea*), Nelson Johnson (*Boardwalk Empire*), Ovid Demaris (*The Boardwalk Jungle*), Bill Kent, Robert E. Ruffolo, and Lauralee Dobbins (*Atlantic City: America's Playground*), Martin Paulsson (*The Social Anxieties of Progressive Reform: Atlantic City, 1854–1920*), Frank Deford (*There She Is*), Gigi Mahon (*The Company That Bought the Boardwalk*), Lee Eisenberg and Vicki Gold Levi (*Atlantic City: 125 Years of Ocean Madness*), Sally Denton and Roger Morris (*The Money and the Power*), Mike Weatherford (*Cult Vegas*), Bethel Holmes Van Tassel (*Wood Chips to Gaming Chips: Casinos and People at North Lake Tahoe*), David Johnston (*Temples of Chance*), William N. Thompson (*Legalized Gambling*), George Sternlieb and James W. Hughes (*The Atlantic City Gamble*), John L. Smith (*Running Scared*), Anthony Summers (*Goddess: The Secret Lives of Marilyn Monroe*), Richard Ben Cramer (*Joe DiMaggio: The Hero's Life*), Nick Tosches (*Dino*), Shawn Levy (*King of Comedy* and *Rat Pack Confidential*), J. Randy Taraborrelli (*Sinatra: Behind the Legend*), Nancy Sinatra (*Frank Sinatra: An American Legend*), Tom Kuntz and Phil Kuntz

(*The Sinatra Files*), Judith Exner (*My Story*), Gus Russo (*The Outfit*), Martin Gosch and Richard Hammer (*The Last Testament of Lucky Luciano*), Seymour M. Hersh (*The Dark Side of Camelot*), Ronald A. Farrell and Carole Case (*The Black Book and the Mob*), William Howard Moore (*The Kefauver Committee and the Politics of Crime*), Dan B. Fleming, Jr. (*Kennedy vs. Humphrey, West Virginia, 1960*), Donald Bain (*The Control of Candy Jones*), and Carole Conover (*Cover Girls: The Story of Harry Conover*).

Three very important thank yous to: my friend Bill Tonelli for the book's title; my beloved, brilliant agent, Todd Shuster, for knowing that *this* was the one and for making me write twelve drafts of the proposal; and last, but not least, my fabulous editor at Crown, Doug Pepper, for knowing exactly when to step in, when to leave me alone, and when to say something really nice. Also at Crown: thanks to Amy Boorstein, Bill Adams, Juleyka Lantigua, Jason Gordon, and especially Sona Vogel for taking such extra good care of my book with her exquisite copy editing. Also, thank you to Mike Jones at Bloomsbury.

Thank you to my researcher and fact checker Kerrie Mitchell, who not only unearthed strange and dusty documents that changed the book in fundamental ways, but found her birth family while we were working together, including a grandmother who once worked as a go-go girl at the 500 Club! Thank you, Jim Agnew, for sending me all those mob files, weird paperbacks, endless faxes, and for pushing me down the Lucky Luciano trail and for making me prove to myself that Skinny wasn't a gangster. Also, a thank you to Jeanne Dewey Donahue for digging up the D'Amato clip file at *The Press of Atlantic City*. A heartfelt thank you to my nieces— Barbara "Wawa" Blackmore and Margaret "Madge" DeVico—for their brilliant and speedy transcription skills. Also thanks to Janice Duschlebauer and Mary Donaghy for same. Thanks a million to my readers: Richard Snow and Carol Smith, Roz Lichter, and Liz Swados.

Thanks to Lisa DePaulo for hiring me as an intern at *Atlantic City Magazine* lo those many years ago and for always being available when I'm in the "pain cave"; Fran Freedman for publishing a great magazine and for knowing *everyone*; Liz Logan for "discovering" me; and all those editors from whom I've learned so much over the years: Alan Halpern, John Marchese, Jill Feldman, Ronnie Polaneczky, Jodie Green, Penelope Green, Eric Etheridge, Will Dana, Carol Kramer, Pat Towers, Don Shewey, Gil Rogin, Alan Light, Maer Roshan, Bruce Handy, Vicky Ward, Susan Morrison, Wayne Lawson, Laurie Jones, Richard Story, Sally Singer, Valerie

Steiker, Eve MacSweeney, Eric Banks, Ariel Kaminer, and Marc Smirnoff. A special thanks to Adam Moss, for teaching me how to write a good story, and to Anna Wintour, for her support, loyalty, and enthusiasm and for encouraging me to write when I needed it most. Thanks to Bill Zehme and Lucy Kaylin for being helpful and kind, and to Rosemary Ahern for the single best piece of advice: think of a good title.

A great, big thank you to Nancy Kaufman for my fifty minutes every Tuesday. I could not have gotten through this without you. You're a genius.

Thanks to Quang Bao and Hanya Yanigihara for hooking me up with my office and to everyone at the Asian American Writer's Workshop for not bothering me for two years while I rattled around the hallways late at night.

To those who made life in Atlantic City fun: Cristine Faunce, Joan Siracusa, Donna Palamero McCarthy, Kitty Marciniak, MORTIMER!, Michael Callahan, Ginny Moles and everyone I met at the Studio VI: Wayne, Jeremy, Roland & Kathy, David, Joseph, Carl and Dennis. A special thanks to Tim Bellew for creating The Bay Club, where I met Paulajane.

Thank you to all of my dear, dear friends for listening to me yammer on about Skinny for three years: Mo Gaffney, Ellen Fanning, Diane Cardwell, Eric Nonacs, Hilton Als, Marisa Bowe, Bart Everly, Spike Gillespie, Ellen Stewart, Darcy Tozier, Ricky Lee, Sally Chew, Joe Berinato, Matt Stewart, Sean Wicker, Derek Nash, Jim Holbrook, Joan Rivers, Kelly Ward, Gene Solomon, Natalie Valentine, Plum Sykes, Casper Grathwohl, Alexandra Kotur, Jill Demling, Jennifer Gersten, Caroline Palmer, Anne Fahey, Hyatt Bass, Josh Klausner, Melanie Ross, Andrew Rosenberg, Lia Braaten, Hellyn Sher, Edward Mapplethorpe, Camille Sweeny, Rob Mackey, Julie Weiss, Craig Stuart, Jeff Cranmer, Susie Park, Diana and Matthew Weymar, Naomi Despres. A special thanks to Arty Nelson for knowing who Skinny D'Amato was on Christmas night in that stupid bar in Pittsburgh, and to Aimee Mann for being my D.I.Y. role model. Deep, unconditional love and thanks to Louis Mazza and Stefan Campbell for being such willing participants in the noble experiment of staying friends despite everything. A special thanks to Rob Van Meter, Chaz Van Meter, and Bob and Debbie Young.

Thanks to Chuck, Johanna, Jeanne, and Kate—the best, weirdest, funniest, most loving bunch of siblings a boy could hope for. But most of all: thank to my parents, Norman and Judy, for loving me (and each other) so much and so unconditionally. You're my heroes.

In memory of Steven Izenhour and Kay Van Meter. May they rest in peace.

Index